de Gruyter Studies in Organization 47

Management in Western Europe

de Gruyter Studies in Organization

International Management, Organization and Policy Analysis

An international and interdisciplinary book series from de Gruyter presenting comprehensive research on aspects of international management, organization studies and comparative public policy.
It covers cross-cultural and cross-national studies of topics such as:
— management; organizations; public policy, and/or their inter-relation
— industry and regulatory policies
— business-government relations
— international organizations
— comparative institutional frameworks.

While each book in the series ideally has a comparative empirical focus, specific national studies of a general theoretical, substantive or regional interest which relate to the development of cross-cultural and comparative theory are also encouraged.
The series is designed to stimulate and encourage the exchange of ideas across linguistic, national and cultural traditions of analysis, between academic researchers, practitioners and policy makers, and between disciplinary specialisms.
The volumes present theoretical work, empirical studies, translations and 'state-of-the-art' surveys. The *international* aspects of the series are uppermost: there is a strong commitment to work which crosses and opens boundaries.

Editor:

Prof. Stewart R. Clegg, University of St. Andrews, Dept. of Management, St. Andrews, Scotland, U.K.

Advisory Board:

Prof. Nancy J. Adler, McGill University, Dept. of Management, Montreal, Quebec, Canada
Prof. Richard Hall, State University of New York at Albany, Dept. of Sociology, Albany, New York, USA
Prof. Gary Hamilton, University of California, Dept. of Sociology, Davis, California, USA
Prof. Geert Hofstede, University of Limburg, Maastricht, The Netherlands
Prof. Pradip N. Khandwalla, Indian Institute of Management, Vastrapur, Ahmedabad, India
Prof. Surendra Munshi, Sociology Group, Indian Institute of Management, Calcutta, India
Prof. Gordon Redding, University of Hong Kong. Dept. of Management Studies, Hong Kong

Management in Western Europe

Society, Culture and
Organization in Twelve Nations

Editor: David J. Hickson

Walter de Gruyter · Berlin · New York 1993

Editor
David J. Hickson
Research Professor of International Management and Organization, University of
Bradford, Management Centre, Emm Lane, Bradford, England

With 17 tables and 3 figures

Library of Congress Cataloging-in-Publication Data

Management in western Europe: society, culture and organization in
   twelve nations / editor, David J. Hickson.
      p.   cm. — (De Gruyter studies in organization ; 47)
   Includes bibliographical references.
   ISBN 3-11-014174-4 (cloth)
         3-11-012710-5 (pbk.)
   1. Management—Europe—Cross-cultural studies.   2 Industrial
management—Europe—Cross-cultural studies.   I. Series.
HD70.E8M36   1993
658′ .0094—dc20   92-42234
                                                                CIP

Die Deutsche Bibliothek Cataloging-in-Publication Data

Management in Western Europe: society, culture and
organization in twelve nations / ed.: David J. Hickson.-Berlin;
New York: de Gruyter, 1993
(De Gruyter studies in organization; 47)
ISBN 3-11-014174-4 (geb.)
      3-11-012710-5 (brosch.)
NE: Hickson, David J. [Hrsg.]; GT

∞ Printed on acid-free paper which falls within the guidelines of the ANSI to ensure
permanence and durability.

Preface

This is a book of its time, insofar as it is occasioned by the development of the European Community in Western Europe. It is also a book whose content will last far beyond this time, as long as these twelve societies of the E.C. last with their variety of cultures and styles of management, whatever the future of the E.C. may be. It is a book that reaches back many centuries to the origins of these societies.

Apart from the opening and closing chapters, which give a general overview across Western Europe, each chapter links the form and practices of management and organization in one of the twelve societies to its social, political, and economic history and its present circumstances. This is a book, therefore, that draws together management studies, organization theory, sociology, political science, and economics in a way that is a tribute to the professionalism and knowledge of those who have written it.

I myself came to an awareness of the European medley gradually over the years. It happened as I taught specialist courses in Britain, Canada, and the United States on cross-national differences in management and organization, and when I joined in founding E.G.O.S., the European Group for Organizational Studies (the word "Group" being now a misnomer for what has become an extensive international network of researchers), and again whilst I was first Editor-in-Chief of the European-based research journal *Organization Studies*. Though never did I understand as much as I understood when I had the privilege of being the first reader of this book. I hope that it will help all subsequent readers as much as it has helped me.

All the chapters have been written specially for the book, except that by Geert Hofstede who had already unwittingly written the perfect opening chapter in the form of a conference paper. The chapters have a great variety of style and format, due both to the diversity of nations they describe and to the wonderful personal diversity of their authors. As editor of the book, I did not impose a standard framework on the chapters. Had that been possible, the result might have been dull, but in any case it would have been impracticable, for some deal with larger nations, some with smaller ones, some with older nations and some with the newer. Most importantly, some chapters deal with nations on which there is substantial relevant published research material, and others with nations on which there is very little, so some authors have achieved masterpieces of succinct synthesis and selection, whilst others have achieved masterpieces of creativity.

The majority of chapters are unique, in the full meaning of that word. There is no other analysis of management and organization in that country available in the English language, and usually not in any language. Each chapter has its own index, since it is the features of each nation that are most likely to be sought and these would be lost in a general index.

The aim is to introduce the characteristics of each society, in sufficient detail to meet the immediate needs of many students, practising managers and administrators, and to provide a basis for those who wish to go further. A single chapter on such a topic cannot be, and none pretend to be, all-encompassing. There must be many half-truths within these covers. Each author will have felt anxious, as I have, that a single chapter may not give a full and balanced view of their fellow men and women in the Continent we share. Yet I must say that as an Englishman I feel keenly, and at times uncomfortably, the truth of what Monir Tayeb writes about me in her chapter on the English!

I apologize to Luxemburgers that I found no way of including a chapter on their attractive land. This left a gap which was filled by Sweden, partly because Sweden is well up in the queue for E.C. membership, and partly because its distinctive Nordic features, together with those of Denmark, provide an informative contrast with those of the nations of Southern Europe.

It is most difficult of all to write dispassionately about one's own country, and so most chapters have been written by authors who, by nationality or origin, are from elsewhere. It took an Irishman, though, Brian Leavy, to write about Ireland, and whilst James Georgas who writes about Greece is American born and holds an American passport, he is Greek at heart and has lived much of his life in Greece. There are also chapters which reap the advantage of authorship shared between a non-national and a national of the country concerned, so Egil Fivelsdal, a Norwegian writes on Denmark with a Dane, Iette Schramm-Nielsen. There are three British co-authors, Barry Turner who writes on Italy with Pasquale Gagliardi, an Italian, Maurice Punch who writes on The Netherlands with Nic van Dijk, a Dutchman, and David Weir who shares authorship on Portugal with his Portuguese colleague Afonso Pereira Inacio.

Of the other authors, the Dutchman Albert Mok writes on Belgium, Monir Tayeb who writes about the English is by origin Iranian (and is now domiciled in Scotland), Arndt Sorge who writes on France has returned from The Netherlands to his native Germany, Malcolm Warner and Adrian Campbell who write the chapter on Germany are British, Max Boisot lives in Spain and writes about Spain but is so cosmopolitan that it has to be remembered that he, too, is British, and Barbara Czarniawska-Joerges combines Polish and German names and so betrays the Polish origin that enables her to write more easily about Sweden, where she now lives. As for the authors of the opening and closing chapters, Geert Hofstede and I are respectively the typical multilingual Dutchman and the monolingual Englishman.

My own experience of life has been enhanced by knowing all these authors, both before and during the writing of this book. I admire their accomplishment in composing these vignettes of the nations, and the positive way in which they all accepted and tackled the extraordinary task that was put to them. All of us very much appreciate the dedicated efforts of Susan van der Werff in constructively editing and co-ordinating such diverse contributions.

I must also thank my several secretarial colleagues at Bradford each of whom, at different times and in different ways, played a part. They are Chris Barkby, Hazel Crabb, Gill Sharpley and Pam Waterhouse.

Finally, Bianka Ralle of our publishers Walter de Gruyter has given unswerving support.

Since this is not *my* book but *our* book, I have no mandate to choose a dedication for it, but were I to give a dedication it would be *to managing mutual understanding*. Despite our different cultures—or is it because of our different cultures—I believe that every one of us who has shared in writing this book would subscribe to that.

David Hickson
Bradford Management Centre

Table of Contents

Chapter 4: England

English Culture and Business Organizations   47
Monir Tayeb

Chapter 8: Ireland

Managing the Economy of a Newly Independent State   125
Brian Leavy

Chapter 9: Italy

Aspects of Italian Management   149
Pasquale Gagliardi and *Barry A. Turner*

Chapter 10: The Netherlands

Open Doors, Closed Circles: Management and Organization in
the Netherlands
Nic van Dijk and *Maurice Punch*

Chapter 11: Portugal

Management in Portugal
Afonso Pereira Inacio and *David Weir*

Chapter 12: Spain

The Revolution from Outside: Spanish Management and the
Challenges of Modernization
Max H. Boisot

Chapter 13: Sweden

Chapter 14:

Chapter 1: Europe

Intercultural Conflict and Synergy in Europe*

Geert Hofstede

Culture: The National Component

The fact that the word "culture" is used in two quite different senses often leads to confusion. We can notice this in discussions as well as in journalistic publications. There is culture as "civilization": arts, craftsmanship, and scholarship, which we could call "culture in the narrow sense", and there is culture as acquired patterns of thinking, feeling and acting: "culture in the wider sense". In this chapter and throughout this book, we deal with culture in the wider sense, which is the way the word is used by anthropologists. A practical working definition of "culture" in this sense is that it represents the "collective programming of the mind which distinguishes one category of people from another". We all belong to several categories at the same time, each of which contributes a component to our mental programming: our nation, region of origin, language group, generation, sex, religion, education, occupation and even the organization for which we work. Thus, our cultural baggage is composed of these various components, completed by our personality, which is the truly unique part of our programming, not necessarily shared with members of any category to which we belong.

As mental programming, culture is *software*; it is invisible by itself but becomes visible in its consequences, which may be hard enough. Of particular interest these days is *organization culture*, the component of mental programming common to people working for the same organization. Organization culture is supposed to be a major factor in explaining the effectiveness or ineffectiveness of an organization, and many managers wonder how to change and re-create it. When organizations move abroad, such as in the case of multinationals, we recognize that their culture has partly been shaped by the nationality of their founder or founders, so that organizational and national cultures do, in fact, overlap. Managers or students sometimes want to know which is more powerful, the national or the organizational component of culture. However, this question cannot be answered; apart from the fact that they may overlap, they also affect different programmes in our minds. For example, ways of dealing with authority carry primarily a national component which the organization can modify but not entirely change; ways of dealing with innovation carry primarily an organizational component, secondary to the national presence.

In all cases, the origins of the mental programming which we call culture lie in the past: culture, whether national, regional, occupational or organizational, represents the crystallization of history in the thinking, feeling and acting of the present generation. It is transferred to future generations through education and socialization. In this book, the subject is Europe, which means we focus on the national component.

National Cultures in Four Dimensions

Our empirical research on national culture differences at the Institute for Research on Intercultural Co-operation at Maastricht began with a study of the distribution of work-related *values* among 53 national subsidiaries of a large multinational business corporation (Hofstede 1980, 1991). Values represent the most stable element in mental programming. They are semi-conscious feelings about good and evil which are usually acquired in early childhood and are then difficult to change as adults. Values represent the stable core of culture. Measurements by skilful pencil-and-paper questions of the values of similar people in these different national subsidiaries showed a strong national component. Comparison with studies by other people, comparing some or all of the same countries, confirmed the existence of such a national component. Statistical analysis showed that the differences between the dominant values in the national subsidiaries were linked to four different factors, four *dimensions of national culture*:
– individualism versus collectivism
– large versus small power distance
– strong versus weak uncertainty avoidance
– masculinity versus femininity
Each country could be given a score on each of these four dimensions.

In *individualist* cultures, people are supposed to look after their own interest and that of their immediate family (husband, wife and children). In *collectivist* cultures, on the other hand, people remain, throughout their lives, members of larger but close-knit in-groups which protect them in exchange for unquestioning loyalty, and which compete with other in-groups (families, tribes, clans or villages).

Power distance represents the extent to which the less powerful people in a culture accept and expect that power is distributed unequally.

Uncertainty avoidance represents the extent to which people in a culture become nervous in unstructured, ambiguous situations, and try to avoid such situations by strict rules of behaviour, intolerance of deviants, and a belief in absolute truths.

In *masculine* cultures, men are expected to be ambitious, assertive, concerned with money, and to admire whatever is big and strong. Women are supposed to care and serve. In *feminine* cultures, men and women are both expected to be non-competitive, modest, concerned with relationships, and to sympathize with whatever is small and weak.

The people in the 53 national subsidiaries studied varied considerably on these four dimensions, which occurred in virtually all possible combinations. The countries have been given scores on each dimension, and these scores can be shown to relate to phenomena in the various societies in which these subsidiaries operate, such as:
– political systems and political priorities
– educational systems and priorities
– management methods and objectives
– negotiation behaviour between individuals and organizations.
For example, individualism can be shown to relate to freedom of the press in a country; high power distance to income inequality among citizens; uncertainty avoidance to a belief in the competence of experts and the incompetence of lay people; and femininity to the percentage of its Gross National Product spent by a rich country on its development assistance to poor countries.

European Heterogeneity

Among the 53 subsidiaries studied, 18 were established in different European countries; the other 35 all around the world, in Africa, Asia, the Americas and the Pacific, excluding, however, the former Comecon countries and China. Among the 18 European countries were 11 out of the 12 present EC countries (excluding Luxemburg), and therefore also 5 out of the 6 original EC countries, plus Sweden which is included in this book. In Table 1, for each of the four dimensions of national culture described above, the range (highest score minus lowest score) among European countries found in our research is expressed as a percentage of the worldwide range.

Table 1 shows clearly that even the initial EC countries show considerable differences in cultural values, especially on the dimensions of uncertainty avoidance and masculinity. Adding six more countries has extended the heterogeneity to all four dimensions, to the extent that,

Table 1. Range of Country Scores on 4 Culture Dimensions Expressed as a Percentage of the Total World Range, for 3 Levels of European Country Subjects

Countries		Individualism–Collectivism	Power Distance	Uncertainty Avoidance	Masculinity–Femininity
EC of the 6	(5)	26	35	57	56
EC of the 12 plus Sweden	(11)	73	54	68	65
All European countries	(18)	73	70	86	82
Total World	(53)	100	100	100	100

Table 2. Relative Position of 11 EC countries and Sweden on 4 Culture Dimensions, Among All 53 Countries Studied

	Individualism–Collectivism	Power Distance	Uncertainty Avoidance	Masculinity–Femininity
Upper third (18)	Britain Netherlands Italy Belgium Denmark Sweden France Ireland Germany	France	Greece Portugal Belgium France Spain	Italy Ireland Britain Germany Greece
Middle third (17)	Spain Greece Portugal	Belgium Portugal Greece Spain Italy	Italy Germany Netherlands	Belgium
Lower third (18)		Netherlands Germany Britain Sweden Ireland Denmark	Britain Ireland Sweden Denmark	France Spain Portugal Denmark Netherlands Sweden

depending on the dimension, between half and three-quarters of the range in values found worldwide is now present within the EC. Culturally, "Europe" does not exist: Europe, and the EC within it, is a cultural microcosm.

This will come as no surprise to experienced EC officials, but it does go against the initial optimism of the founders of the EC, who believed in cultural convergence through economic unity. It is still in conflict with the assumptions of many national politicians, some journalists, many members of the public, and particularly, many non-Europeans. The misleading fact is that Europeans *look* more or less alike, but this does not mean they are culturally alike. Similarly, ethnic groups that do *not* look alike (for example, those with different skin colours) are not necessarily culturally different. Comparing Europe to North America, we find that:

Europe is   genetically more homogeneous,
                   culturally more heterogeneous
North-America is genetically more heterogeneous,
                   culturally more homogeneous
having gone through a melting-pot phase which Europe has never known.

Table 2 shows the relative positions of the EC 12 countries on the four dimensions, among the 53 countries studied worldwide. The one dimension on which the nine EC countries, before the latest additions, were more or less homogeneous was individualism, but the entry of Spain, Greece and Portugal has also introduced heterogeneity on this point.

Origins of Intra-European Cultural Differences

If culture is the crystallization of history in the thinking, feeling and acting of the present generation, how can European countries, which have shared such a lot of their history, be so culturally heterogeneous today?

Did we not share the influence of the Roman Empire? Well, the fact is that some countries were part of Rome, whereas others were not. The Roman inheritance, besides that of the Romance language, is visible in relatively high power distances and uncertainty avoidance, reflecting the centralized authority and universal legal systems of Roman civilization. However, the "barbaric" countries of Europe to the North and the West lack this inheritance.

Were we not all converted to Christianity? Yes, we were; and the Church of Rome extended to where the Empire had never penetrated, to the farthest extremities of the continent. However, religion is not equivalent to culture: cultural values modify the forms religion takes. It is striking that after 1000 years of Roman Catholicism, the countries that

broke away from Rome were precisely in those parts of Europe where the
Roman Empire had not left its cultural inheritance, and not in the Latin
part. This shows that the Church was still firmly founded on the values of
the Empire.

Did we not, in ages past, send our scholars to the same universities in
Bologna, Salamanca, Paris, Leyden and Oxford? Did not my namesake
Geert Geertsz of Rotterdam, who changed his name to Desiderius
Erasmus, write his booklet "In Praise of Folly" for his friend Thomas
More in England and, did not their friend Hans Holbein in Germany make
the illustrations? Did not our royal families intermarry, and our courts
model themselves along the lines of the French court, spreading civilized
habits which were subsequently taken up by the better-off, more privileged, sections of the population?

All this is true. Elias, a truly European scholar, carried out a thorough
and revealing study on the diffusion process of civilized habits in Europe
from approximately the year 1000 (Elias 1980, 1969, 1936). Many of our
present civilized habits originated and spread from the French courts.
However, it is striking how often Elias in his historical references points to
differences between parts of Europe as far back as the fourteenth or
sixteenth century, differences which seem quite modern today. Take, for
example, an observation made in 1546, that no people in Europe were as
obedient as they were in France (*op.cit.* 2:304). Take another look at Table
2, based on data from around 1970, showing France as the European
country scoring highest on power distance, i.e., the extent to which the less
powerful people accept and expect that power is distributed unequally.
French obedience, obviously, did not spread to the same extent as did
French table manners and French cuisine. The various European revolutionary waves illustrate the same point, from the 14th century farmers'
revolutions to those on university campuses in 1968. Though revolutionary
fire did spread from one country to another at times, it found very different
fuel in each one, both in quantity and quality.

The stubbornness of cultural differences can be understood if we realize
that mental programming manifests itself at different levels, some of them
superficial, others much deeper. On the scale superficial to deep we find
symbols, heroes, rituals and values, respectively. Symbols are words,
gestures and objects whose meaning has to be learned. Symbols are easily
transferred and our speech, manners and dress reflect the influence of
other countries; they could most easily be labelled "European". Values
represent the other end of the spectrum: they are feelings of right and
wrong, good and evil, beautiful and ugly, rational and irrational which are
often unconscious and cannot be so readily recognized and discussed.
Research indicates that values are acquired early in life, reinforced by
social systems, and are very resistant to change in an adult. For this reason,
values tend to be transferred from generation to generation, and so do the

differences in values dominant in one country or region as compared with another.

In the same way as an individual's values are formed early in life, a society's values are also formed early in its history, and that is probably why the long shadow of the Roman Empire is still visible in our twentieth-century research data, more so than that of more recent political events.

The survival of cultural differences is maybe less surprising if we remember the survival of language differences. The 12 countries of the EC, in addition to their 10 official languages, host another 10 minority languages (such as Frisian, Welsh, Basque, Catalan), making a total of 20. Language is the vehicle of culture, and it is an obstinate vehicle: any particular language shows a preference for certain trains of thought. If the diffusion of European civilization has not eradicated language differences, why should it have eradicated culture differences?

European Cooperation as a Laboratory for the World

At one time there seemed to be a fairly widespread "Europessimism" over the lack of progress in European integration, which appears to ebb and flow. In view of the heterogeneity of the partners, what has been achieved so far is impressive. The EC has become an economic block, recognized as such by the outside world, profoundly affecting the economic decision-making of its member countries. As an example of voluntary cooperation among a group of sovereign nations, it probably has no parallel. If a culturally and linguistically mixed community such as Europe can be made to cooperate, this is a source of hope for the development of voluntary cooperation elsewhere in the world.

Yet the visible results do not show the cultural assimilation that the EC founders had expected. We are *not* becoming more similar (in fact, comparative research data over a four-year period indicates that we are becoming more different; see Hofstede 1980, Chapt. 8), but we have learned to collaborate in spite of, maybe sometimes even thanks to, our differences. It is not cultural assimilation, but cultural synergy that has come within reach.

Cultural and linguistic heterogeneity which, from the outset, was a liability for Europe, becomes an asset, once we have learned to master it, when dealing with other heterogeneous parts of the world such as Africa, Latin America and, in particular, the Middle East and Asia. Europe's main competitors there, the U.S.A. and Japan, lack the multicultural experience and, usually, the linguistic skills of many Europeans. If we have learned to manage intercultural cooperation within Europe, and within politics, business, and education, we should be able to manage inter-cultural cooperation anywhere. History has made Europe into an inter-cultural laboratory for the world: perhaps we can use it to the world's benefit.

Note

*Developed from a paper originally presented at a conference in Maastricht, The Netherlands, 1986, on "Cultural Aspects of Economic Co-operation in Europe".

References

N. Elias (1980, 1969, 1936): *Über den Prozess der Zivilisation: soziogenetische und psychogenetische Untersuchungen*, Vols. 1 and 2. Frankfurt/Main: Suhrkamp.

G. Hofstede (1980): *Culture's consequences; international differences in work-related values*. Beverly Hills, CA: Sage.

G. Hofstede (1991): *Cultures and organizations: Software of the mind*. London: McGraw Hill.

Chapter 2: Belgium

Management and Culture in a Pillared Society*

Albert L. Mok

Does Belgium Exist?

If one asks whether there is a specific management culture in Belgium, one is in fact asking the question: does Belgium exist? "For centuries Belgium was a distant dependent province of foreign powers (successively of Spain, Austria, France and the Netherlands) and only gained its independence in 1831" (Hofstede 1980: 337). Hofstede rightly observes that the Dutch/ French language split is a hot political issue in Belgium, although according to his data the Dutch and French speaking parts largely share the same (French) culture. He explains this by their common history and the fact that, when Belgium separated from Holland in 1831, French was the language of government, the upper classes and education. This has remained so for over 100 years. Hofstede's findings are, however, somewhat contradicted by Aiken and Bacharach (1980: 240), who argue that Walloon organizations are more like typical French bureaucracies (rigid and hierarchical), as described by Crozier (1963), than their Flemish counterparts, which are more open and flexible. The difference is ascribed to historical circumstances, but Aiken and Bacharach admitted they were unable to specify them, due to lack of empirical data. Although I by no means wish to imply that I can do their job better, I hope to shed some more light on this intriguing country named Belgium, where I have been a "guest worker" for over twenty enjoyable years and in the Northern part of which they speak my own language (Dutch), only a little differently. Mine is a view "from the north" (The Netherlands, also called Holland). I am sure that someone with a different frame of reference would see other things and give explanations which differ from mine.

Resourceful Survivors

Whether this is due to their history of foreign domination or not, the fact is that Belgians today are resourceful survivors and staunch individualists.

When, for instance, in 1990, the King of the Belgians for religious reasons refused to sign the Bill which would, under certain restricting conditions, legalize abortion, the then Prime-Minister Wilfried Martens invented the cunning solution of the King abdicating for the duration of the parliamentary debate and the signing of the Bill (by ministers, instead of by the Head of State). After two days the King resumed his reign. In any other Western constitutional democracy this would have caused a major crisis, as a result of which the hereditary monarch would probably have had to relinquish his or her throne. Not so in Belgium. It did, however, start a discussion about changing the constitutional role of the Head of State into a mere figure-head, as in Sweden. However, in Belgium, the King has a very useful role as a mediator in conflicts between the two communities, and in reality cannot be missed. A Senator in 1911 uttered the now famous words to King Albert I of the Belgians: "Sire, il n'y a pas de Belges" ("There are no Belgians, Sir"). There is a Belgian state, but there is no Belgian language, no "ethnicity" to which Belgians refer as their source of reference. The King is, so to speak, the only one who is unquestionably "Belgian". Belgians always tell me that they feel a Belgian identity only when they are abroad or when the national soccer team plays against Holland. There is a national anthem and a national flag, but at least in Flanders there exists a very ambivalent attitude towards these symbols and the "Flemish lion" is always raised and sung alongside the Belgian tricolor and the "Brabançonne".

The Ethnic Split

Belgium is a small country of about 30,000 square kilometres, clenched between Holland in the north, Germany in the east, France in the south and the North Sea in the west. There are 10 million people living in Belgium, about 5 million of which live in the northern part called Flanders, where they speak Flemish. Flemish is Dutch, but with small differences. About 4 million people live in the southern part called Wallonia, where they speak French, and about 1 million live right in the middle of the country, in the capital Brussels, with its surrounding 19 communities. On the eastern border there are 80,000 Belgians whose native language is German.

It is perhaps symbolic that Walloons are less proficient in Dutch than the

Flemish are in French. It signifies the dominant position which French culture has always enjoyed in Belgium. Not anymore. Language, however, is only a means of expressing the real issues which lie behind it. The religious, political and economic divisions in the country are "ethnic" facts which dominate every aspect of life. In a sense Flanders is more "ethnic" than Wallonia, which only became aware of a separate identity after Flanders started breaking away. Is culture in Wallonia Walloon, Belgian or French? It is significant for this Walloon cultural ambivalence that there are two regional governments in the southern half of Belgium, one for the Walloon region, and one for the French-speaking community, which is a wider concept. There is only one Flemish regional government in the northern half, and Brussels has a regional government of its own. The state structure is at this moment (1992) only partially devolved, because until now there have not been separate elections for the regional governments. Such elections will probably be held in 1994, if the many parties involved can come to an agreement. From then on, Belgium will be a federal state.

History of Belgium

Belgium is part of what is usually called the Low Countries or the "Benelux" (Belgium, Netherlands and Luxemburg). During the eighteenth and nineteenth centuries this region underwent profound political and social changes (Dhont and Bruwier 1973: 329 366; Van der Wee 1972: 168 ff.). Originally, it was made up of four areas: the northern United Provinces (the modern Netherlands), the southern or Austrian Netherlands, the principality of Liège (under the rule of a prince-bishop) and the sovereign abbey region of Stavelot–Malmédy. The last three regions make up modern Belgium (the Grand-Duchy of Luxemburg belonged to the Dutch Crown until 1890). The Northern and Southern Netherlands have ancient ties and so became one kingdom in 1815 under the Dutch king, William I. However, their economic and religious differences were too great: the North was protestant and concentrated on commerce, the South roman-catholic and industrial. At the time of the industrial revolution there were few important industries in Holland, while in the South, thanks partly to the presence of coal and steel in Wallonia, Belgium became the first industrialized country on the continent of Europe (Van der Wee 1972: 168; Mokyr 1976: 228), but there were other factors involved. Dhont and Bruwier (1973: 331) point to motive power. Thanks to the sharp contours and swiftly flowing rivers in Wallonia there was power for the many water mills. A third factor was the industrial policy of King William I of the United Kingdom of the Netherlands. As lack of capital can retard industrialization (Van Schelven 1984: 224), the King founded a holding company cum bank in 1822, in Belgium: the *Société Générale de Belgique* "pour favoriser l'industrie aux Pays Bas". It was the first mixed bank of its kind in the world, and it applied the "banking pattern" of industrialization (whereby banks have financial hegemony over industry) long before the Germans did (*Gedenkboek* 1972: 16; Scott 1985: 117). Two years later, in the northern Netherlands (Holland), the king founded the Netherlands Trade Society, with the specific objective of stimulating and financing trade with the colonies in the East Indies (now Indonesia). William I himself supplied three-fifths of the founding capital of the *Société Générale*. Thanks to his active industrial policy and his development of Belgian infrastructure, Belgium (i.e. Wallonia) industrialized very rapidly. Eight hundred kilometres of paved roads were built and the railway network was already well advanced by the time the Belgians formally seceded from the United Kingdom of the Netherlands in 1839.

In 1831, after a ten days war with Holland, Belgium became a kingdom of its own, with Queen Victoria's uncle, Leopold of Saxe-Coburg, as the first King of the Belgians (not of Belgium, for officially that state was not founded until after the treaty with Holland was formally signed in 1839).

The French speaking bourgeoisie considered Flanders as a kind of conquered country, very much as other countries viewed their colonies (Roosens 1981: 39). The dominant pattern in the nineteenth century was the finance capitalism of the holding company *Société Générale*, dominated by its bank, the *Générale de Banque*, led by a French speaking bourgeoisie, based on the control of Walloon coal mining, steel, glass, textiles, engineering, machine building and other heavy industries, and the exploitation of the riches of the Belgian Congo (now Zaïre) in Africa (Daems 1978). This remained so until after the First World War, when the economy of Belgium had to be restructured. The depression which followed led to banking failures as industrial empires collapsed. A law of 1934 (effective from 1935) made direct bank investments in industry illegal. As a consequence, the relationship between the banks and their holding companies was reversed: instead of the banks controlling the holding companies, the holding companies controlled the banks (Scott 1985: 134). In that way the holding system was consolidated as one of the main features of the Belgian economy, at least on the Walloon side. In Flanders things were quite different, as we shall see.

History of Flanders

The history of Flanders in the latter half of the nineteenth century speaks of "Poor Flanders" (Daems et al. 1981: 25), where alcoholism and child labour prevailed, where tens of thousands of people travelled daily on "working men's trains" to and from the industrial centres of Wallonia and northern France to earn a minimal wage. The significance of the railways as a means of transporting cheap labour for Wallonia's industrial regions was underlined by the introduction of the cheap working man's ticket in 1870 (Van Isacker 1978). Important in all this was an over-population in Flanders compared with Wallonia. In the nineteenth century, Wallonia had the "French" demographic pattern (early marriages, few children), while Flanders had the "Irish" (agricultural) pattern: late marriages and a very high birthrate. The "Irish" pattern makes for a crooked distribution of the means of existence, with great poverty and a lack of adequate employment.

A Deep Recession (1880–1900)

A period of relative prosperity after the Franco–Prussian war of 1870–71 was followed by a deep recession in the 1880s, which lasted well into the 1890s. Wages were lowered, production declined, prices rose. As a result, violent clashes occurred in many Walloon enterprises. Strikes and riots were rife. Rebellion of the workers was ruthlessly suppressed by the Army, with much loss of life (Kympers 1980: 175).

Against this background of extreme poverty, unemployment and dependence on a violent Wallonia it is small wonder that the industrialization of Flanders was initiated during the worst years of depression (1880–1900), by enterprising people who made the most of what their *local* environment had to offer, using their savings as capital and their (large) families as labour. The flourishing family firms which sprang up all over Flanders during this period were very much a product of the factors named above as constituting the social climate of the day. The most important was the absence of a substantial industrial sector. This made Flanders more vulnerable to economic depression than Wallonia, especially in rural areas. Around the turn of the century an increasing number of Flemish entrepreneurs came to the conclusion that Flanders could only emancipate on a solid basis of Flemish capitalism. A great boost to that end was the discovery in 1901 of coal in the soil of Flanders and its exploitation (since 1917). (The last coal mine in Belgium closed down for good in 1992.) For Flemish nationalists like Lodewijk De Raet, the problems of Flanders were caused by the dominance of holding company capitalism, led by French speaking financiers (Roosens 1981: 115).

The Flemish brand of capitalism rested on small and medium sized firms, run by a business elite much inspired by political militantism, and financed partly by the small savings of the Flemish people. To that end a Flemish bank was founded (*Kredietbank*). In rural areas the *Boerenbond* (Farmers' Association) was active as a savings bank. In 1908 Flemish entrepreneurs founded the Flemish Trade Association (VHV), which in 1926 became the Flemish Economic Association (VEV). After the gradual devolution of Flanders, it became a Flemish Employers Association, taking its place in the industrial relations system on the regional level. In 1926, Lieven Gevaert (1868–1935), the famous Flemish industrialist, became its first president, until his death in 1935. The list of his successors as VEV presidents reads like a directory of Flemish "familial" entrepreneurs.

Language as well as the industrial backwardness of Flanders were the inspiring motives. The VEV, together with other pressure groups, was successful in its battle to do away with French and to make Dutch the sole official language of Flanders and in its drive to attract foreign investment with the help of so-called expansion laws from the 1950s onwards. Thereafter the balance of (economic) power shifted gradually from Wallonia to Flanders (Quévit 1978), although the holding companies did not lose their grip on managerial enterprises, even in Flanders. From then on, Flemish cultural identity rested on a firm economic base. One wonders whether and to what extent the lack of a clear Walloon identity contributed to the decline of Wallonia as an industrial region.

Belgian Industrial Structure

There are three kinds of enterprise which constitute Belgian industrial structure: the familial enterprise, the managerial enterprise and the transnational enterprise. Each of the two parts of Belgium show what Clark and Staunton (1989) have called a "typical variety". The "typical variety" in Wallonia was dominated by the managerial enterprise and the holding company, in Flanders by the familial enterprise, at least until well into the twentieth century.

The familial enterprise is established by the personal entrepreneurship of the founder of the firm and his successors. In this kind of enterprise, capital is furnished and control is exercised by a small and limited number of entrepreneurs who are related by family ties. The firm is in a sense an extension of the family and, in the beginning, business is conducted from the drawing room, as it were. The wife of the founder has an important role to play, especially with regard to book-keeping and the financial aspects of the enterprise (Scase and Goffee 1980). Relations with staff are on the same level, with no sharp division between firm and family (Stokvis 1989: 34). Trade unions have very little grip on this kind of enterprise.

Weber (1925) called this the patrimonial organization. Personnel call the male members of the family by their first name, respectfully preceded by "Mr.": Mr. Marc, Mr. Patrick.

For this phenomenon, the Dutch sociologist F. van Heek (himself a scion of a well-known Dutch family textile firm) used the word *"familism"* (Van Heek 1945: 241). It existed predominantly in rural areas, around the many small Flemish towns, was characterized by intergenerational, "dynastic" continuity and a tendency to steer clear of salaried managers from the outside, and depended on the local labour market for workers. Individual paternalism predominated. There was "tacit knowledge" of local customs (Polanyi 1967). The profit motive was and is less important than being able to hand the firm over to the next generation (Stokvis 1989: 97). Even in the judicial form, familistic attitudes can be noticed. In conjunction with financing by family capital and nonpayment of dividends, most family firms in Flanders remained a "firm" for at least the first generation, and some for even longer. Only when the growth of the enterprise made the acquisition of outside capital compulsory did these family businesses change the judicial form of "firm" into "limited liability company", though not necessarily with outside managers entering the board rooms. At least during a transitional period, business policy and the control of the labour process remained in the hands of the original owners.

Many Flemish firms which sprang up during the last quarter of the nineteenth century were characterized by this local family pattern. Examples are Santens (textiles), Van Den Avenne (animal food), Lannoo (printing), Bekaert (steel wire) and Gevaert (photo chemicals). The histories of these firms make fascinating reading for students of management. The Roman-Catholic heads of these family firms stress the communal and local leadership role of the family. The liberal entrepreneurs in Flanders have likewise contributed to Flemish industrialization, but they were more "managerial" than "familistic" in their leadership style (e.g. Sucres de Tirlemont).

The managerial enterprise is characterized by the presence of managers from the outside, who take control of the production process away from the formal owners, who lack the necessary know-how to conduct the technical and economic affairs of the firms. Galbraith (1967) has coined the term "technostructure" for this kind of power system in the enterprise. Some have rightly criticized Galbraith for being too rigid in this matter. As was said above, there is at least a transitional period in which the (family) owners remain (partly) in control, even when "outsiders" have taken over the board room. The coming of the judicial form of the public limited company was of crucial importance in the birth of the managerial enterprise, which in Wallonia happened as early as 1833, but in Flanders much later.

Transnationalization, according to Van Dijck (1992: iv), is the process whereby a firm which started as a national enterprise assumes the status of a transnational enterprise through a series of steps: exports, gaining international standing, multinationality. The transnational enterprise, in the case of Belgium, is predominantly a local familial or managerial firm which has founded productive and/or commercial subsidiaries in one or more foreign countries. Many multinational companies are active in Belgium, but they are mostly firms of foreign origin with offices and plants all over the world. There are only very few Belgian multinational companies in the sense given here.

Three Stages

Thus the pattern of industrialization in Flanders becomes clear. Although in the nineteenth century some industrial establishments did exist, mainly in textiles, food stuffs and building materials (Roosens 1981: 40), the real take-off of Flemish industrialization appears to have taken place in three stages: between 1880 and 1900, between 1900 and 1945 and after 1945.

As was described above, after 1880 a multitude of family firms came into existence. Some of these grew into managerial enterprises, with further growth into transnational companies. One famous example (Bekaert) will be treated in some detail later in this chapter, but there are many Flemish companies which made their way successfully to the transnational scene, e.g. Hansen Transmissions at Edegem near Antwerp.

The second way in which Flanders became industrialized was by Walloon industrialists establishing important, but sometimes environmentally polluting production processes on Flemish soil (like copper, zinc, lead and other metal processing and glass), led by French speaking engineers and usually owned by that ever present *Société Générale*. Some examples are Métallurgie Hoboken-Overpelt (Hoboken, Olen and Overpelt), Poudreries Réunies de Belgique (now closed down), Vieille Montagne (Balen) and Glaverbel (Mol). The managerial enterprise became the dominant pattern after the turn of the century. Gradually, from the 1950s onwards, French speaking managers were replaced by Flemish ones, first in the personnel departments (the language laws are very strict on the use of Dutch in education and in labour relations), later in the board rooms.

It was only after the Second World War that the big multinational companies (U.S., German, British, Dutch) discovered the many advantages of Flanders, especially Antwerp, as an important gateway to Europe's industrial regions (Germany, France and beyond). For example between 1950 and 1970, 10 per cent of all U.S. investments abroad came to Belgium, especially Flanders (Roosens 1981: 97). During the fieldwork preceding the writing of this chapter I noticed that even in the Flemish subsidiaries of multinational companies a "Flemish" management style prevails (e.g. Samsonite in Oudenaarde, Monsanto in Antwerp), characterized by a flexible way of dealing with people and problems, a pragmatic attitude, and a readiness to compromise, in the context of a "flatter" hierarchical organization than found in, for instance, French companies (Maurice et al. 1980: 66ff). Indeed, resourceful surviving and pragmatism is a way of life which characterizes management style as well as other aspects of the Flemish existence.

Local Politics

Many of the founders of family firms in Flanders had close ties with their local community. Lieven Gevaert, for instance, founded Flemish catholic schools, which exist to this very day. Their offspring in the second, third and sometimes fourth generation became local politicians and mayors of their towns. Some played and still play a role in national politics, for example as a member of Parliament. After the 1991 general election, 40 of the 396 members of the Belgian parliament were professional entrepreneurs (report by L. Puylaert, VEV). On the ideological level, many family entrepreneurs were and still are faithful sons of the Roman-Catholic Church and would heartily embrace the motto "Everything for Flanders—Flanders for Christ" (the motto of the Flemish Front Movement, which was started during the First World War as a protest against the Walloon–French domination of the Army).

Foreign Takeovers

The takeover of Belgian companies by foreign capital, of which Agfa-Gevaert and the Bekaert Group are well-known examples, and concentration tendencies have gained momentum since 1960. In 1988 the *Société Générale* became part of the French Suez group of companies. Foreign control of Belgian finance capital became the normal pattern (Vincent 1990: 360). For that reason, holding companies, and especially the capital rich insurance companies, have become a favourite target for takeovers. According to Aiken and Bacharach (1980: 240), Walloon organizations resemble French ones more than Flemish organizations and that makes French acquisitiveness understandable.

The reader will by now not be surprised that the gradual conquest of Belgian capital by French interests is much resented in Flanders (German or Dutch takeovers are viewed less suspiciously) and constitutes the basis for debates, for example in the case of the privatization of the Belgian airline Sabena (to Air France or KLM?).

Small and medium-sized companies, especially in Flanders, together with the holding companies (especially in Wallonia), remain the backbone of the Belgian economy, although the number of small companies is decreasing.

Industrial Relations

By the end of the nineteenth century Wallonia had a strong industrial proletariat, whose militancy was feared by employers and the authorities. In 1896 there were already 400,000 industrial workers in Wallonia (40 per cent of the working population), while in Flanders there were only 184,000 (10 per cent of the working population) (Roosens 1981: 39). Until well after the Second World War, that is after the coming of the bulk of the multinational enterprises, Flanders remained the reserve labour pool for the Walloon economy. Wallonia had, as was already mentioned, much larger companies than Flanders, and concentrated on heavy industries like coal mining, iron and steel, engineering and machine building, glass and textiles. This, by the way, also determined the industrial relations model, which became institutionalized after World War Two, in 1944–1945. What could be called the "mining model" laid much stress on worker representation on the shop floor, which, in combination with representation on the sectorial and national bargaining levels, made for a strongly institutionalized industrial relations system (Slomp and Van Mierlo 1984).

Unions in Belgium came into being in the 19th century as mutual support associations, which mobilized working class families around mutual assistance: sickness, accident and unemployment benefits, pension funds, widow and orphan funds, and child benefits. Community life centred on the "circle" (catholics) and the "people's house" (socialists). The neo-corporatist model until this day forms the cement of the Belgian political system, which is characterized by the so-called "pillars".

The mining model and the neo-corporatist model together make the trade unions and their representatives very visible to the workers. Their role in the social security system, and their being the backbone of the so-called "pillars", make it possible to set up a "spoil system", or system of "clientelism" as it is sometimes called. This binds members to their union and their "pillar" (Huyse 1986). As a result, union density in Belgium rose from 30 per cent in 1945 to 70 per cent in 1989, against the trend in many countries.

Pillarization

This "pillar" thing has to be explained. Society can be seen to be composed of semi self-contained vertical slices or pillars. There are roughly three of these national collectivities or, to use another term again, "families" in Belgium: a catholic one, a socialist one and a liberal one. (There are political parties outside these "families", such as the Flemish nationalists and the green party, but their strength is limited.) Each consists of a political party, a labour movement with unions for blue and for white-collar workers separately, including a liberal trade union, youth movement, women's committees and mutual sickness funds, each with their "own" members of parliament. Some have newspapers, there is a Christian employers' federation, there are catholic and state schools.

There are catholic, anti-clerical ("free"), state-owned and "pluralistic" universities. For example, the University of Antwerp consists of three campuses, one catholic, one (non-catholic) state-owned and one "pluralistic", each with their own governing body, coordinated by a central committee. The Board of the "pluralistic" university institute where I teach must, by law, have a balanced membership of catholics and non-catholics (only the Board, thank God). This is decided on by people's behaviour, not by their religious beliefs: if you have attended a Catholic school and university, are a member of a Christian trade union and a Christian sickness fund but never go to church, you belong to the Catholic pillar. Protestants, whether or not they are faithful Christians and church attenders, are considered to adhere to the anti-clerical tradition.

Each of the "pillars" has its own traditional pattern of community life, with a relatively strong social closure (Weber 1925). The catholic pillar organizes the local community around the church, its priests and the local notables, and their ideology centres on the nuclear family. The socialist pillar is centred on the working class quarters of the cities (the *cité*), with the ideological cement of a common fate and a dislike of the clergy. The liberal pillar is only slightly less anti-clerical, consisting of emancipated and (sub)urban bourgeois families, with an ideology stressing private ownership and individualism.

This pillarization of society, which in a less rigid form also exists in The Netherlands, is complicated in the case of Belgium by the language split. There are two varieties of each pillar, which sometimes cooperate across the language border and sometimes combat each other. The socialist family is strongest in Wallonia, the Christian family has the most adherents in Flanders and the liberals (especially in Brussels and other urban conglomerates) are inclined, more than the others, to have similar viewpoints across the language barrier, being more downright "economic" in their ideology than the others. As a result of national bargaining practices, the

central trade unions are bi-lingual national associations, with the exception
of the Christian white collar union, which is split in two. Central bargaining
on the employers' side is done by the Confederation of Belgian Enterprises, which is equally bi-lingual.

An Example: The Bekaert Group

The wire-drawing firm of Bekaert, now a transnational company, constitutes a good example. It was founded in 1880, by the verger/ironmonger
Leo Leander Bekaert (1855–1936) in the little West-Flemish town of
Zwevegem, not far from Kortrijk, then a very rural area. Because, among
other things, he sold wire to the farmers, he noticed their need for wire
which could more effectively prevent cattle escaping from the meadows.
Thus the idea of barbed wire was born: twined wire with a little nail every
10 centimeters. The novelty was not only the new product, but also the
locality. Starting a metalworking industry in the midst of farm houses, far
from the industrial centres of Wallonia, was risky, but proved to be a
brilliant idea. "Produce where there is a market", was Bekaert's motto.

> In a wooden barn—covered with tarred paper and temporarily erected in the
> garden behind the Sint-Amand rest-home at Zwevegem—a man with a box
> of nails hanging from his belt walks alongside three steel wires. Every 10 to
> 20 cm, he twists a nail between the wires. The steel wires are fixed at one end
> to the wheel of an upturned wheel-barrow and, at the other end, attached to
> hooks in the wall. (Kympers 1980: 249)

That is how the now transnational firm of Bekaert was founded. "Under
the strong hand of Leo L. Bekaert, the business developed empirically,
pragmatically. Work was done quickly, diligently and carefully, without,
however, obeying any really strict rules" (Kympers 1980: 300). A perfect
description of Bekaert's management style! Tribute should be paid,
however, to Miss Honorina, Leo's sister, who was the "organization
woman", while Leo built up the firm (Kympers 1980: 225).

The driving forces behind the later expansion of Bekaert's firm after the
first quarter of the twentieth century were L.L. Bekaert's two sons, L.A.
and M. Bekaert, one the "empire builder", the other the "organization
man", as is so often the case, for instance Gerard and Anton Philips, C. &
A. Brenninkmeyer, etc. (Chandler 1962). They took over the management
of the factory after the First World War, during the period in which it had
suffered severe damage. This proved to be a blessing in disguise, because it
forced the brothers Bekaert to buy new machinery and motivated the
workers to put their shoulders to the wheel. Productivity rose accordingly.

A diversification of products was achieved. In addition to barbed wire Bekaert started to manufacture bed-springs, wire netting, steel wire and staples. Exports to France, Germany and Holland increased. Many new machine shops were put into use and the number of workers rose gradually. (At Zwevegem alone the number rose from 13 in 1880 to over 6,000 in the 1980s. Until 1924 the business at Zwevegem was "a one-man show".)

The first milestone in Bekaert's development from a family via a managerial into a transnational firm was its reorganization in 1924, 44 years after its founding, into a *société anonyme*, a limited liability company, although this did not affect its family character and shareholders were all members of the family. When it became a legal possibility in 1935, the judicial form was changed to a "personal limited company", which was more suited to the medium-sized enterprise Bekaert then still was. The present day Group structure was not adopted until 1969, when the Bekaert Group became a Public Limited Company with quotation on the stock market. The "Creed" they then adopted strongly bore the seal of the family origins, stressing the community character of the firm (Kympers 1980: 318).

In the literature on the industrialization of Flanders there is often a laudatory note on the family firm expanding "without the participation of outside capital" and thanks to the restraints of the family members, when female, often unmarried. This was the case with Bekaert, which held out for almost 90 years. Gevaert, the photographic firm in Mortsel (near Antwerp), founded in 1890 as a one-man business by Lieven Gevaert, became a "firm" in 1894 but did not attract outside capital until 1920, when it became a limited liability company (Davidsfonds 195: 55). Santens, Van Den Avenne, Lannoo and others held out longer than Gevaert, but exact figures for these latter companies are not available. Of course, there is another side to this. Dhont and Bruwier (1973: 342) have pointed to the fact that the application of the Limited Company form, as early as the first quarter of the nineteenth century, in fact much earlier than in other industrializing countries, did much to stimulate the industrialization of Wallonia. The holding company is a direct application of it. In Flemish family firms this judicial form could not be applied at the start because of the small size of the businesses and the unwillingness of family members to share power with outsiders.

Management Culture

Hofstede (1980) has defined culture very aptly as "the collective programming of the mind which distinguishes one category of people from another". I take this definition to include the following elements: (1) shared values, (2) a common history and (3) the possibility of cultural transmission (socialization). This is important in the case of the family firm in Flanders, for even if it grows into a managerial and transnational enterprise, we can still recognize the cultural birthmark of the founders. Flemish managers are individualists and realists, more so than their Walloon counterparts. "Culture's Consequences", as Hofstede has called them, in the case of Belgium, can largely be explained by the history and structure of Belgian society and the differences between Flanders and Wallonia as described above.

In comparison with other European countries Belgium as a whole, in Hofstede's analysis, scores high on *uncertainty avoidance*, and this factor scores even higher in Wallonia than in Flanders, as is confirmed by Aiken and Bacharach (1979: 240). Institutionalized rules and rituals, culture in the "objective" sense (Lauwers 1985: 6), serve to cope with the uncertainty which belongs to the cultural heritage of Belgian society, and are transmitted to the members of this society by the basic institutions, the family, the church and the school, and are then applied in the workplace. Each of these has its own traditional brand of rules and rituals, into which new members are socialized, and which determine the way people relate to other members of their society. Within their own "pillar" people find the security which society-at-large does not provide. People without a "family" are floaters, especially those who have left their pillar, been cast off, or foreigners who have not been in the country long enough to join.

In Hofstede's scheme, Belgium also scores very high on *power distance*, almost as high as France. Power distance in organizations is indicated by a reluctance to let subordinates interfere with the decision-making by the manager, a tendency of subordinates not to disagree with the boss and in general an acceptance of social, financial and legal inequality in organizational settings. The most interesting aspect of power distance is the way in which it is justified (Bendix 1956). In the typical Flemish family firm, authority is legitimized by the "*pater familias*", and all power derives from him (Weber's traditional type of authority). In the managerial and transnational enterprises, authority, in principle, is more of Max Weber's legal–rational kind, but Culture's Consequences are such that in Belgium, even in rationally organized hierarchies, boss and subordinate both share the traditional faith in authority which is transmitted through the family, the schools, the church, the youth movement, etc. This is more so in Flanders than in Wallonia, because Flemish people seem to manage their firms differently from Wallonians, in a way that is more closely linked to the catholic family than to the socialist and liberal ones. Authority and obedience are two of a kind, as Hofstede rightly observes. All Belgians, whether Flemish or Walloon, know much about it.

Conclusion

We started this chapter by calling the Belgians staunch individualists and resourceful survivors. This has much to do with people's identities; with how they see themselves in relation to others. In Belgium the relation with the national collectivity has always been difficult. Time and again researchers point to the animosity of Belgians towards the state and state interference in their lives and in the economic aspects of their existence in particular (Clerinx 1992). Having a business of your own is not a bad way to gain independence. Belgians strongly believe that their prosperity is the result of their own efforts, without outside help (Mok and Van Goethem 1992), whereas, for instance, Dutch people are closer adherents to the collective ideal. Dutch people seem to be of the opinion that their welfare is a result of societal processes on which they have very little influence, and they are proud to have a state which cares for them (Berting 1991: 134). In a certain sense, Belgians are too cynical to believe in the welfare state, however much they make use of it when necessary.

These staunch individualists make living in Belgium very pleasant. To be able to go about doing things in your own way with little outside interference, seems supreme freedom. Perhaps the paradoxes are not so negative after all: if social, economic and corporate life is extremely ritualized as is the case in Belgium, people's reaction is likewise extreme, and individualism is the result. Or is it the other way round? Belgium, if it does exist, remains an intriguing enigma.

Note

*I would like to thank Professor Jan Lauwers of Antwerp University for his advice and valuable suggestions for the improvement of this chapter, and the Flemish managers whom we interviewed for their willingness to give us their views.

References

Aiken, M. and S.B. Bacharach (1980): "Culture and organizational structure and process: a comparative study of local government administrative bureaucracies in the Walloon and Flemish regions of Belgium" in C.J. Lammers and D.J. Hickson (eds.), *Organizations alike and unlike. International and interinstitutional studies in the sociology of organizations*, 215–250. London, Boston and Henley: Routledge and Kegan Paul.

Bendix, R. (1956): *Work and authority in industry. Ideologies of management in the course of industrialization*. New York: Harper.

Berting, J. (1991): "Nederlanders over de betekenis van individuele arbeidsprestaties" in L.J.M. d'Anjou and A.P.J. Bernts (eds.), *Presteren en verdelen in Nederland: over individuele belangen en sociale solidariteit*, 129–150. Meppel and Amsterdam: Boom.

Chandler, Jr., A.D. (1962): *Strategy and structure. Chapters in the history of the industrial enterprise*. Cambridge, MA: MIT.

Clark, P. and N. Staunton (1989): *Innovation, technology and organization*. London: Routledge.

Clerinx, R. (1992): *Ingenieur—cultuur—ethiek*, Brussels: Instituut van de Onderneming.

Crozier, M. (1963): *Le phénomène bureaucratique*. Paris: Seuil.

Daems, H. (1978): *The holding company and corporate control*. Leiden and Boston: Nijhoff.

Daems, H. et al. (1981): *De Belgische industrie. Een profielbeeld*. Antwerpen and Amsterdam: DNB.

Davidsfonds (1955): *Lieven Gevaert. De mens en zijn werk*. Leuven: DF.

Dhont, J. and M. Bruwier (1973): "The Industrial Revolution in the Low Countries 1700–1914" in C.M. Cipolla (ed.), *The emergence of industrial societies I*, 329–366. London: Fontana/Collins.

Galbraith, J.K. (1967): *The new industrial state*. Harmondsworth: Penguin.

Gedenkboek (1972): *Société Générale de Belgique 1822–1972*. Brussels: SG.

Hofstede, G. (1980): *Culture's consequences. International differences in work-related values*. Beverly Hills, CA: Sage.

Huyse, L. (1986): *De gewapende vrede: politiek in België na 1945*. Leuven: Kritak.

Kympers, L. (ed.) (1980): *Bekaert 100. Economic development in south-west Flanders*. Tielt: Lannoo.

Lauwers, J. (1985): *Op zoek naar cultuur. Grondslagen voor een verantwoord cultuurbeleid*. Leuven and Amersfoort: Acco.

Maurice, M., A. Sorge and M. Warner (1980): "Societal differences in organizing manufacturing units: a comparison of France, West Germany and Britain". *Organization Studies* 1/1: 59–86.

Mok, A.L. and W. Van Goethem (1992): "Werken in de prestatiemaatschappij" in J. Kerkhofs et al.(eds.), *De versnelde ommekeer. De waarden van Vlamingen, Walen en Brusselaars in de jaren negentig*, 69–91. Tielt and Brussel: Lannoo/KBS. Also published in French: "Le travail: au-delà de l'instrumental" in L. Voyé et al. (eds.), *Belges, heureux et satisfaits. Les valeurs des belges dans les années 90*, 85–118. Brussels: De Boeck/FRB.

Mokyr, J. (1976): *Industrialization in the Low Countries*. Newhaven and London: Yale University Press.

Polanyi, M. (1967): *The tacit dimension*. Garden City, NY: Anchor Books.

Quévit, M. (1978): *Les causes du déclin Wallon*. Brussels: Vie Ouvrière.

Roosens, A. (1981): *De Vlaamse kwestie. "Pamflet" over een onbegrepen probleem*. Leuven: Kritak.

Scase, R. and R. Goffee (1980): *The real world of the small business owner*. London: Croom Helm.

Scott, J. (1985): *Corporations, classes and capitalism*. London: Hutchinson.

Slomp, H. and T. van Mierlo (1984): *Arbeidsverhoudingen in België*. Utrecht and Antwerpen.

Stokvis, R. (1989): *Ondernemers en industriële verhoudingen. Een onderneming in regionaal verband (1945–1985)*. Assen and Maastricht: Van Gorcum.

Van Dijck, J. (1992): "Transnationalization of economic and social life in Europe" in J.J.J. van Dijck and A.A.L.G. Wentink (eds.), *Transnational business in Europe. Economic and social perspectives*, iv–xiii. Tilburg: Tilburg University.

Van Heek, F. (1945): *Stijging en daling op de maatschappelijke ladder. Een onderzoek naar de verticale sociale mobiliteit*. Leiden: Brill.

Van Isacker, K. (1978): *Mijn land in de kering, 1830–1980*. Antwerpen: DNB.

Van Schelven, A.L. (1984): *Onderneming en familisme*. Leiden: Nijhoff.

Van der Wee, H. (1972): *Historische aspecten van de economische groei*. Antwerpen and Utrecht: DNB.

Vincent, A. (1990): *Les groupes d'entreprises en Belgique: le domaine des principaux groupes privés*. Brussels: CRISP.

Weber, M. (1925): *Wirtschaft und Gesellschaft*. Tübingen: Mohr.

Chapter 3: Denmark

Egalitarianism at Work: Management in Denmark*

Egil Fivelsdal and Iette Schramm-Nielsen

Introduction

In this chapter we will interpret Danish managerial behaviour in terms of values, institutional context and history, assuming that there are broad value themes in Danish culture, which are rooted in the history of the country and institutionalized in social, economic and political structures.

From a sociological point of view, Denmark is a remarkably homogeneous society. There are no religious, ethnical or language cleavages. As in any society, there is a stratification system on the basis of economic, educational and cultural criteria, but this stratification is softened by a policy of equalization, which expresses some basic values in Danish society.

The chapter will be divided into three main parts: first we shall venture a description and an interpretation of the contemporary Danish managerial values and behaviour tendencies that we and others have registered. Next will follow a short description of the societal context in which Danish management operates. Finally, we will attempt to link some of the phenomena that we have registered with some of the historical deep-structures, which, in our opinion, have contributed to shape norms and values and thereby also institutions.

Danish Managers and Their Shared Values

Managers are an important occupational category in the economic system, since Denmark has a very large service sector, an extensive foreign trade, and many small and medium-sized companies. Middle managers are especially numerous and play important roles as coordinators, motivators and decision-makers. As in many other national contexts they serve as a basic link between the strategic and the operative level of the organization.

The importance of managers is also reflected by the fact that the Danish business education system is highly developed, heterogeneous in nature, and has a large capacity relative to the size of the population.

Denmark being a small and homogeneous country, most of its managers will tend to share a number of broad value orientations, of which we have chosen to treat three key concepts which are distinctive, and which will explain a number of related values and behavioural tendencies. They are egalitarianism, consensus/cooperation, and professionalism.

Egalitarianism

It has often been said by foreign observers that Danish management style is characterized by soft, indulgent and participative behaviour. These characteristics can be related to the hierarchical relationship and the organizational structure.

In Denmark the ideal is a flat organizational structure with as few layers of hierarchy as possible, making the distance from top to bottom as short as possible. Also, there is often a gradual transition of authority between the layers, as there is no canonized definition of what authority is inherent at each level; it depends on the job, the manager himself and the capabilities of the employees surrounding him.

Furthermore, and this is perhaps the crucial point, decision-making is usually delegated to a large number of people, all of whom can make decisions on matters related to their area of responsibility. Thus the sphere of authority is spread over a great number of people in each layer of the hierarchy, thereby also spreading power, or responsibility as Danes would put it.

An eloquent point can be made in this connection, namely that Danes generally resent the word "power", which has all the negative connotations of superiority, force, domination, and coercion. No Danish manager would refer to the power he (she) has, but he (she) would willingly speak of his (her) responsibilities, a word which has positive connotations of work, competence, and obligations towards others. In consequence, what is important in a Danish setting is less who has authority over whom as who is responsible for what.

When many people have decision-making authority, each within their domain, managers have to work in constant cooperation with lower layers of the hierarchy, making all parties interdependent. In such a context, decision-making becomes a mixture of top-down and bottom-up decisions. This is what Hofstede (1984) would call a short power distance, and his findings on this dimension seem most convincing (Denmark is extremely low, number 37 out of 40 countries).

Also, in a Danish setting, there is little or no personal control of subordinates' work, since they are supposed to be responsible for their sphere of work. They are self-directed, and control systems on the personal level are only enacted if something goes wrong. It is also important to note that it is acceptable for employees to make mistakes. The assumption is that if a person makes a mistake, it is because he or she has misunderstood, and therefore mistakes are generally not hushed up. This is in line with another basic attitude, namely that lying is unacceptable.

Having and delegating responsibility is one of the strong motivational factors for managers and employees alike, and the one that is most often used as an argument for the management style practiced. At the same time it also works as a compensation for earnings, which by European standards are not only rather low for the managerial group but also fall within a relatively narrow band.

The interpersonal relationships are characterized by a basic egalitarianism, which is cultivated by all parties concerned, and respect must be shown for each individual person whatever his or her rank. Indeed there are strong tendencies towards universalistic treatment in many situations. Deference as a value and behaviour pattern is rapidly disappearing, be it towards age, status or sex. There is a strong expectation that people should be treated alike as much as possible, and that differentials in treatment, if any, should be explained, i.e., be defended on a rational basis.

This egalitarianism entails or is preceded by an anti-hierarchical and an anti-authoritarian attitude. A hierarchy is considered a necessary evil for the functioning of an organization, but not a goal in itself, and the general opinion is that it should be kept to a strict minimum.

The anti authoritarian attitude is a natural complement to egalitarianism, which implies the value of human equality, but it also has to do with the ability of individuals to make independent assessments of situations and phenomena, an ability which is expected at all levels.

Egalitarianism of the sexes is a widespread ideology, and women are non-dependent and non-deferring towards men, but so far hierarchical egalitarianism has been difficult to implement in the face of traditional behaviour. There are still typical female occupations, and a division of work according to gender. Many women have administrative jobs, but only a few of them have reached the higher echelons of management. However, this pattern is likely to change rapidly as new generations of well-educated females are now entering the labour market.

Two further and related points should be made. The first is that an egalitarian and anti-authoritarian attitude may explain the informality, which is the norm in personal interaction both within and between all levels of the hierarchy. Informality in social behaviour is a way of disguising the differences that do exist in occupation, education and earnings. Informality can be observed in style of language as well as in dress, which tends to be more than relaxed compared to the standards in most other countries.

It follows from this that most people make a point of paying as little attention as possible to rank and status. On the other hand status symbols do exist. To take some obvious examples: a manager is expected to live up to certain standards in choice of car, office size, furniture, private consumption, etc. A person's title is an important status symbol, because it is considered to be the expression of proven performance, but at the same time such status symbols are often the object of jokes which serve to release tensions in this area of contradictory value themes.

The second point is that the egalitarian ideology has fostered anti-competitive norms. Indeed, the American idea of individual competitive achievement and the division of people into "winners" and "losers" is not popular in Denmark.

We would suggest that this is one of the many effects of "The Jante Law" (pronounced Yante). The "Jante Law" is probably one of the most significant characteristics of Danish culture. This "law", in point of fact an unwritten social code, was put into print before the middle of the century by the Danish–Norwegian author Aksel Sandemose (1899–1965). Jante is the fictional name he gave his home town in Denmark, where—according to Sandemose—the "Jante Law" was especially dominant. However, it probably dates centuries back, as Danish literature and cultural history abound with examples of its manifestations.

According to Sandemose, the key words to the Jante Law are adaptation, uniformity and envy, and the author coined ten commandments of which the first four read as follows:

1 Don't think that you are somebody.
2 Don't think that you are worth as much as we are.
3 Don't think that you are wiser than we are.
4 Don't think that you are better than we are.

It is generally accepted that this unwritten social code has profound implications for relationships and behaviour in the workplace as elsewhere.

One of the implications for management is the risk of repression of managerial initiative, since leaving the ranks in order to distinguish oneself at the expense of others is frowned upon. Another is that charismatic leadership is precarious, but then again it is acceptable if it is played down or exercised in a humourous way. This social norm may also lead to a certain self-censorship, as people have to consider how a certain action might be regarded.

It follows from this that the "Jante Law" probably exerts strong social control and entails a tendency towards uniformity and conformity. On the other hand Danes are increasingly conscious of its negative effects on performance and social interaction and they are inclined to condemn it.

Consensus and Cooperation

Any understanding of Danish management necessarily implies the realization of the strong impetus for consensus and cooperation. This attitude implies an emphasis on discussion and bargaining as participants work towards an acceptable compromise. However, in contrast to what may be seen for instance in France, where discussions seem to play an even more important role, Danes tend to formalize the procedure in regular meetings (Schramm-Nielsen 1991).

This can be explained by the very notion of cooperation which, in a Danish context, means working together towards a common goal. In consequence, the compromise has to be the result of negotiations between all parties concerned or the result has to be explained to and accepted by all parties concerned. This is exactly where the notion of delegation of responsibility becomes of crucial importance since, ideally, everybody concerned is supposed to have their right of expression before a decision is made.

The negative side to this consultative mode is of course that it is time-consuming, and also that it does not necessarily lead to the best decisions from a managerial point of view. Foreigners often note this collective dimension of Danish social life, for whereas individual ambition is seen somewhat negatively, collective ambition is well accepted and so are collective reward systems. The bourgeois government (1982–Jan. 1993) tried to introduce more individual differentiation in salary systems, but in popular discourse this is often called "rewards for ingratiation"!

An important point related to the notion of informality is that the general ethos of Danish management must be characterized as deeply anti-bureaucratic. This is not to say that there are no rules, but the heart of the notion is that formal rules should be kept to a strict minimum. We would like to suggest that one consequence of the general animosity to formalized, written rules and procedures, is the extensive meeting activity, which compensates for formal bureaucracy. Danish work culture abounds with implicit rules, which are negotiated and reinforced during meetings and other collective activities. To sum up, managerial work in Denmark requires the ability to explain, argue, persuade, conduct meetings and cope with the questioning attitude of employees.

Professionalism

Traditionally, Denmark was a society of farmers, craftsmen and merchants dominated by a guild system. This is still visible in the structure of unions and other organized interest groups (interest organizations). These traditions have a number of implications for Danish managerial culture.

The first is a pragmatic attitude and "trained intuition". Danish managers tend to look for pragmatic solutions and to be action and outcome-oriented. By trained intuition we mean to suggest a preference for solutions on the basis of practical experience. Also, problem-solving is seen as a whole including all the necessary steps from start of operation to implementation, a holistic pragmatism (Schramm-Nielsen 1991).

A pragmatic attitude also means that the persons involved and the methods at hand will determine the objectives to be attained. In other words Danes generally do not start with the formal objectives, but with the resources at hand (Holt Larsen 1987).

The strong emphasis on experience, application and practicality entails flexibility in daily work, but it has its drawbacks in being sometimes a barrier against visions and bold innovation. This penchant for utility and practicality may be labelled "*Praktizismus*" using a German term.

The second implication is the ethos of craftmanship and professionalism. We may hypothesize that "achievement" in Denmark is strongly related to the idea of excellence in occupational performance. In Denmark performance criteria are very clear, and weak performance is sanctioned, so the average level of performance is high. This is supported by a well-developed system of craft training and vocational schools, a system which has a long history.

The values of craftmanship have been generalized in the work culture on the national level, and there is a strong feeling in Denmark that national survival in international competition must be based on very high standards of performance. The craft culture and the ideals of quality may be defined as an important part of the cultural capital of the nation. What does this mean for managers? It means that a manager must be clearly competent to really deserve his position. In Denmark, authority flows from competence, not from titles, postures and status symbols.

It also means that there is no cult of theory in management circles. Pure theory is considered a waste of time. Theory has to be coupled with practice to be valuable (Wegens 1992). This can also be seen in the fact that educational schemes for budding managers which combine theory and experience are very popular and are now being further developed by several schools, which compete for students on this score.

It would not be wrong, we think, to speak of a certain anti-intellectualism in some quarters, and there is certainly less esteem for intellectual brilliance than one would find in other European countries such as France

and England. If we combine this lesser veneration for intellectualism with
the anti-authoritarian attitude that has been mentioned earlier and the
ability expected of everybody to be able to make independent assessments
of situations and phenomena, we might have a clue to another attitude
often encountered, namely a negative attitude towards the authority of
experts. Well-reasoned technocrats may be respected, but less so in
Denmark than in the neighbouring countries of Norway and especially
Sweden. This of course is related to the value theme we have called
Praktizismus.

Finally, the merchant tradition means that there is a strong emphasis on
trading activities including the mastery of several foreign languages, which
is a must for any Danish manager. Openness and flexibility are also characteristics often attributed to Danish managers.

It is well documented that work is a central life interest in Denmark,
which has the largest work force and the largest work volume in the EC,
relative to the size of the population (Petersen et al. 1991), but there is also
a widespread attitude that life is more than work.

In concluding this section it should be added that all cultures have
variations and contradictions. Clearly, some Danish managers do not fit
the above description. Thus, we may find at the top and at the bottom of
the size distribution of Danish companies more autocratic tendencies, for
instance among owners of small-scale production companies or in the
large, old, family-owned corporations, such as those that have been started
as shipping companies where the "captain" traditionally has preserved
centralized decision-making power, but then again, the latter examples are
very small in number.

Let us now turn to the societal background of management which
shapes, and in turn is shaped by, management.

Aspects of Danish Society

Denmark is one of the small Western democracies. Its area is 43,000
square kilometres—about the same size as Switzerland. The population is
5,146,000. From an historical and cultural point of view, Denmark is a part
of Scandinavia and has many ties to the other Scandinavian countries.
Denmark controlled a large part of Southern Sweden until 1658 and all of
Norway until 1814. The Scandinavian languages (Danish, Norwegian,
Swedish) are closely related to each other in structure and vocabulary.
Mutual understanding is fairly easy, especially since the spread of television. Cultural, social and political similarities between the Scandinavian
countries are striking, in spite of great differences in geographical structure

and resources. The welfare systems are highly developed, and in many quarters the well-developed welfare state is regarded as a Scandinavian invention. The Scandinavian countries have a common labour market, and they coordinate some of their political and administrative activities through the Nordic Council (established in 1953), of which Finland and Iceland also are members.

The distribution of the labour force in major economic sectors is a good indicator of the economic level of a country.

Table 1.   The Danish Labour Force in 1990   (in %)

Agriculture	5.8
Extraction of raw materials	0.1
Manufacturing	20.3
Electricity, gas	0.7
Construction	6.6
Market-oriented services	35.3
Non-market services	31.2
Total	**100**

Source: Statistical Ten-year Review 1991: 103

The picture is very clear: Denmark is an industrialized country with a highly developed service sector. The primary sector occupies only about 6 per cent of the labour force, while as much as two thirds of the labour force work in various services. The category "market-oriented services" includes trade, postal services, communications, transport (5 per cent), finance (4 per cent) and business services (5.5 per cent). Non-market services are mostly public services (public administration, public hospitals, education, etc.). The public sector is very large no matter which economic measure is used.

There is a high degree of female participation in the labour force—76 per cent of women between the ages of 16–66. This creates a need for services like nurseries and kindergartens. Public expenditure is among the highest in the world, and the government regards rationalization of the public sector as the "alpha and omega" of Denmark's ability to compete for labour and new industries in Europe (Finansministeriet 1992).

Denmark is highly dependent on foreign trade and now exports about 35% of the GNP. Denmark's trading partners are concentrated in the EC. In 1990 51.9 per cent of the export went to EC countries, with Germany alone accounting for 19.7 per cent. Outside the EC, Sweden and Norway, together, accounted for 18.5 per cent (Statistical Ten-year Review 1991). Denmark's export has increased considerably during the last ten years and the country now has a comfortable surplus on the balance of payments after many years of deficits.

The "raw material" of Denmark is arable land and considerable energy resources in the North sea. Sixty per cent of the land is under cultivation and 12 per cent is forested. There are now about 77,000 farms with an average size of 35 hectares. The number of farms is rapidly decreasing because of amalgamation into larger units. Danish agriculture is highly rationalized and has a very high productivity. Agriculture is at the centre of an agro-industrial complex delivering supplies to the sector and processing its output (dairies, slaughterhouses, food processing, etc.). There are extensive education and consultation services for the farmers. Cooperatives are common in some parts of the agri-business while most farms are family-owned. About 75 per cent of the agricultural production is exported, and Denmark is one of the world's largest exporters of bacon. The economic significance of agriculture makes it a strong force in Danish politics, despite the small proportion of the population that it employs.

Industry in Denmark dates back to the middle of the last century, but it developed slowly due to the lack of raw materials—coal and iron had to be imported. Only in the 1950s did industry become a dominant economic activity. Manufacturing now employs about 20 per cent of the labour force.

The size distribution of companies according to employment shows that Danish industry has many small units, only 1.1 per cent of the companies (81) units have 500 or more employees. Among these may be mentioned well-known companies such as Carlsberg Breweries, Lego Systems, Bang & Olufsen, Danfoss, Royal Copenhagen and Novo Industries. Danish industrialists and government are worried that the size distribution will make industry vulnerable to the increasing competition and to hostile takeovers in the new European market. It is often maintained that Denmark needs "large industrial locomotives" which can create growth and employment (Finansministeriet 1992). On the other hand, it is also argued that the size distribution makes Danish industry highly flexible in the face of rapid changes in international markets. Many of the successful companies may be described as "niche industries", e.g., in pharmaceutical products, hospital equipment, electronics, machinery and measuring instruments. Another characteristic of the manufacturing sector is the relatively low percentage of R&D expenses due to the size distribution. Government tries to stimulate the development of advanced technology processes and products, but it is doubtful how successful the various public projects have been. Another aspect of government policy is attempts to develop "networks" of smaller companies for the pooling of resources in the development of technology and export projects.

The size factor is often mentioned in economic and political debates in Denmark—as a resource and as an obstacle. Size does not determine social values directly, but the size distribution is related to the anti-bureaucratic ethos we have mentioned. "Small is beautiful" is a well-known expression in Denmark, also in managerial circles. Decentralization and divisionalization are in vogue in the larger companies, and this is in keeping with the general cultural ambiance.

An important sociological feature of the size distribution is the employees' closeness to the owners of the companies. In the smaller companies, the owner (or a family member) will often be the chief executive. "Family capitalism" is well developed in Denmark, but it is running into difficulties in some of the larger companies (e.g., because of family dissent, lack of capital, stagnation and conservatism). Closeness to the owners may increase the sense of personal responsibility for running a profitable business and provide training to cope with strategic issues. On the other hand, the manager's career may come to an abrupt end in family-owned companies when younger family members have received an appropriate education and come to take control. This situation seems to be quite common in the Scandinavian countries, but there are no studies of it. It reminds us that professional managers are also employees (Roomkin 1989) and in important respects are more vulnerable than many other occupational groups in modern society. Protection against dismissals is not well developed in Denmark.

Politics and Interest Groups

Denmark is a society with strong democratic values and strong democratic institutions. The Danish political system is based on the formal three-partite division of powers well known in all modern constitutions, but there are power bases in the economy which carry much influence in the political process. Therefore, the political system is often described as leaning towards "corporatism", i.e. a system in which interest organizations have regular and strong influence on political parties, parliament and bureaucracy. This system is institutionalized in a network of formal and informal councils and committees which serve as coordinating, controlling and bargaining mechanisms (Fivelsdal et al. 1979; Christensen 1991). Stratification and sectoral interests are basic to the system. Agriculture is the sector with the most articulate and integrated interest system, but most other sectors and strata are well organized and politically alert. Bargaining and political consensus-seeking are fundamental aspects of the political processes in general. Political attitudes are, of course, related to interests and structural resources, and it is striking that few issues are related to "ideology" in the sense of abstract principles of interpretation and action. Political culture in Denmark has a strong strain of *Praktizismus*!

A characteristic feature of the Danish organizational system is that there are neither religious nor cultural–ideological cleavages as in other European countries, where labour unions may be split along religious or political lines. The degree of organization (density of membership) is generally very high—labour union density is about 80 per cent (Scheuer 1992). Employers and industrial interests are also well organized. This makes for strong, unified interest organizations which have a long tradition of peaceful bargaining and cooperation.

Many unions and white-collar associations have occupation or profession as their membership criterion across sectors and industries. Professional associations for engineers, lawyers, economists and business school graduates are well developed, but their bargaining activities are mostly concentrated on the public sector. Incentives for membership include a range of educational activities, publications and various services. Of special importance for managers belonging to these associations is the extensive range of courses on managerial problems.

Labour unions and some of the white-collar unions (especially in the public sector) in Scandinavia have a long tradition of close cooperation with the Social Democratic Party (The Labour Party). The party was established in Denmark in 1871 and was first represented in Parliament in 1884. After 1900 the party grew rapidly in membership and influence, especially on the municipal level, which served as a school for democracy. In 1924 it formed the first Social Democratic government, and it has held political power in many consecutive periods. Because of its numbers, strong organization and political discipline, the labour movement has made a strong impact on Scandinavian societies. One may even speak of a Social-Democratic hegemony from the middle of the 30s until the middle of the 70s.

This hegemony which has been practiced in collaboration with some of the small non-socialist parties has developed and consolidated the Danish welfare state. An important part of the programme was a strong emphasis on the values of equality and democracy. "Denmark for the people!" was one of the earlier slogans, and this expresses the core value of a broad modernization programme which appealed to many groups in Danish society. Many economic institutions, the public administration and the school system have been gradually transformed in a more egalitarian direction, but no hegemony lasts forever. Since 1970 the Social Democratic programme has been under attack, and the economic problems of the 70s and the 80s led to the upsurge of new political strategies and changes in government. A Social Democratic coalition government was established in January 1993.

The new goals may be summarized under the headings of tax cuts, budget cuts, privatization, environmental goals and the rationalization of the welfare state. Private management practices are often presented as ideals for the public sector. Public administrators are being retrained to think in terms of efficiency, decentralization, service levels and market mechanisms (Coninck-Smith 1991).

Nowadays, political discourse is dominated to a high degree by economic terminology and economic arguments. To a large extent the political agenda is set by economists and the mass media. In the political parties, most of the top people now have an academic background in contrast to the situation twenty years ago, when farmers and union leaders held prominent positions in their respective parties. Perhaps we could call it a "managerial revolution" in parties and interest organizations.

For ten years, from 1982 to January 1993, Denmark had a non-socialist coalition government under Poul Schlüter as Prime Minister. This government was critical of many aspects of public administration and public spending, but it was unable to implement large tax cuts, and so far all the welfare rights have been preserved. The balance of payments have improved considerably, but the other side of the coin is increasing unemployment. In early 1993 there was over 10 per cent unemployment. The government (among others) believes that education will be one of the important ways to combat unemployment, that is, educating the unemployed as well as the new generations entering the labour market. This policy has put the educational system under strain in recent years, and the professional associations are increasingly worried that there is an overproduction of university and professional school graduates. Let us now take a look at the educational system.

Aspects of Education

Perhaps we get closest to the operative values of a society when we study its educational system. There are many factors involved: the organization of the system, the curricula, standards of performance, evaluation systems, relations between students and teachers, manifest and latent connections to the economy and the power systems (Archer 1979). Basic national values and the "cultural capital" are reproduced and developed through the educational system. In industrial societies, long education is a major prerequisite for the functioning of the economic and political system. To understand managers and managerial values, we should also look at education.

The Danish educational system is based on egalitarianism and democratic values. It does not attempt to develop "samurais", but young people who have social as well as cognitive skills and who are set on developing themselves further, according to their own talents and inclinations. It is basically a liberal–pragmatic view of the goals of education in a highly developed society.

The purpose of the primary and lower secondary education (*Folkeskole*) is expressed as follows:

> The aim of the Folkeskole is—in cooperation with parents—to give pupils a possibility of acquiring knowledge, skills, working methods and ways of expressing themselves which will contribute to the all-round development of the individual pupil. In all its work, the *Folkeskole* must try to create possibilities of experience and self-expression which allows pupils to increase their desire to learn, expand their imagination, and develop their ability for making independent assessments, evaluations and opinions. The *Folkeskole* shall prepare pupils for taking an active interest in their environment and for participation in decision-making in a democratic society, and for sharing responsibility for the solution of common problems. Thus, teaching and the entire daily life in school must be based on intellectual liberty and democracy. (Ministry of Education 1988)

This formulation is presently under revision, but it gives in a nutshell the legitimation of the basic part of the national school system. On the operative level there are differences in performance between schools and between teachers, but the main theme is clear enough. Foreign observers are often impressed by the good social atmosphere in Danish schools, where there are few grades and no streaming.

Priority is given to functional training rather than formal learning, and teachers should prepare pupils for life in society and for taking part in economic life. Ways and means include appeals to the pupils' reasonableness and interests instead of moralizing and coercion, and laying emphasis, when teaching, on dialogue and the narrative style. One of the aims of this pedagogy is to foster a relaxed atmosphere of tolerance, cooperation, and harmony rather than an atmosphere of competition and elitism.

After finishing the *Folkeskole*, students may engage in vocational training or continue theoretical work at the "Gymnasium", i.e., the 3-year course of general upper secondary education which is a platform for university entrance. Students now compete for entrance to the university or professional school level. The budding manager will either choose a technical or a business education—or he/she may study law, economics or political science at university.

Depending on the line chosen, vocational training is by no means a blind alley as far as a managerial position is concerned. Many small firms promote from within, and there are many opportunities for further training in managerial disciplines. It should be added that some companies prefer to select trainees at an early stage and expose them to an internal or branch management training system. This is true of banks, among others.

Universities and professional schools develop occupational specialists. Civil engineers may take some courses in economics and organization, but the primary concern for them is still the technological specialty chosen.

Business schools have previously been controlled by economists with a university background, and their main goal has predictably been to train micro-economists or functional specialists (accountants, marketing specialists, finance specialists, export managers, personnel managers, etc.) Business schools are themselves organized along such functional or disciplinary lines, which cause strong institute identification, tensions between disciplinary groups and problems in developing new fields.

The major directions in business education were established many years ago. First, the 3-year Bachelor of Business Administration (BBA) with a broad selection of economic sub-areas. Second, on top of the BBA, a 2-year Master of Science (M.Sc.) programme which, so far, has been offered with a broad range of electives. Third, there is the extension programme, a 4-year night school course mostly attended by people who have jobs. After 2 years of macro-economics, business, statistics and law, the students sign up for 2 years of special studies in one of the functional specialties (e.g., accounting, marketing, finance, organization, etc.), for which a thesis is required. It is a rather tough programme with a high drop-out rate. It is interesting to note that, in addition to people with no academic background, many engineering graduates choose to take this line, as it makes them more eligible for managerial positions.

As stated earlier, the Danish business education system has a very large capacity. At the time of writing at least 20,000 students are enrolled at the main schools, to which can be added students attending other types of business education or combinations of theoretical studies and on-the-job training. This is a large proportion for a population of just over five million, and it reflects the importance of business and trade.

Almost all education in Denmark is public, all education is state funded, and there is practically no paid tuition. There are no elite schools, elitism being against the credo of egalitarianism. However, the demand for higher education has long exceeded the available means, and a numerus clausus, i.e. restricted admission, has had to be practised, making some routes elitist as far as academic prerequisites are concerned.

Another characteristic is that the educational infrastructure is kept as open and flexible as possible, allowing people to "go back to school" at any stage of life. This obviously also means that age is unimportant. This is in strong contrast to for instance the French system, where students get a minus if they do not complete their education according to standard schemes. A great variety of schemes for part-time studies makes it possible to both study and stay on the job.

Over the past ten years, a host of new lines of business education have been created to compensate for the functional specializations, which many felt had become too narrow and out of step with business needs. These new lines of business education combine business economics with other disciplines like engineering, law, computer science, mathematics and languages and culture, and they are all extremely popular with students. In line with the *Praktizismus* orientation of Danish business life, several new lines also combine business economics with built-in practice.

With a traditionally large foreign trade, many Danish managers have been used to coping on foreign markets, but with the growing internationalization of Danish business life, the understanding of foreign cultures was given higher priority, and this element is now increasingly becoming part of business school curricula along with extended programmes in foreign languages. After many years of secluded life, the humanities are now seen as a complement to business life.

Another feature of business education which has emerged recently is the use of project work built into the curricula. While working on such a project, the students form self-directing study groups supported by a tutor, and given the tradition of independence and autonomy of Danish students, this formula has gained in popularity, making the aspiring manager self-reliant as well as sensitive to problems of cooperation.

From Squirearchy to Social Welfare

Danish society has not always been as democratic and egalitarian as it is today. If we go back to the 18th century, the societal structure was that of a squirearchy, i.e., a small class of landed proprietors dominating a poor peasantry. In the late 18th century, a top-down government decision enacted important structural land reforms, which gave emancipation to the Danish peasant and a gradual transition from copyhold to freehold tenure. This was to prove of crucial importance, since it was the start of a long modernization process, economically and politically.

In the early decades of the 19th century, there was a growing concern for individual rights and freedom of expression, and the first steps were taken towards representative government. The first liberal constitution was introduced in 1849, when the king was persuaded to relinquish his absolute rule and hand over power and responsibility to the National Liberal Party. This was also the period when the medieval system of town trade was abolished and liberty of trade and economic reforms opened the door to a modern capitalistic development. Early 19th century also saw another great reform, when, in 1814, general compulsory education was introduced. From the middle of the century, education played an increasing role in Danish economic and political life, and one outstanding person who contributed to this was Grundtvig, clergyman, poet, historian, educationalist, and opinion former.

For Grundtvig, the main enemy in pedagogical matters was the classical Latin culture with its drill, rigorous discipline and abstract learning.

Instead of just imparting knowledge, education, he thought, should inspire personal, national and Christian endeavour, and to Grundtvig the word, not the book, is the best means of education. He was convinced of the paramount importance of dialogue, and today, one would say that he considered it of vital importance to avoid one-way communication. In Church matters as well as in education Grundtvig played an enormous role in the struggle against authoritarian ways of life, and in both fields he pleaded for freedom, democracy and dialogue.

This critical attitude towards authorities and authoritarian methods was taken up by several political parties, not least the Social Democratic Party which grew in importance from the turn of the century. There is much evidence to suggest that today's democratic and humanistic attitude of the Danish educational system can be ascribed, to a large degree, to the efforts of the Social Democratic Party which was almost uninterruptedly in power, alone or in various coalitions, from the 30s to 1982, and whose political and ideological goal was to promote egalitarianism via the education system.

Thus, from an originally autocratic society, by means of reforms, debates and gradual changes, Danes have developed their egalitarian and participative style in political, economic and social life. As has been indicated above, this did not come about overnight. Actually, autocratic tendencies were present up to the period after the Second World War, when the modernization process, in the present meaning of the word, took off.

It follows from this that democratization has been a slow, gradual, step-by-step process, and we would like to suggest that this is also a characteristic of Danish society: although social life has not been devoid of clashes between interest groups, for instance on the labour market, there have been no abrupt changes, no revolutions, and in recent history no civil wars. In fact, Denmark is basically a non-violent country. This, we believe, can be attributed to the homogeneous nature of the society, where the basic values are shared by the greater part of its members, making variations relatively small. In such a society, the degree of consensus tends to be strong (Enz 1986). This, we would suggest, might explain the attitude of cooperation, consensus and compromise that we find at the societal as well as the organizational level.

However, democracy does not altogether explain the anti-authoritarian attitude of the Danes, since many other countries can rightly claim to be democratic without having a similar aversion to authorities. Here we would venture to bring into the picture the importance of Protestantism, although the importance of this dimension may not be so easy to establish. One reason is that Danes are generally not active believers, church attendance is extremely low, and Danes seldom speak of religious matters. However, the vast majority of Danes do adhere to what we would call a Lutheran–Protestant ethic.

At the core of the Protestant movement of Luther, Calvin and their followers was the protest against the use of power in questions of faith. The message of the Protestant leaders was that faith and faith alone would lead to salvation, and faith cannot be forced upon a person or salvation bought for that matter. Only in a state of freedom can the individual choose to be a believer. One of the implications was to reject the authority of the Church of Rome in spiritual as well as in mundane matters and to reject the entire church hierarchy. Instead Protestantism stresses the importance of a direct contact between the individual human being and God, without mediators of any kind. In the Protestant ethic, this direct, non-mediated contact with the highest authority is of crucial importance (Weber 1958). Another central concept in Protestant thinking is personal and independent judgement in moral and religious matters. Modesty is also part of the Protestant value system, potentially the source of the "Jante Law".

What we wish to imply here is that anti-authoritarianism is as central and fundamental a value in the Protestant ethic as it is in Grundtvigian thinking, and that this has had a profound impact on the reforms carried out in the Danish educational system.

Given the impact of education as a socializing agent we can now re-establish the links between important principles of Danish education and Danish managerial attitudes. The fact that Danish managers tend to prefer pragmatic, comprehensive solutions in problem-solving may be ascribed more to functional training in primary/lower secondary education than to formal learning. In Grundtvigian terms, theoretical abstractions were replaced by pragmatic usefulness (Schramm-Nielsen 1991).

When Danish managers practice soft management, i.e., delegate responsibility and employ light control, the reason may be that education insists on independent assessment, evaluations and opinions and on participation in decision-making—in the Grundtvigian philosophy the importance of dialogue, vertical as well as horizontal between all parties concerned. The fact that employees are allowed to openly disagree with their superior should be seen in the light of the principle of intellectual liberty and democracy of the Danish *Folkeskole*, and the Protestant principle of confidence in the judgement of the individual, for both Grundtvigianism as well as Protestantism represent an anti-authoritarian and anti-hierarchical ideology.

Concluding Remarks

At the outset we assumed that there are broad value themes in Danish culture, which are rooted in the history of the country and institutionalized in social, economic and political structures.

The picture we have painted, admittedly with a very broad brush, has allowed us to see that contemporary Danish managerial practice has not come about accidentally, but, in fact, is the consequence of historical evolution, and that it represents a consistent set of values reproduced over time. In other words, the surface structures that we can register today are rooted in historical deep-structures. Seen in an historical perspective, such a penetration of shared understanding may be a confirmation of the stability of fundamental cultural traits; their consistency over time points to their endurance, and they will therefore probably be very slow to change.

Note

*The first part of this chapter is based on some of the few studies that have been made on Danish managers (Holt Larsen 1990; Lindkvist 1992; Schramm-Nielsen 1990, 1991; Wegens 1992). It especially draws on Schramm-Nielsen 1991, which is a qualitative study that inquires more specifically into the Hofstedian cultural dimensions (Hofstede 1984). It is also inspired by a workshop on Scandinavian Management held at the Copenhagen Business School in May 1991. Last, but not least, it draws on the authors' own professional experience and their knowledge of managerial practice in other countries. For a well-documented survey of the Scandinavian countries, see Fullerton and Knowles (1991). Problems of innovation in Denmark are discussed in Borum and Kristensen (1989). Topical problems of Danish business are presented in *Business Denmark* (1992). Empirical work on Danish politics is published in English in the political science journal *Scandinavian Political Studies*. Important sources of statistics on Denmark used in this chapter are *Statistical Ten-Year Review* (1991) and *Statistical Yearbook* (1991).

References

Archer, Margaret S. (1979): *Social origins of educational systems*. London: Sage.
Borum, Finn and Peer Hull Kristensen (eds.) (1989): *Technological innovation and organizational change. Danish patterns of knowledge, networks and culture*. Copenhagen: New Social Science Monographs—Nyt fra Samfundsvidenskaberne.
Business Denmark 1992, The yearbook of Danish business. Copenhagen: Business Denmark Publications.
Christensen, Jørgen Grønnegård (1991): *Den usynlige stat*. Copenhagen: Gyldendal.
Coninck-Smith, Niels de (1991): "Restructuring for efficiency in the public sector" *McKinsey Quarterly* 4: 133–150.
Enz, Cathy A. (1986): "New directions for cross-cultural studies: Linking organizational and societal cultures" in Richard N. Farmer, (ed.), *Advances in international comparative management* Vol 2, 173–189. Greenwich, Conn.: JAI Press.

Finansministeriet (1992): *Finansredegørelse 92*. Copenhagen: Finansministeriet.

Fivelsdal, E., T. Beck Jørgensen and P.E. Daugaard Jensen (1979): *Interesseorganisationer og centraladministration*. Copenhagen: Nyt fra Samfundsvidenskaberne.

Fullerton, Brian and Richard Knowles (1991): *Scandinavia*. London: Paul Chapman.

Hofstede, Geert (1984): *Culture's consequences*. London: Sage.

Holt Larsen, Henrik "Made in Scandinavia" in *Børsen* [newspaper] May 6, 1987.

Holt Larsen, Henrik (1990): *Lederudvikling på jobbet*. Copenhagen: Valmuen.

Lindkvist, Lars (1992): "Management in the Nordic countries—differences and similarities". Unpublished paper. Copenhagen: Institute of Organization and Industrial Sociology, Copenhagen Business School.

Ministry of Education (1988): *The Folkeskole. Primary and lower secondary education in Denmark*. Copenhagen: Ministry of Education.

Petersen, Eggert et al. (1991): *De trivsomme og arbejdssomme danskere. Krisen og den politisk-psykologiske udvikling 1982–90*. Aarhus: Psykologisk Institut, Aarhus Universitet.

Roomkin, Myron J. (ed.) (1989): *Managers as employees*. New York: Oxford University Press.

Scheuer, Steen (1992): "Denmark: Return to decentralization" in Anthony Ferner and Richard Hyman (eds.), 168–197. *Industrial relations in the new Europe*. Oxford: Blackwell.

Schramm-Nielsen, Iette (1990): *Relations de travail franco-danois dans les entreprises privées*. Copenhagen: Integrated Modern Languages and Economics Centre, Copenhagen Business School.

Schramm-Nielsen, Iette (1991): *Dansk-fransk samarbejde i erhvervsvirksomheder. En komparative undersøgelse*. Copenhagen: Center for Sprogøkonomi.

Statistical Ten-Year Review 1991. Copenhagen: Danmarks Statistik.

Statistical Yearbook 1991. Copenhagen: Danmarks Statistik.

Weber, Max (1958): *The Protestant ethic and the spirit of capitalism*. New York: Scribner.

Wegens, Jesper (1992): "Seniorlederen". (Unpublished project paper). Copenhagen: Institute for Organization and Industrial Sociology, Copenhagen Business School.

Chapter 4: England

English Culture and Business Organizations

Monir Tayeb

Introduction

This chapter is intended to demonstrate how the business climate of English organizations is influenced by their societal culture, political environment and economic context. The relationships between these parameters are of course interactive and very complex. The assumption here is that the political and economic factors interact with societal culture, and societal culture causes the business climate and approach to management.

The structure of the chapter follows the same sequence. The first section briefly discusses the salient societal cultural characteristics which are attributed to the English. The second section elaborates on those characteristics which are more likely to be relevant to business activities and business organizations. The third and fourth sections discuss England's political and economic systems. The last section details how the English business climate is shaped by these several influences.

Societal Culture

England—The Country

England is a part of the United Kingdom of Great Britain (England, Wales, Scotland) and Northern Ireland, an island nation to the west of the continental mainland of Europe. England is predominantly a lowland country and has a generally mild and temperate climate.

Britain emerged into recorded history with the arrival of the Celts in the British Isles. It was occupied by the Romans in the first century AD and an ordered civilization was established under their rule for about three hundred years. The Romans withdrew completely from Britain by the fifth century to be followed by a long period of increasing disorder caused by raids—mainly Angle, Saxon and Jute—on the island from northern Europe. In the following two centuries, the raiders established settlements and a number of small kingdoms were created. In the ninth century, further settlers arrived from Europe and the Vikings from Scandinavia pillaged the east coast and established settlements there. The last successful invasion of England took place in the eleventh century, when Normans from the coast of Northern France took complete control and imposed a full feudal system.

Immigration from Europe over the centuries has led to the establishment of Irish and Jewish communities in many of the larger cities. In the latter part of the twentieth century, immigrants from the South Asian countries and the Caribbean also formed distinctive urban communities. This chapter deals only with the English among the various peoples of Britain because it is their cultural characteristics and their political system which predominate and have the greatest influence on business performance. Nevertheless, the United Kingdom is a multi-cultural society and in Wales, Scotland, Northern Ireland and those parts of England where Asian and Afro-Caribbean communities predominate—or in companies elsewhere in the U.K., whose entrepreneurial bases originate from them—the values of these communities fuse with those of the English to create nuances in business style and practice, which can be significant.

England—The Culture

A seminal and perhaps the first comprehensive empirical survey on the subject was conducted by Gorer (1955) among the readers of a popular national newspaper. His findings characterized the English as aggressive, shy, reserved, class conscious, and law-abiding, having high ideals of conduct both for themselves and for others.

This was followed by Terry (1979), who made an extensive survey of the literature on the English and their cultural values and attitudes written by both English and non-English writers, and other observers. He identified thirteen significantly English characteristics which go beyond those found by Gorer. These are conservatism, tenacity, compromise, rural focus, liberty and individualism, violence and aggression, class consciousness, love of sport and fair play, pragmatism, reserve, lack of ambition, chauvinism, and orderliness and discipline.

Later still, Tayeb (1984) identified, from her occupationally representative sample, thirty major characteristics attributed to the English, in order of significance. Table 1 lists these attributes from most significant to least, as seen by her 100 English respondents.

Table 1.   Major English Characteristics

Characteristics	Rank Order
Strong sense of responsibility	1
Trustworthy	2
Cope well with set-backs	3
See things through	4
Honest	5
Self-control	6
Self-confidence	7
Independence	8
Law-abiding	9
Cope well with new and uncertain situations	9
Disciplined	10
Friendly	10
Not afraid of powerful people	11
Prefer to work on their own	12
Obedient to their seniors	13
Tolerant	14
Trusting	15
Rational	16
Not open to bribery	17
Interested in community affairs	18
Respect the law to the letter	19
Fair play	20
Aggressive	21
Prefer to be in a group	22
Respect powerful people	22
Reserved	23
Hate to be dictated to	24
Class conscious	24
Opposed to change	25
Prefer to merge with the crowd	26
Willing to take account of others' opinion	27
Play safe	28
Modest	29
Do not believe in fate	30

The characteristics that are most significantly present in English culture and which are more likely to have a bearing on English business climate and approach to management are individualism, deference and acceptance of inequality, self-control and reserve, conservatism, xenophobia, honesty and trust, regard for liberty, and class consciousness. These will be discussed below in some detail. However, given the stratified nature of

English social structure, one needs to examine first if there is such a thing as English culture.

Social class differences are a well recognized feature of English life, and the literature on English culture shows that middle-class and working-class people are different from one another in terms of the degree to which they hold certain values and attitudes. Gorer (1955) argued that middle-class people participate in voluntary and charity activities and fund-raising functions to a greater extent than their working-class compatriots, because they have a guilty conscience about their poorer countrymen. Raynor (1969), commenting on working-class people, states that they like to exhibit their aggression and physical toughness. Tayeb (1984) found that working-class people seem to regard others in their walk of life as being less interested in community affairs, more modest, less rational, less law-abiding, and possessing less self-control.

On the whole, however, the similarities between working and middle classes are far greater than the differences between the two. Although members of the two classes experience a different family upbringing, they are more or less equally exposed to other social institutions such as school, religion, mass media and the like. The advanced communications systems within the society have also facilitated the fusion of values and attitudes among people. It may therefore be safe to assume for our purpose here that the two broad classes of English society are sufficiently alike to talk about an English culture.

Organizationally-relevant Attitudes and Values

Individualism

Child-rearing practices and the religion of the English appear to be the major sources of their individualism. Although the present middle-class family in England is a loosely-knit and nuclear one, and the English working-class family is a network of comparatively closely-knit and dense relationships, autonomy and independence are inculcated in the children from an early age in both classes. Children in middle-class families are regarded as independent individuals and are "pushed" towards independence at an age as early as two or three. Parents do not interfere with their children's affairs, at least not directly, especially after the age of puberty. Children have great freedom in matters like further education, marriage, social intercourse with people and the choice of a job, but parents very subtly and indirectly dissuade them from, say, becoming involved with partners of a lower class than their own, and engaging in jobs and general affairs considered undesirable and radically deviant from the norms of their own social class.

Life for the working-class child is harsher, on the whole, than that of his/her middle-class counterpart. Attitudes are more authoritarian, the father is the head of the household and demands obedience from the child. Even so, in common with middle class practice, the independence of the children is valued and they are literally "pushed" out of home at an early age (Rose 1968; Roberts 1978).

The main religion of the English is Christianity. A vast majority of those who claim any church membership (a minority of the population) belong to some organized Protestant Church, especially the Church of England, rather than to the Roman Catholic Church. Protestantism, which came to England during the reign of Henry VIII (1509–1547), both as part of the wider protest against the interposition of the Church between God and the believer, and as an expression of nascent English nationalism, tended to replace those patterns of the society into which the institutions of the Church were integrated, with a more individualistic system.

Weber (1930) considered that the change from feudalism to capitalism and private ownership in English economic structure took place in the sixteenth century, and he saw Protestantism as the driving force behind capitalism. In Weber's view, Protestantism was instilled into the modern economic person from the cradle onwards, stressing personal responsibility, ability and initiative. Thus, although modern capitalism was derived from the peculiarities of Western social structure, it was inconceivable without it, for it "had the psychological effect of freeing the acquisition of goods from the inhibitions of traditionalistic ethics" (p. 171).

It seems, however, that the origins of individualism and the "capitalist ethic" in England can be identified long before the sixteenth century. Macfarlane (1978) argues that "the majority of people in England from at least the thirteenth century were rampant individualists, highly mobile both geographically and socially, economically 'rational', market-oriented and acquisitive, and ego-centred in kinship and social life" (p. 163), and from the thirteenth century onwards "it is not possible to find a time when an Englishman did not stand alone. Symbolized and shaped by his ego-centred kinship system, he stood at the centre of his world" (p. 196). Protestantism appears to have encouraged and reinforced this individualism and the spirit of capitalism.

However, it has to be added that the "Protestant ethic and the spirit of capitalism", which once were the major driving forces behind the Industrial Revolution, seem to have declined among the English since then (Barnett 1972; Roderick and Stephens 1978, 1981, 1982; Wiener 1981). Nor do the English seem to be as highly individualistic as, say, the Americans (Jamieson 1980; Wiener 1981).

Deference and Inequality

Deference and obedience to seniors are held strongly as a virtue by the English. Further, English people are said to respect those in power. Yet at the same time, they do not like to be ordered about and hate to be dictated to. In effect, they respect authority when it is used well.

The English, wrote Bagehot a century ago, are a deferential nation.

> Certain persons are by common consent agreed to be wiser than others, and their opinion is by consent, to rank for much more than its numerical values. We may in these happy nations weigh votes as well as count them. . . Instead of resenting the assumed superiority of a relative few, many Englishmen defer to those they regard as legitimately superior. (Bagehot 1963: 141)

Although leaders enjoy special advantages in English politics by virtue of this deference to people in positions of authority, this same attitude also reflects the expectation that leaders will pay attention to the needs and the desires of their followers. Democratic elections are the main institutional restraints upon leaders, and regulate their activities. A sense of trust is also pervasive in the attitudes of the people towards political leaders and government. Rose (1965: 43) points out that "the ancient legal maxim, 'the Queen can do no wrong', suggests the viewpoint that the government is not a menace to English men [and women]" (see also Almond and Verba 1963).

Self-control and Reserve

The English are a disciplined people, with control over both themselves and their emotions. To me, as a person from an emotional culture (Iran), the English at first seemed unemotional and without feelings, but once I got to know them better, I found that they are indeed emotional, beneath the surface. The difference between the English and the Iranians is that the former refrain from expressing their emotions in public, which may have something to do with their love of privacy, whereas the latter are, in general, less inhibited in showing their finer feelings and emotions in the company of others.

Conservatism

The English are widely seen to be a nation with a love for the past, traditionalism and conservatism, and a reluctance to change. These characteristics are clearly manifested, for instance, in the careful preservation of old buildings and monuments, and in the detailed attention to public ceremonies such as the annual pageantry surrounding the opening of the Parliament, which has its roots in centuries-old traditions.

Xenophobia

The English are a tolerant, friendly people who believe in fair play, have a high public spirit and take an active interest in community affairs. These fine feelings, however, do not seem to be extended towards foreigners to the same extent as they are to fellow Englishmen and women.

England's geographical insularity has been a mixed blessing. As an island, the country has been sheltered to some extent from expansionist invaders. Also, because of this relative immunity, the country, unlike many landlocked countries, has never needed a strong standing army; as a result, the armed forces have not become a tool in the hands of rulers nor have they been used to suppress the people.

However, the other side of the insularity coin has meant that the English have developed relatively insular and xenophobic attitudes towards non-English people. The construction of the Channel tunnel linking England and France illustrates this point well. The English and French intended to build the tunnel as early as 1802, but whenever England seemed tempted to link itself physically with the Continent, history and xenophobia intervened (*Time* 1990). For instance, in 1858, the then Prime Minister, Lord Palmerston, in response to renewed interests in the tunnel, said "What! You pretend to ask us to contribute to a work, the object of which is to shorten a distance which we find already too short?" Lord Randolph Churchill, arguing against a Channel-tunnel bill in 1889, is reported as saying "The reputation of England has hitherto depended upon her being as it were, *virgo intacta*". As recently as November 1990, the opening of the first minuscule connection in the tunnel to France brought out insulting headlines in one of the most popular English newspapers.

Honesty and Trust

The English are in general trustworthy, honest and trusting (Rowntree and Lavers 1951; Almond and Verba 1963). Having come from a different culture, Iran, where the state of trust among people in general is lower, and having conducted research in India, where the public administration is bedevilled by corruption, I personally perceive the English to be more

honest and trusting than the Indians and Iranians. As a research student at
Oxford in the mid-1970s, one of the things that struck me most at the
Centre for Management Studies was the fact that students and fellows alike
could use the photocopying machine as frequently as they wished without
any control, counter key or supervision. All you had to do was to write
down in a little book the number of the photocopies taken each time. I can
think of many countries where this would be unthinkable!

Liberty

Among the rights of Englishmen and women, liberty is considered pre-
eminent. Traditionally, individual liberty has been protected by Common
law against Crown and State. As has already been pointed out, the absence
of land frontiers has meant that the country has not needed a large standing
army, and so she has avoided the threat posed to public liberty by the
presence of an ever-ready agency for use by the executive power. Today,
respect for the liberty to speak, act and travel where one pleases is so
deeply inculcated in the individual that there are few statutory guarantees
for liberty: it is taken for granted. However, the enjoyment of liberty may
sometimes be curtailed by the activities of government departments, and in
the conflict between the claims of an individual for libertarian rights and
the claims of a government department, the individual is often the loser. It
must be added, however, that one of the basic principles of the unwritten
English constitution is the rule of law and the equality of individuals before
the law.

Class Consciousness

The English are said to be obsessed with class differentiation (Terry 1979).
Almost everybody one speaks with can place themselves in one class or
other. According to Gorer's survey in 1955, nine out of ten English people
felt no hesitation in assigning themselves to a social class (Gorer 1955). In
1971 he found that 35 per cent of the people whose attitudes he surveyed
thought they belonged to the middle class and 65 per cent to the working
class (Gorer 1971).

Family background, education, and even accent, betray people's social
class. The class hierarchy broadly consists of upper class (a very small
proportion of the total population), middle class and working class, but
there are subtle gradations within the classes rather than sharp and rigid
divisions and, moreover, the structure is a dynamic one in that there is

movement between classes. This stratified structure is not regulated by laws, as were the estates of medieval times, or by rituals, as are the castes in India, but is based on the way the different members of society regard their own position and that of others.

The values and attitudes of the society are dominated by those of the middle class, since, by definition, they occupy most of the positions of power and persuasion—in Parliament, the civil service, universities, mass communication media, financial and commercial institutions and the church.

How Do the English Compare With Other Western Europeans?

To put this sketch of the English into perspective, we can turn to Hofstede's (1980) massive study of cultural dimensions across 40 countries, which covers 11 of the EC countries, including Britain. The British sample may include also non-English respondents (Scots, Welsh, etc.), but given the size of English population as a whole (over 50m out of 56m), the majority will have been English. Table 2 was constructed using Hofstede's results. The nations are listed in alphabetical order.

Table 2.   Comparison of Cultural Dimensions Across 11 EC Countries

Country	Power Distance	Uncertainty Avoidance	Individulism	Masculinity
Belgium	65	94	75	54
Britain	35	35	89	66
Denmark	18	23	74	16
Eire	28	35	70	68
France	68	86	71	43
Germany	35	65	67	66
Greece	60	112	35	57
Italy	50	75	76	70
Netherlands	38	53	80	14
Portugal	63	104	27	31
Spain	57	86	51	42

As the table shows, the British (and quite probably the English) perceive less power distance, are better able to cope with uncertainty, are more individualistic and more ambitious and aggressive (have a masculine culture) than most of their continental counterparts. Hofstede attributed the differences between his samples on these dimensions to cultural, historical and geographical factors.

Political System

The present political culture reflects a range of values and philosophies. Traditional Tories believe in a corporatist economy, managed by a technocratic élite, and moderated by the controls of party government and parliamentary democracy. The "Thatcherite" Conservatives sought to move the burdens of social choice from government and politics to the market. Following 1979, the Conservative government pursued policies of free enterprise, competition and less state intervention and its top priority was to furnish a framework within which private business can succeed. Over the same period, the Labour Party abandoned many of its socialist policies, such as nationalization, unilateral nuclear disarmament and hostility to the European Community. It shifted its emphasis towards "caring capitalism" with both private and "social" ownership. The Liberal Democrats see their position as that of a party of the middle ground. The Greens place their emphasis on the overarching importance of the natural environment, and to some extent have succeeded in influencing public opinion and the policies of the major parties.

In the absence of an electoral system based on proportional representation, in the past sixty years or so governments have been formed either by the Conservative or Labour parties only.

Economic Context

England was the home of capitalism, which determined its evolution (Weber 1930, 1961), even though capitalism developed slowly. As early as the end of the Middle Ages there was a system that could be called "commercial capitalism". This system changed to "industrial capitalism" in the eighteenth century and for nearly two hundred years took on a *laissez faire* character, which implied opposition to government interference and a belief in free competition and the unrestricted liberty of the individual (Dore 1973; Macfarlane 1978).

The contemporary economy can hardly be called a pure version of capitalism since it is characterized by a mixture of freedom and control, and of private and state enterprise. The emphasis on freedom or control shifts from time to time depending on the policies of the government of the day. Since the 1920s, Labour governments have tended to use direct powers to control the economy, in addition to using fiscal measures to regulate growth. Conservative governments, on the other hand, have tended to rely mainly on fiscal policy, or what has recently been called "monetarism", rather than direct intervention.

Since 1979 the economic scene has been dominated by "Thatcherism", labelled after the former Prime Minister, Mrs Thatcher. In the pursuit of her policies, over two-thirds of the state-owned companies were privatized, control over foreign exchange was lifted, taxes were reduced, industry was deregulated and companies were left on their own to compete in a free market with domestic and foreign competitors. As a result, higher productivity and an "enterprise culture" returned to the country and wealth creation became respectable. However, a price had to be paid for all this in terms of high interest rates, unemployment, companies going out of business, and strains in the state education and health services.

The Resulting Business Climate and Approach to Management

Attitudes Towards Industry and Business

On the surface, as some commentators (*The Economist* 1989) point out, the 1980s saw a resurgence in the desire of Britons to do well in business and to get rich. The so-called "enterprise culture" made money-making more respectable. The City of London lured people from all classes to enjoy its telephone-number (i.e. six-figure) salaries, Porsche cars and insider-dealing trials. Something happened to revive the work ethic and pep up ambitious managers to work long hours, to stay sober at lunch, and to feel it was again possible to become rich through work. Nevertheless, the English display little love of business. This may be traced to the English educational system and its dominant values and priorities.

A major feature of the English educational institutions is their greater emphasis on arts and classics and the relatively low priority given to engineering and technology. This, as many writers have pointed out, betrays a significant influence of middle-class values in which arts subjects are still favoured, relatively speaking, and anything concerning industry and technology is disdained (see for instance, Barnett 1972; Jamieson 1980; Wiener 1981; Roderick and Stephens 1981).

Moreover, it is still not clear whether those with the best education want to go into business. In 1979 the proportion of new graduates from Cambridge University going into "industry", a category which includes manufacturing, civil engineering and some services, but not the City or banking, was 16 per cent. By 1988 it had fallen to 9 per cent. On the other hand, the proportion going into "commerce", which includes stockbroking, other financial services, advertising and management consultancy, rose from 8 per cent to 13 per cent, probably partly at industry's expense. Nevertheless, the combined total dropped from 24 per cent to 22 per cent. The picture is much the same using the figures for all university graduates (*The Economist* 1989).

Trade Unions

Although the origins of the trade union movement can be traced back to the craft guilds of the Middle Ages, the modern trade union is essentially a product of the Industrial Revolution (Irwin 1976). Union membership is industry- and craft based and cuts across firms and organizations. As a result, there are likely to be several unions in the same factory or office, bargaining not just with employers but against each other. Overall information on this is sketchy, but according to the latest Workplace Industrial Relations Survey, 35 per cent of manual workers and 61 per cent of non-manual workers still had more than one union at their place of work in 1984, compared with 35 per cent and 57 per cent, respectively, in 1980 (*The Economist* 1989). Most large plants are still organized by a cluster of separate, partly competing unions. There are some companies, especially those owned by Japanese multinationals, however, which have managed to sign single-union agreements with their workforce.

English unions, unlike their counterparts in some other European countries such as Poland and France, are more pragmatic in their approach and fight for better pay settlements and better working conditions within the present economic and social system rather than engaging in class struggles and ideological battles for the overthrow of the system. They see their role as one of representing the workforce, pushing for objectives that are consciously desired by the workers themselves.

Since the establishment of the Labour Party in 1906, which grew out of the trade union movement, unions have been able to use the Party to further their interests as well as themselves being its major source of finance. However, in recent years, a combination of decline in membership because of mass redundancies caused by economic recession and the introduction of new technology, and anti-union legislation (e.g. banning secondary picketing, ending closed shop practices, allowing the courts to seize unions' assets in case of illegal action) have eroded the powers of the trade unions.

Them and Us

Tayeb (1988) in a study of a sample of English manufacturing companies found that the differences between shopfloor workers and white-collar employees, especially managers, inside the participating organizations appeared to reflect the social structures and systems of the society. The managers considered themselves to be members of the middle class, which shares in the ownership and participates in the control of the means of production, and the manual workers saw themselves as members of the working class, exploited by the former. In most cases, the relationship between management and workers was ridden with mistrust and hostility, emanating from a conflict of interests between the two classes.

The managers and other white-collar employees had great advantages over the manual workers in many respects, such as power, status, pay, physical working conditions, eating places, rules for lunch and tea breaks, and holidays. Shopfloor workers were subject to a tighter control at work. They had to clock in and out at specific times, and in some of the companies which produced chemicals and drugs, were subject to physical search every time they left the company premises.

It seems now though that there is a trend to diminish these differences. In a survey of British business, *The Economist* (1989) reported that many of the symbols of division between classes—between worker and manager, them and us—have been dismantled. Many firms have got rid of their ranks of corporate dining rooms and substituted one, modern single-status canteen. Some have got rid of their segmented car parks, where bosses were less likely than workers to get their hair wet in a rainstorm. This new trend, if trend it is, has affected most obviously the several thousand workers who work for Japanese firms operating in Britain.

English Business and 1992

The English have always been a trading people, and firms have developed considerable competence in dealing with export markets, responding to foreign competitors and to a flood of imports without going bust or requiring immediate trade protection.

The Channel tunnel and the fall of remaining non-tariff trade barriers in the EC after 1992 expose English business even further to international pressures. It remains to be seen how it will cope with the new situation. Various surveys conducted by the Confederation of British Industry showed that English firms were not prepared for 1992 and were reluctant to embrace this new and volatile market wholeheartedly. Of the 12,000 companies questioned, "10,000 companies appear to be sleepwalking towards 1992". This may have something to do with English managers' conservatism. As *The Economist* (1989) points out,

> [English] firms are more comfortable spending their cash in buying American firms than European ones. Despite the hype about 1992, that is not necessarily a mistake; it is surely better to invest in a country you understand and where markets are open and transparent than in areas less well understood but temporarily fashionable.

The government, too, has customarily been closer to the United States and has been a "reluctant European", opposing such proposals as the monetary and political union of the EC member states.

English Managers and Organizations

English managers are very polite, tenacious, resourceful, reserved, and self-disciplined (Terry 1979); but at the same time, they have generally ethno-centric attitudes towards their foreign counterparts, and can hardly speak a foreign language—it doesn't matter, they all speak English, anyway!

Simon Newitt, a senior manager of a management consultancy firm, sums it all up thus: "Purely and simply we still have an ignorant, arrogant, narrow minded colonial, nationalistic attitude . . . We were a great country once, ruling a fifth of the earth's surface and a quarter of the world's population . . . One Brit is worth 10 foreigners?" (*Executive Post*, No. 460, 27 Sept 89, p. 3.).

As would be expected from their conservative individualism and xenophobic tendencies, English managers are said to have too short-term a perspective in their business planning (at least relative to the Japanese), to spend too little on R & D and on training, to have a conservative approach towards new technology, and to place more emphasis on the production rather than on the marketing side of their business, relative to their major competitors such as American, Japanese, German and French managers (see for instance, Jamieson 1980; Locke 1985; Handy 1988; Reid 1989; Gordon 1990).

There are also non-cultural as well as cultural explanations for some of these attitudes. Take the managers' short-term perspective, for example. The City is one of the major sources of capital for most English companies.

Above all, investors, both individuals and institutions, seek a quick return on their investment. This puts managers under immense pressure to go for a "quick buck" (to use an Americanism). They do not have the luxury of the long-term financial support that their Japenese counterparts enjoy in their cosy relationships with banks and government. R & D is an obvious victim of this situation. Employee training is another. Product quality is the third. The list can go on.

Managers' reluctance to allocate a great deal of time and financial resources to employee training also has a foot in the societal culture. English employees, like many other individualistic people, and unlike the Japanese "company man", pursue occupational advancement through their career rather than their work organization. Job-hopping and moving from company to company are the rules of the game, rather than life-time employment and cradle-to-grave commitment to one company. As a result, English managers see expenditure on training as a waste of their precious capital, and not as an investment in human resources.

The relatively poor quality of some English products (Trought 1989) is not unexpected given the economic context of the firms. Within the decade between the early 1980s to the early 1990s, recession hit English firms twice. Moreover, the government's open-door policies subjected these firms to fierce competition from Japanese, German and American rivals, among others. Many managers were forced to go for lower quality in order to keep their prices down. A speech by the chairman of a large jewellery retail-chain firm, in which he told his audience that his company sells rubbish to customers at cheap prices (BBC Radio 4 news and commentary programmes, 23 April 1991), illustrates how some companies were left with precious little alternative.

Turning to the leadership style and management–employee relation ships, one can also trace many of their features to the cultural, political and economic characteristics of English society. Deference to authority (culture) plus a high level of unemployment (economy), for instance, could together explain the absence of serious trade union challenge to manage-ment's prerogatives and right to manage. As was mentioned earlier, English unions pragmatically seek better working conditions and wage settlements, rather than engage in an ideologically-based class struggle against their bosses (Gallie 1978).

Love of privacy and individualism may be behind English managers' preference for formal and clearly defined job territories and regulations (Tayeb 1988). The idea of territory is also present in the physical structures and designs of the buildings in which the organizations are housed. If you visit any English university, for instance, you will see that most lecturers have their own offices—little personal territories. In collectivist Iran, most university departments have only senior common rooms in which lecturers get together during the breaks between lecturing periods. The open-plan office is an imported phenomenon which has been adopted by only a few English firms whose managers are keen to learn lessons from their Japanese counterparts (Tayeb 1990).

Individualism can also be expected to influence the relationships between employees, their bosses and their work organizations. English employees, unlike their collectivist counterparts, do not expect their superiors to look after them and to help them with their personal difficulties. This would be an invasion of their privacy. To them a manager who is concerned with the employee's well being is one who, for instance, provides them with up-dated equipment so that they can perform their tasks better. In other words, managers and workers have an impersonal and task-oriented relationship with one another (Tayeb and Smith 1988).

Concluding Remarks

History, ecology and a long drawn-out evolutionary process have created a culture and social climate in England which stand English managers and their companies in good stead in many respects, but handicap them in some others.

Their honesty, frankness, trust, self-control, self-discipline, and politeness are their major cultural assets. Their individualism, professionalism and reserve give an impersonal and formal air to business dealings, which are interpreted as what they are and respected as such by colleagues from similar Western cultures. This can be misunderstood, though, as arrogance, detachment and "coolness" by businessmen and women from more emotional and group-oriented cultures, such as India and Japan. Also, the explicit xenophobic tendencies displayed by some English managers are bound to work against their business interests, especially when there are more receptive competitors across the Channel.

A vast majority of English firms, thanks to the economic climate and the government's open-door policies, are willing and quite competent to deal with competitive markets. At the same time, they are hampered in their efforts by unhelpful and sometimes downright harmful aspects of their culture and their society. These include capital market short-termism, less-than-favourable attitudes to business, traditionalism and reluctance to embrace new technology wholeheartedly, antipathetic industrial relations, and ill-prepared school leavers and university graduates. To an outside observer, the situation resembles a perfectly decent vehicle whose driver has put his feet on the accelerator and brake pedals simultaneously! It is a tribute to the resourcefulness and resilience of the English businessmen and women that, in spite of this, their country occupies such a high rank among the league of the industrialized nations.

References

Almond, G.A. and S. Verba (1963): *The civic culture*. Princeton: Princeton University Press.

Bagehot, W. (1963): *The English constitution*. London: Fontana/Collins.

Barnett, C. (1972): *The collapse of British power*. London: Eyre Methuen.

Dore, R. (1973): *British factory—Japanese factory*. London: George Allen and Unwin.

The Economist (1989): "Business in Britain", 20 May (a survey).

Gallie, D. (1978): *In search of the new working class*. London: Cambridge University Press.

Gordon, C. (1990): "The business culture in the United Kingdom" in C. Randlesome (ed.), *Business cultures in Europe*, 58–106. Oxford: Heinemann.

Gorer, G. (1955): *Exploring English character*. London: The Crosset Press.

Gorer, G. (1971): *Sex and marriage in England today*. London: Nelson.

Handy, C. (1988): "Great Britain" in C. Handy, C. Gordon, I. Gow and C. Randlesome, *Making managers*, 163–185. London: Pitman.

Hofstede, G. (1980): *Culture's consequences*. Beverly Hills, CA: Sage.

Irwin, J. (1976): *Modern Britain*. London: George Allen and Unwin.

Jamieson, I. (1980): *Capitalism and culture: A comparative analysis of British and American manufacturing organizations*. Farnborough: Gower.

Locke, B. (1985): "The relationship between educational and managerial cultures in Britain and West Germany" in P. Joynt and M. Warner (eds.), *Managing in different cultures*, 166–216. Oslo: Universitetsforlaget.

Macfarlane, A. (1978): *The origins of English individualism*. Oxford: Basil Blackwell.

Raynor, J (1969): *The middle class*. London: Longman.

Reid, D.M. (1989): "Operationalizing strategic planning". *Strategic Management Journal* 10/6: 553–567.

Roberts, K. (1978): *The working class*. New York: Longman.

Roderick, G. and M.D. Stephens (1978): *Education and industry in the nineteenth century: the English disease*. London: Longman.

Roderick, G. and M.D. Stephens (1981): *Where did we go wrong?: industry, education and economy of Victorian Britain*. London: The Falmer Press.

Roderick, G. and M.D. Stephens (1982): *The British malaise; industrial performance, education and training in Britain today*. London: The Falmer Press.

Rose, G. (1965): *Politics in England*. London: Faber and Faber.

Rose, G. (1968): *The working class*. London: Longman.

Rowntree, B. S. and G. R. Lavers (1951): *English life and leisure: A social study*. London: Longman.

Tayeb, M.H. (1984): "Nations and organizations", Ph.D. thesis, Aston University.

Tayeb, M.H. (1988): *Organizations and national culture: A comparative analysis*. London: Sage.

Tayeb, M.H. (1990): "Japanese management style", in C. Daily (ed.), *Organisational Behaviour*, 257–282. London: Pitman.

Tayeb, M.H. and P.B. Smith (1988): "A survey of management styles in four capitalist countries". Paper presented to the Fifth Workshop on Capitalist and Socialist Organizaitons, Brdo Pri Kranju, Yugoslavia, August.

Terry, P. (1979): "An investigation of some cultural determinants of English organization behaviour". Unpublished Ph.D thesis, University of Bath.

Time (1990): "1066, 1993 and all that", 12 November, p. 16.

Trought, B. (1989): "A comparison of the work activity of quality assurance and production managers". *International Journal of Quality and Reliability Management* 6/2: 25–30.

Weber, M. (1930): *The Protestant Ethic and the spirit of capitalism*. London: George Allen and Unwin.

Weber, M. (1961): *General economic history*. New York: Collier.

Wiener, M.J. (1981): *English culture and the decline of the industrial spirit: 1850–1980*. London: Cambridge University Press.

Chapter 5: France

Management in France

Arndt Sorge

France on a European Map

In the "Greater" Europe between the Ural mountains and the Atlantic
Ocean, and from the Arctic to the Southern tip of Gibraltar, Sicily and
Crete, the centre is somewhere in Poland, Czechia or Slovakia. Although
the Communist ice age is receding, our present-day concept is still very
much focused on Western Europe, where France clearly occupies a central
position.

Other countries in Europe also have a central position in the sense that
they have been surrounded by envious or restless neighbours. In history
lessons in countries such as Poland, Czechia, Slovakia, Germany and others,
pupils will be told that their country lies in the middle of bisecting lines of
migration, trade and other movements of a friendly or unfriendly nature.
This sort of experience seems to be very European. To avoid the less
pleasant sides of this experience, France has striven, throughout history, to
achieve "natural borders", and she has pretty well succeeded in obtaining
them. The Atlantic Ocean and the Channel (or should one say *La Manche*)
in the West and Northwest, the Pyrenees in the South, the Mediterranean
Sea in the Southeast, the Alps and the Rhine river in the East are as close
as one can get to the notion of natural borders. French history is a model
example of state consolidation, dominated from a Parisian centre whose
strength has steadily grown through countless conflicts of consolidation
with regional entities, notably the duchy of Burgundy which once extended
as far as the Dutch North Sea Coast.

On the eve of the French Revolution, the Kingdom of France was the
most integrated and coherent political entity in Western Europe. It had the
largest population and army and was the cultural centre of modern government by absolutist rule. French language, culture and commerce radiated
throughout Europe. The centrality and dominance of France increased
further after the 1789 Revolution, culminating in the Continental
European empire of Napoleon I. Even after the Battle of Waterloo,
France continued to influence Europe culturally to such an extent that the
French language remained the *lingua franca* of international diplomacy for

a century. The last exclusive remnant of this radiance is the World Union of Postal Services which retains French as the official language.

The success of governmental consolidation in France was mainly due to two things. First, as always, it was a matter of luck: the monarchy happened to defeat its internal arch-rivals, the Dukes of Burgundy; it held its own against England in the Hundred Years' War and profited from rivalry between independent rulers in Germany. Second, France was a distinctive heir to Roman statecraft, public administration and law. This provided the essential tools for the central control of larger social aggregates. The country blended this heritage successfully with Germanic feudalism and belligerence, and Celtic ingenuity and pleasure in the nice things of life. Fortunately for the socio-cultural coherence of France, the conquering Germanic tribe which gave it its name, the Franks, probably took the same interest in the good life as the Gallic inhabitants, in contrast to their more austere and stern North Germanic colleagues.

Much as France is usually styled as a Latin nation, it is, in fact, very multi-cultural. Even today, cultural heterogeneity is far from negligible in France, and it has been exacerbated by the influx of immigrants from Poland, Italy and other countries and, after World War II, from North Africa. From the French Revolution onwards, though consolidated within reasonably "natural" borders, French identity gained a sophistication of international allure. France was seen as the home of those who cared for liberty, equality and brotherliness, its social order transcending long-established systems, such as feudalism, which were based on privileges and duties linked with status and origin. The simultaneous occurrence of effective consolidation within quasi-natural borders and international radiance and colonialism brought with it a trait that was to become characteristic: a desire for European self-sufficiency which coincided, alternated or conflicted with internationalism. However, French consolidation and expansion within Europe absorbed so much energy that colonial expansion remained rather limited, compared to that of Britain, Portugal and Spain, the major seafaring and colonializing nations. Thus, in becoming the most important and most integrated country in Europe by the eighteenth century, France did pay a high price. Most of its earlier colonial endeavours were hindered by the Seven Years' War (1756–1763) against Prussia in Europe and England in the colonies, and by the aftermath of the Battle of Trafalgar which frustrated Napoleonic empire-building, except in North Africa.

As a result, France reached a half-way position between Germany, almost a non-entity where colonial empire-building is concerned, and Britain and Spain, the most avid and successful colonists. It achieved a blend of national self-sufficiency, cultural–diplomatic radiance in Europe and moderate colonialism. Internally, it developed the largest and most integrated domestic market in Europe and a very good infrastructure of rivers, canals, roads and railways. From the French absolutist kings down

to the Fifth Republic, the success story of France as a polity, and, as an economic force, has consistently been based on the following recipes:
– make the same institutional arrangements apply all over the country and standardize laws and other regulations;
– create the infrastructure which is needed to facilitate economic and social exchange between different regions;
– use the best brains of the country in a technocratic civil service, in order to augment the capacity of private merchants, artisans and industrialists.
These recipes are clearly of Roman ancestry, but whereas the Roman empire had fallen apart, conflicts in France had a clear centripetal outcome, asserting a central and universalistic authority. The revolutionaries of 1789 came to consider universalistic values, authority and law, as coinciding with Frenchness.

France could afford to be self-sufficient in Europe because it had a singularly large domestic market, well integrated at an early stage by infrastructure, rules and regulations. Its ingredients—the metric system, the *Code Civil*, rational structuring of public bureaucracies and straight country roads pointing from one village church spire to the next one, are, next to army tactics and regulations, the country's most important institutional export items. This part of the country's cultural radiance, which appears North American in character, was related to the build-up of France's self-sufficiency. However, France never left business success to the chance events of completely unguided free enterprise. Its economic order has consistently been more mercantilist than in other countries. In the Third Republic (from 1872 onwards), a protectionist variant of mercantilism was used to conserve social peace.

Self-sufficiency in this kind of national economy—a mercantilistic business system, orientation towards national rather than international markets—led to a certain stagnation relative to other competitors (Lévy-Leboyer 1979). However, European integration and the abandonment of world-wide economic nationalism after World War II gave France a powerful push towards international markets, particularly after de Gaulle's rise to power and the end of the Algerian War. Indeed, the period after 1963 probably changed the social and economic landscape more than in the neighbouring countries. France emerged from behind its quasi-natural borders to form, with Germany, an informal political alliance which gave the main impetus to European integration in the EC. At the same time, France shed its colonies. All told, it thus became more European and less self-sufficient in outlook.

However, throughout this transition, France by no means drifted away from the principles which had constituted its earlier rise to power. De Gaulle stood in a long line of continuity, dating back to François I, Louis XIV, Napoleon I and III. France did not need socialists to bring in national plans. Which other West European country could have conceived of giving prominence to a *Commissariat Général du Plan* under a definitely non-socialist government? This phase of modernization and Europeanization continued to be dominated by the cherished principles of rational technocracy at the service of charismatic leadership, mercantilistic government–industry interaction and a clear sense of public missions to be achieved. The same holds for the socialists; the similarities with Gaullist and centrist concepts strike both the foreign and the domestic spectator.

This amazing continuity, across the vicissitudes of revolutions, rebellions, civil, colonial and European wars, changes of parties in power and alliances with foreign countries, has given French business life a particular profile. Europeanization has by no means weakened this French profile but helped to carry it to new forms. De Gaulle always insisted on *"l'Europe des patries"*. Even if the French have doubts about what their "patrie" really is, the distinctiveness of their business, management, organization and regulatory arrangements is unlikely to dwindle.

Mapping Work-related Attitudes

Work-related values and attitudes form a convenient starting-point for the discussion of management and organization in any country. The available research results on work-related attitudes very often follow a standardized format and thus make it easy to map the position of a country on a world chart. Starting with work-related attitudes, therefore, does not imply that everything follows from the cultural, mental programmes instilled in individuals.

Let us then try to locate France on a larger map of attitudes related to management and organization. Hofstede's analysis of work-related values in different countries, which is also presented in the first chapter of this book, puts France in the middle of a cluster of countries with higher power distance and stronger uncertainty avoidance (Hofstede 1980: 316). French people may argue about who should wield power in society or in the enterprises, but they quite willingly accept an unequal distribution of power. To them, centralization of decision-making is a more unquestioned feature than to Northern Europeans. Here, we see the effects of a long history of centralization and concentration of public and private functions. Not only is government very centralized in France, but so also is business life; most larger groups and companies have headquarters in Paris, for instance. Even if people constantly grumble, in the provinces, about remote control from a distant Parisian centre, they hardly do anything to change this.

Governmental and business centralization go hand in hand, historically. Public works (mines, road-building) and governmental armouries also played an important role in business development, and they were under the control of the capital. Similarly, the production of luxury goods drifted towards Paris because the French kings encouraged the aristocracy to spend as much time as possible at the royal court and to engage in conspicuous consumption, to divert their minds from rebellious or treacherous intrigues to bring about regional independence. This illustrates the Franco-Romano-Gallic variant of French nation-building: centralization and concentration tempered with the good life, in the interest of the body politic.

Infrastructure was designed in such a way that major roads and railways invariably pointed towards Paris. Interconnections between regional sub-centres are much more difficult. Paris is the most convenient and time-saving meeting-place, rather than a town between a number of locations farther to the South of Paris. Anyone who has tried to go by car or train from, say, Marseille to Nantes on the West coast will realize that. The infrastructure, with the possible exception of regional airports, helps to maintain governmental and business centralism in Paris, despite increasing regionalism since the end of de Gaulle's presidency. The famous fast train, TGV (*train à grande vitesse*), is but another step in this direction, giving Paris an even more prominent central place.

Next to the power distance, where, according to Hofstede, France is comparable to Belgium, Portugal, Spain and Greece, the country is distinctive for uncertainty avoidance. Uncertainty-avoiding cultures emphasize control of risk and uncertainty in many ways. One of them is through the family: creating and maintaining diffuse kinship or quasi-kinship structures which buffer and support individuals in the face of risk. Although this method of uncertainty avoidance is most evident in Greece, it is nevertheless important in France. Indeed, even some large French groups are still largely under family control, such as Peugeot or Dassault, the aircraft manufacturers.

In the microcosm of business life, familial relationships are also very much in evidence, specifically paternalistic ones. The French language uses many derivations from the Latin word *pater*=father in a neutral–factual or approving manner, much more than do Germanic languages, even German. The employer or boss is "*le patron*". His wife or a female employer is "*la patronne*", a curious word if you consider it etymologically. Imagine an English employee addressing his female owner–manager as "fatheress"! The larger community or the function of employers is "*le patronat*". A French head of a company would feel insulted if called an "*employeur*", to try on some *Franglais*. The cultural and agricultural heritage is "*le patrimoine*". Note that this is not necessarily an indication of masculinity. According to Hofstede (1980: 324), France is rather more to the feminine side; somewhere between Scandinavia and the Netherlands on the feminine side and the Anglo-Saxon/Germanic cluster on the more masculine one. This does not imply overt masculinity, but more a concern with familial lineage and social patterns, which, in most of our cultures, run through the father. There is, of course, some affinity between this dimension and power distance. Familial relations in France imply the presence of power distance, sometimes in a subtle and sometimes in violent forms. Foreign visitors have been known to tell stories such as that of a restaurant apprentice being slapped in the face by *le patron* for a mistake, with restaurant guests looking on in bewilderment.

However, uncertainty avoidance more often takes on a less familial and more modern form. France is the pioneering country and exemplary model for the use of generally applicable, formalized, written, strict rules, schemes, algorithms, scales, frameworks, etc. There is a great endeavour, also in business life, to invent and apply such modern, rational instruments. This is the very pronounced Cartesian bent in French culture — always on the look-out for ways of compressing an unwieldy, uncertain reality into neat, orderly and often complicated schemes. The social hierarchy of streams in secondary education is, for instance, closely related to the mathematical and formal logic content and level taught in each stream. Correct logical inferences are very highly rated, as is correct use of the language which, even in the most subtle paradoxies, uses both in order to explore an underlying logic. This is the way socially selected and highly educated civil engineers, administrators, military planners and statute law specialists think, especially when their profession is rooted in a large, impersonal public body.

With the importance of such bodies in France, this way of thinking has percolated down, through the centuries, to workers, clerks and farmers. This has been achieved by *"l'éducation nationale"*, a particularly important, cohesive, centralized and laicistic body in France. The largest sector-specific trade union in France is the teachers' union, *Fédération de l'Education Nationale*. At this point, it can be seen how familial and abstract-logical uncertainty avoidance reinforce each other, in France. Abstract schooling has achieved a remarkable synergy with familial patterns, which fuels the engine of the French economy and society. Despite its inherent dangers of scholasticism and risk-averseness, this is one of the most powerful social integrators and effort motivators in French life. The French are motivated by families to excel in doing things the correct and logical way, *"comme il faut"*. In this posture, the figures of the goldsmith, military engineer, higher civil servant and lawyer merge, and they set an example which has become valid everywhere, far beyond the original confines of the royal court, the officer corps, higher administration and public works.

Usually, scores on the two "Hofstedean" dimensions of power distance and individualism are correlated. From the table in his major book (Hofstede 1980: 223), it emerges that countries which have larger power distances are usually also more collectivistic, emphasizing the importance of the social collectivity more than that of the individual. This makes sense to the North European reader. After all, what is the function of a strong central power, if not to subdue the individual and make him or her function as a member of a collectivity, be it the nation or the enterprise. However, the interesting thing now is that France—and Belgium—are very clear exceptions to that rule, if it is one. The French combine above-average acceptance of power distance with higher individualism. By the same token, they also combine individualism with uncertainty avoidance. This also flies in the face of North European prejudice which cannot help but conceive of the individualist as an Anglo-Saxon risk-taker.

Nothing could be more informative about France than this eccentric position with regard to power distance and uncertainty avoidance on the one axis and individualism on the other. The conflict between individualism and other culture dimensions sometimes leads to unpredictable and violent rebelliousness. More than in other countries, newspaper readers in France barely blink an eyelid when it is reported, as often happens, that a bunch of farmers have dumped a great mound of dung on the portal of the local *préfecture*; or that lorry drivers have clogged up the most important motorways at the beginning of the holidays in what they call *opération escargot* (snail) in true military slang, causing a tail-back up to Paris and the Belgian border; or that a company head-office is occupied and board members are symbolically held hostage. In short, in France there is constant tension between the demand for strong authority, and individualistic assertion against it.

Crozier (1970) has suggested that temperamental and even furious outbursts alternate with schematic orderliness because the latter leads to a blockage of individual manoeuvre. Outbursts result as the only way of bringing about individual adaptation and change, after which things settle down again in an orderly fashion and a new cycle begins. This, in a nutshell, is how the conflict between individualism and the other dimensions is handled. The same author has also shown that bureaucracy in the French mould may actually be the perfect safeguard of the individual sphere (Crozier 1963). By defining the rights and obligations of its members in precise and formal terms, French bureaucracy, whether in public service or in private enterprises, also protects organization members from unpredictable or unwarranted intrusion. Thus, French people in formal organizations strike a bargain. They protect their individuality by conforming with formally laid down rules and regulations, preferring formally circumscribed individualism to ambiguous and therefore contestable individualism.

Hence, in terms of French culture, there is not only conflict but also coalescence between individualism, power distance and uncertainty avoidance. Again, this has to be seen as a result of historical processes. It was the king, or the emperor, or the republic that looked after brilliant individuals, giving them a function and influence in the public services which they could otherwise not have aspired to. The hierarchy has more than a purely oppressive ring to it in France, because it is suffused with a meritocratic ethos, and because individual talent and individualistic aspirations are cast more in terms of striving after performance *comme il faut*. In an interesting dialectical twist, individualism in France is concerned with excellence in the emulation of general norms of taste, logic and professional practice. Whereas the Anglo-Saxon individualist tries to do his or her "own thing" and considers hierarchy a dirty word, the French individualist tries to achieve a perfection within a protective niche provided by a stable organization.

In that way, business motives have acquired a particular slant in France. Business enterprises are certainly not disinclined to make money, but sheer profit maximization is rather frowned upon, as something vulgar. The "honour" of the businessman, the engineer and the administrator is an important factor (d'Iribarne 1989). It is constituted by his or her ability to achieve high professional standards and to do justice to norms of taste, sophistication and logical rigour. Thus, behaviour in business firms has a fairly aristocratic undercurrent, especially in the motives of the bourgeoisie. Once again, it has to be seen as an historical result of the way in which the court and the republic built up an important service class and in which this was intertwined with private enterprise.

When considering French values, the bystander first thinks of the famous triad of *liberté–égalité–fraternité*. From the above, dependence–hierarchy–vested interests would seem to be more accurate.

Barsoux and Lawrence (1990: 10) have described these contrasts in a suggestive diagram, picturing *liberté* opposite dependence, *égalité* versus hierarchy and *fraternité* against vested interests. The French Revolution had three dominant values as its motto; hence the diagram which indicates these and their opposites becomes a hexagon. By a nice coincidence, the French often refer to their country as *l'hexagone* because it looks like one on the map. They also use the derived adjective, for instance, when referring resignedly to typical national conditions or problems. Barsoux and Lawrence are quite right to point out the conflict between a number of espoused values and actual values-in-use. Let us look now at what they would probably call *notre dilemme hexagonal*.

It does seem as if values-in-use and the espoused values of the French Revolution are poles apart. On the other hand, it would be too simple to describe the relationships between opposite categories as merely conflictual and declare that, apparently, the French Revolution did not affect working and business life.

First, with regard to liberty, it has already been shown that the dependence of individuals on formal rules and precise obligations and

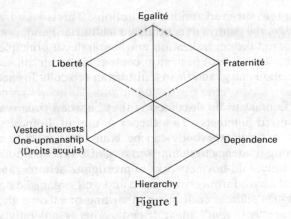

Figure 1

rights is the French way of demarcating individual liberty. Second, let us deal with the poles of equality–hierarchy. Arguably, people must be treated equally if they are treated impersonally, and only on the factual merits relevant to a particular problem. Thus, when selecting candidates for a hierarchical organization or for promotion, equality of chances and success based purely on merit or performance serve to stabilize the hierarchy rather than destroy it.

The principle of applying for entry or promotion in a large, open competition (*concours*) is very much adhered to. End-of-school exams are set to nationally standardized tasks and marked totally impersonally. Entry into selective higher education, civil service careers and a number of large firms takes place by means of a country-wide *concours*. This is the chance for the brilliant candidate to prove his or her mettle in the important, culturally conditioned professions mentioned earlier on. The process should not be confused with competition for advertised jobs, which also occurs in many countries. A professorial job in a French university, or a research position at the prestigious CNRS (*Centre National de la Recherche Scientifique*), or the post of administrative head of a public authority, are not available as posts to be filled independently. One applies for professorial jobs in a specific discipline, vacant throughout France; one applies for a career in the CNRS country-wide, and so on. One indicates where one would like to work, but one does not apply for a specific post.

Such processes guarantee equality of access, and the *concours* provides a democratic foundation for hierarchical structures. This is indeed the long-term effect of the French Revolution. It has democratized or equalized formal entry conditions, and in that way has helped the proliferation of hierarchical principles. Particularly in France, but also in other countries, equality is interpreted more in terms of equality of entry conditions than in equality of results. Unequal distributions of income, power and life chances have thus survived various revolutions. This is because revolutions have focused on the control of centralized institutions and, one may argue, have exacerbated the centralization and hierarchical principles which follow from it. These are perfectly compatible with an emphasis on bureaucratic anonymity, and this is, in turn, a typically French expression of equality.

The third conflict to be discussed is that between *fraternité* (brotherliness) and vested interests. The theory-in-use in France, as in other countries, is that not everybody can be your brother, but, nevertheless, there is a strong tendency to define and organize brotherhoods in order to avoid uncertainty. Old-boy networks of prestigious schools, and colleagues in professorial *corps*, form very effective and well-organized brotherhoods. When colleagues address each other in writing or talking, they will often use the phrase "*cher ami*" (dear friend). This is not only a superficial phrase but a truthful expression of professional solidarity, very much bound up with a modernized feudal notion of honour. There is little sentimentality involved but a clear, though usually latent, willingness to share and support. In social conflicts, the range of true friends is often far greater than formal membership criteria indicate. For instance, despite low membership figures—presently about 10 per cent of the labour force—trade unions or strike organizers can count on much broader active participation than from registered members alone.

It becomes apparent, therefore, that in the French constellation, opposites stabilize and hold each other in place, rather than merely acting at cross-purposes. To that extent, *liberté–égalité–fraternité* are not so much clichés as simply one side of a coin which invariably falls with a different side upwards each time.

Organizing and Managing

Bureaucracies have become associated with a social pathology which frustrates real performance by over-emphasizing division of responsibilities, routine and impersonality. This is a far cry from the way bureaucracy was defined by Weber when he introduced it as a standard social science term. In his idea, bureaucracy was the most efficient way of dealing with large-scale tasks, particularly in a context which stresses legalistic and formal–rational bases of accepted power. Commentators on Weber tend to link this more sober and positive evaluation of the bureaucratic phenomenon with views and traditions ascribed to the—now extinct—state of Prussia. However, Weber was not a Prussian by origin; his appreciation of bureaucracy would have made even more sense had he been French, or had the concept been delivered by, say, the French sociologist Durkheim.

Pugh (1984) distinguished the "full bureaucracy" from other, more moderate, forms as characterized by high centralization of decisions, impersonal forms of control and refined division of labour. International comparisons of organization suggest that this type of bureaucracy, which also underlies the going jokes and complaints about its pathologies, is particularly cultivated in France. However, this does not imply that the French have made their peace with social pathology in organizational life. If anything, it attests to the view that the French are extraordinarily effective, because they do make the full bureaucracy work despite the task environment for which it is thought to be suited, according to organization theory.

They have cultivated the full bureaucracy precisely in those situations where it can be expected to perform better than other types. It was singularly adapted to France at the beginning of modernity, as the largest and most integrated society with the most powerful political centre. This political, commercial and industrial centre was confronted with various tasks on a very large scale indeed, and the pressure to do things in a uniform way was great. There was a constellation, comparable to the explosive development of the American interior market in the nineteenth century, which also led to the emergence of increasingly bureaucratic organizational juggernauts, once the first enterprise pioneers retired. To be sure, there is less of the American cut-and-thrust in French entrepreneurial style. It is more civilized and in keeping with its own code of honour, but, arguably, aristocrats are only vaguely distinguished from capitalist robber barons, maybe because they left that phase behind. In any event, full bureaucracies are clearly there in both cases.

The French style full bureaucracy was highlighted by Crozier (1963). In particular, he traced its origin and social function to the affinity it had with pre-existing patterns of social interaction, notably the desire to avoid or mediate direct face-to-face relationships. This suggested, as pointed out above in the discussion of values, that bureaucracy became a lubricant of social life in France, rather than merely the proverbial fly in the ointment.

Let us now look at how organizing in France is different from other countries. Probably the most detailed comparison of French organization with others was done by Maurice et al. (1982). It was a comparison with West Germany, which was extended to Britain by Maurice et al. (1980). They found that, in France, there are usually more levels in the hierarchy, and that lateral differentiation of organizations into departments, work groups and jobs is intense. Staff and line responsibilities are more clearly separated in the way exhorted by the French engineer and management writer, Fayol.

The hierarchy is more top-heavy in France, with between $1\frac{1}{2}$ and 2 times as many supervisors and managers as in German organizations. The lowest level of the industrial production hierarchy (*chef d'équipe*) is more separate from the workers, enjoys more disciplinary authority, and is counted among the white-collar employees, whereas the equivalent in Germany has blue-collar status and less disciplinary authority. Spans of control at different levels in France are usually smaller, indicating the possibility of tighter supervision.

French organizations also have more non-managerial white-collar specialists in either commercial–administrative or technical functions. Here, the difference with Germany is particularly large; France has about two or three times as many technicians to blue-collar workers. Why this is so, is shown in interviews reported in the source quoted above. There is a pervasive tendency in France to separate technical, planning, administrative and supervisory tasks from execution tasks. The technicians and planners are there to prepare the execution of a job as comprehensively as possible. Production jobs in France, notably under the widespread system of separating operating and machine-setting jobs, offer comparatively less responsibility, remuneration and status to operators.

This shows "Hofstedean" uncertainty avoidance (separate, detailed technical planning) and power distance (more and more intensely supervising superiors) in operation. Everything is suffused with an inclination to segment, parcel out, analyze beforehand, specify and specialize to such an extent that there is also a strong functional necessity to make sure that differentiated bits of the organization form a coherent whole. This management role requires great analytical capability and a certain vigour, to establish the sought-after coherence. The figure of the analytically competent military engineer emerges once again, not just as a mere historical remnant, but as a type which is well adjusted to dealing with modern industrial problems. Indeed, the publications quoted above show that vigour, ability to command and obtain discipline feature more prominently in the role expectations of French supervisors, than they do in their German counterparts. Whereas formerly, the raised voice had been the preserve of the foreman, and the merciless, analytical clarity the domain of the manager, supervision is now being topped up with technical qualifications.

Throughout the organization, written rules, instructions, and communications of all kinds are widely used, in order to make a segmented and complex operation predictable and reliable. Again, this is not simply the cultivation of paperwork and red tape for its own sake, which would be an all too easy caricature. If you strive to reduce uncertainty in a very complex organization, formal procedures are the obvious if not unavoidable solution, at least if reliable uniformity of operation rather than flexibility of adaptation is the most important criterion.

Furthermore, this method of control is particularly relevant where operations carry a large, concentrated risk, and informal step-by-step learning is difficult. Nuclear power stations, for instance, blow up infrequently, but when they do, the damage is catastrophic. French managerial methods seem particularly adjusted to handling concentrated risk by meticulous anticipation and planning. Again, this is not surprising because the strong points of the French economy feature products such as jet fighters and passenger planes, nuclear power station manufacture and electricity generation, aluminium smelting, the manufacture and operation of high-speed trains.

Yet the full bureaucracy does trip over its own feet and is used manipulatively. To strive for such a system is to lay the foundations for predictable blunders. As may be expected, the French press is full of blunder stories and, in a system which breeds personal unaccountability, there is a constant suspicion that cover-ups are being organized to protect the integrity of impersonal hierarchies and personally responsible bosses. This is a standard *topos* in French thrillers, both with a political and a less political line. The air is usually thick with suspicions that a supposed culprit has been sacrificed in order to take the blame off someone higher up.

The scandal and mystique bred by this type of management and organization occurs in both public services and large private enterprises. The clever manipulators, schemers and conspirators are in the high spot in social imagery and reality, much like subtle intrigue and deadly poison in the complicated web of back rooms at the Versailles of Louis XIV.

This kind of drama is usually more subtle and sophisticated than in, for instance, the American TV series, Dallas. Strong-arm stuff does occur, such as in the policing of foreign workers in some large industrial concerns, but it is for the underlings to set this up and carry it out. Top management is relatively removed from the more ferocious side of labour control. Every now and then, an underling who is being sacrificed "spills the beans", but those higher up usually succeed in remaining in the clouds that veil the upper levels of the organization. Full bureaucracy profits from dispersed responsibility, long lines of command and organized unaccountability. This is part and parcel of life in both capitalist firms and public administration, under a socialist president or a conservative company president.

Top bosses of French joint-stock companies are called *Président-Directeur Général*, PDG for short. Even in the abbreviation, the term loses little of its impressiveness, and is a good indicator of the weight of hierarchy and central responsibility rolled into one. In France, the chairman of a board of management is the superior of other board members, whilst he or she is only a *primus inter pares* in, for instance, the Netherlands or Germany. In a conversation with François Sellier, a senior industrial relations scholar, which I shall never forget, I pointed out that my teacher of private law in Germany had illustrated the position of a German chairman of the management board with the following observation: "With respect to other Board Members, the '*Führerprinzip*' does not apply". Sellier instantly replied: "Ah oui, nous l'avons, le Führerprinzip".

Such company bosses wield a type of authority which is frequently paternalistic and charismatic, in the manner of the great generals and field marshals. Barsoux and Lawrence (1990) have shown that the metaphors used in business terminology and slang are very much related to military life and cooking. For instance, advertisements during "battles" between companies in take-over bids have fallen back on images of the "white knight" trying to rescue a damsel in distress. The press relish the jousting of business leaders in tournaments such as these, as much as they do in Britain and the United States. By contrast, unfriendly take-over bids in the domestic economy are very much frowned upon in the Netherlands, Germany or Scandinavia, where people would consider them a frivolous waste of resources and a conspiracy against the public well-being.

Below the level of charisma and tournament jousting, inspired by the military tradition of the *grand chef* and the noble knight, there is a less dramatic level of events which, however, again has clear parallels with military life. Probably more than any other nation, the French have demarcated a class of managers between top management/entrepreneurs and ordinary workers, following traditional military concepts and codes. The term *cadres* for this class of people is hard to translate, but the best translation is probably "commissioned officers in civilian business life". The gulf between *cadres* and non-*cadres* in the workforce is very similar to that between commissioned officers and enlisted men (including non-commissioned officers like corporals and sergeants). Becoming a *cadre* is an important event, much like the ritual of knighting in medieval times. Cultures have a manner of coming up with set, punchy terms for concepts that are important to them. The French have the word *passage-cadre* which denotes entry into the *corps* or *cadres* in an enterprise. *Cadres* have separate unions; even if the *cadre* happens to be a communist and joins the CGT, he or she will belong to a union separate from those to which ordinary employees belong.

For all the status distinctions that surround the *cadres*, it is not a category that evokes glitter and distinction. The definition of *cadres* comprises so many bureaucratic elements that a certain amount of grumbling and disorientation is probably inevitable. The French continuously interrogate themselves about the phenomenon and social position of *cadres* (see for instance Boltanski 1982). It rather resembles complaints in the officers' mess during a protracted time of peace: where is the charisma, all this red tape, one is just a cog in a wheel, things are manipulated by the political top. If you want to raise a topic that will really get French managers involved in a long discussion, the best bet is to mention *l'individualisation*. This refers to an individualization of salaries, working conditions and personnel policy, breaking free from well-established schemes, salary scales and regulations that have come to govern the working life of a *cadre*. His or her dilemma apparently is, increasingly, that they are exhorted to be more entrepreneurial whilst their conditions of employment have become more rigid. The eagerness with which the French would launch themselves into this discussion, thus appears to be a function of the social typeing and regulations which we see applied to management in that society.

It would, of course, be correct to mention that British *managers* are similarly set apart as a highly distinctive category, but the British manager is less tied to his or her company, more likely to change jobs, and has fewer difficulties in bargaining individually over conditions of employment. He is much more of a buccaneer or mercenary in type, who would find it super-fluous to discuss the individualization of his terms of employment: if there was no room for that, he would not be doing the job. Mercenaries are certainly not alien to French traditions, but one of the highest distinctions for a French army officer is to lead the mercenaries of the foreign legion, rather than being a mercenary himself. Similarly, the ethos of French managers is more feudal and rather reminiscent of the Japanese samurai warriors, who also turned their hand to industrial enterprises and infused Japan's business life with feudal elements.

A lot of changes have happened and are still happening in France. Notably, in the wake of the students' unrest after 1968 and various enter-prise law reforms after the *accords de Grenelle*, the authoritarianism of management and organization has been reduced. As in other countries of Europe, there is much more talk about increasing flexibility, motivating individuals and creating flatter organization structures. Counter-currents have been produced, to enrich the French world of imagery and manage-ment practice, such as through the widely popular autodidactic entrepreneur and politician Bernard Tapie, with his emphasis on egalitarian achievement, unaristocratic and unbureaucratic postures. The question is whether, in the midst of this change which has also happened elsewhere, the *relative* position of France has changed. The answer is that it probably hasn't. The figure and posture of Tapie is still typically French in that it displays the force and charisma of the *grand chef*.

Human Resources

Organization and management practices are very interdependent with the way in which a society educates and trains people and constructs occupa-tional careers. In that respect, France is again highly distinctive in Europe. The overall education system is very stratified and elitist. This is not to say that upward mobility is more limited than in other countries; it is, for instance, clearly more evident than in Germany, where blue-collar workers enjoy better wages, more enriched functions and higher social status. Ger-

man workers are therefore socially more stable than their French counterparts, who aspire to escape worker status more quickly. Throughout the
French educational system, there are omnipresent mechanisms to extract
elites by competition on the basis of marks, in the *concours* which have
been mentioned before. The differentiation of this system is such that the
term "elite" is very much a relative notion. Elites are extracted from
relative elites, and they in turn are in line for another process of elite
extraction. Although membership of a relative elite confers advantages,
and provides relative objective or subjective security, it usually leaves
people with the feeling that they have not quite made it, because they
missed out on, or failed in, the next higher process of elite extraction.

The first major step in the elite hierarchy is the choice of secondary
education. Natural science/mathematics streams are more selective than
professional education. University education, however, is not very elitist
because in principle, it is open to all those who finish the grammar school.
Students ambitious to succeed in business life do not go to universities if
they do not have to! Next to, indeed in many respects above, universities,
the French have a tier of specialized higher schools (*grandes écoles*) which
recruit students on a highly selective basis. That tier is again, needless to
say, very much stratified internally. Reputed schools at this level advertise
the fact that they can only admit about one tenth of those who apply.

However, there are few who can apply for such schools as they are
themselves a relative elite, already. In addition to a *baccalauréat*, the
French equivalent of A levels British style or *Abitur* in Germany, they are
required to have had two or three more years of *classes préparatoires*, an
awesome education on top of normal grammar school education. This has
a highly selective function and requires a great deal of effort and per-
severance. It truly is the students' nightmare of relentless cramming,
celebrated in student symbols and sagas of failure and success. Subsequent
education at a *grande école* is easier, by comparison.

Grandes écoles exist mainly in the areas of engineering/technology and
business studies. They are maintained by all sorts of governmental or other
bodies, but mainly by ministries (such as the defence ministry in the case of
Ecole Polytechnique) and chambers of industry and commerce (which support mainly regional business schools, the *Ecoles Supérieures de Commerce*, and more elitist business schools such as ESSEC, HEC, etc.). These
institutions educate most of the future engineers, business specialists,
administrators and managers of the country, whether in public administration or private companies. In comparison with other countries, it is striking
that people who later hold jobs that are rather different, go through courses of studies which are rather similar. French society as a whole has a
tendency to assimilate public administration and private company
management.

For instance, the top school for public administration, *Ecole Nationale d'Administration*, leads students to a highly important but modestly named function: *inspecteur des finances*. Although this is a function in public administration, those who are entitled to it also stand a good chance of being recruited by large, prestigious companies. Companies are typically linked with schools through the old boy network and, sometimes more formally, linked to one of the *corps*, i.e. larger professions and personnel categories in a specific service. The coinciding of public administration and private enterprise socialization, employment and professional practice patterns also implies, however, that the world of management in a large reputed company may be far removed from what happens in a small company, led by *autodidactes* or people who have been through less demanding education and training processes. This world is less publicized and researched, but it is nevertheless quite important.

My impression is that small company personnel are, in France, justified in feeling bypassed and neglected vis-à-vis the glittering prizes of socialization and work careers which become the household names in French industry, commerce and finance. The media make a great display of the rating of *grandes écoles* in terms of the calibre of students and preferences of employers. By comparison, continuous education for working people, the "sandwich" principle of mixing practical training and education at school, and education and training at lower levels of the workforce, are rather undervalued. Apprenticeship by combined training at work and technical school has virtually vanished from the French scene; it has only survived in artisan trades. The technical *collège* and *lycée*, offering full-time education, has supplanted it as a form of basic professional education and training for industry, commerce, finance and other sectors with larger units of employment.

Let us take a look at how qualifications are distributed over managerial and supervisory employees in France and in other countries. My colleagues and I compared a number of plants in France, Britain and Germany which yielded the following table of maximal qualification levels reached by managers and supervisors in three chemical factories in the three countries. These factories were as similar as one could find them, with regard to personnel size, products, technology, ownership and location. In fact, because they themselves considered each other very similar and were partly owned by the same multinational groups, they had themselves started comparisons. We were dealing with manufacturers of ethylene polyethylene, acrylonitrile and similar intermediate synthetic chemicals, in factories larger than 2000 employees. These operations were studied in the late 1970s, when they were already internationally quite similar from the point of view of technology.

The distinctive thing about the French qualification distribution is that it is very top-heavy. There are four times as many people with a university level degree as in Germany, and nearly twice as many as in Britain. Part of

Table 1. Vocational Qualifications of Managerial and Supervisory Staff in 3
Chemical Factories (highest qualification reached by each individual)

France	%	Germany	%	Britain	%
Without formal qualification	19		3		42
		Craft	42	Craft	21
Technique court	11				
Techn. professionnelle	8	Meisterbrief, Techniker	30	City and Guilds, Ordinary National	4
Techn. long	12				
BTS, PST, CNAM	14	Ing. grad.	17	Higher National State (e.g. in engineering, Ministry of Transport—Steam)	8
					4
Supérieur, grandes écoles	36	University degree	8	University degree	21
Total	100		100		100

Source: Maurice et al. 1980: 79

the explanation, of course, is that the French factories have created more
"room at the top". The other is that *grande école* leavers do not start their
careers in very high functions but have to collect experience lower down
the hierarchy, whereas the British and notably the German factories promote a larger number of managers from lower levels, after post-experience
courses in engineering. The contrast with Germany is particularly striking.
The frequency of qualification in a German factory is inversely proportional to its "height", and higher qualifications are often built onto lower
ones. In France however, the frequency of a qualification is almost a
positive function of its "height", and qualifications have usually been
obtained before entry into working life.

What we know from other studies suggests that this also occurs in other
large industry or service sectors. It is of course true that provision of
technician education has expanded greatly, in France. *Grandes écoles* are
less keen to expand because they fear a lowering of selection standards and
of the elitist image.

A different picture might emerge if we looked at smaller companies.
These are traditionally less sought after by *grande école* leavers, and the

companies, for their part, would consider such educational output to be "above their station" and less immediately employable and profitable. Intermediate categories of engineers and business administrators, with both practical training and a good academic grounding, are produced in larger quantities in Germany and are suitable for large and small company contexts alike. These categories do not figure as widely in France. Human resource creation in France is more polarized. Either you aim for a good position in a small company or a subordinate position in a large company, or you go for a good career in a large well-known company. Where you finish up, is very much determined by your initial professional education. In France, disparities of educational provision and career changes are quite clearly related to disparities between concentrated, well-reputed industries on the one hand and dispersed, less reputed ones on the other.

The effect is visible even at the level of craftsmen. The Director of Vocational Education and Training at a large German motor car manufacturer once said to me that they had compared craftsmen according to their performance and work attitude in Germany with a comparable manufacturer in France. They found that the French craftsmen took greater interest in the technological spearheads and knowledge bases of their trade, neglecting the more messy and everyday practical contingencies of shop-floor work. The young German workers, by comparison, were not very keen on technical sophistication but more on competently coping with the day-to-day problems of production work. Therefore, even at this lower level of organization, the French demonstrate relative elitism. Even Frenchmen in less privileged positions often consider themselves, with some justification, to be participants in a noble mission and relative exponents of excellence. This is, indeed, democracy *à la française*. Where the Dutch extol the virtue of behaving in a normal way because this is crazy enough already, the French are encouraged to strive for extravagant things because it would be unusual not to. To that extent, the saying which came up in Napoleon's army, that the common soldier has a field marshal's baton in his knapsack, has an element of symbolic truth to it.

Industrial Relations

Unions and other representative bodies such as works councils and shop stewards (*comités d'entreprise*, *comités d'établissement*, *délégués du personnel*) have got a very powerful competitor in France. The hierarchy French style is not only punitive and encroaching, but it also has something to offer. To an extent which is often forgotten, it offers professional advance on a large scale. The fine differentiation of the hierarchy and an ample provision of supervisory, planning, and management positions, provide means for this. The combination of individualistic and hierarchical principles, a characteristically French phenomenon, clearly works to the disadvantage of unions and other representative bodies. The French employee can, as a rule, expect more from individual loyalty to the enterprise hierarchy than from dedication to collective interests. Organization and management practice in France have, intentionally or unconsciously, decoupled the worker's fate from the fate of the collectivity of workers.

In a way, the unions have even been instrumental in this. For one thing, the union movement is highly fragmented, with three major general union confederations split along ideological lines, a large independent union for *cadres* and supervisors and another large union for teachers. This fragmentation has made workplace and industry-wide bargaining difficult. The ideological split contributed to an emphasis on political, rather than collective bargaining postures. Political demands have focused on easier access to better schooling, and a great deal of attention has been dedicated to that by the French government. This education and training system has been successful in the hands of polarized, hierarchically differentiated and top-heavy organization structures, and these structures have in turn served to demolish the nucleus of working-class identity and solidarity.

The traditional strongholds of union activity in France have, in addition, been subject to severe attrition because of the demise of the steel industry and crises in the motor car industry and in mechanical engineering. Furthermore, the strongest union in France, the *Confédération Générale du Travail* (CGT) has followed what are called democratic–centralist principles shading into communist orientations to some extent, which came under increasing pressure with the decentralization of bargaining and a certain withdrawal of the state from industrial relations. In addition, there was, of course, a chain of electoral defeats of the Communist Party and the bankruptcy of communist countries in Eastern Europe. The combined effect is that union membership in France amounts to only about 10 per cent of the working population.

This outcome did not come from protracted union-busting by a neo-liberal government; quite the opposite. In no other West European country except Scandinavia has a socialist government or president been in power for so long a period during the 1980s. This serves to reiterate the importance of the interrelationship between French organization, human resources and industrial relation patterns.

There is also the government and statute law to consider. Whilst these do have a strong role to play in much of Continental Europe, their role in France is somewhat different from that in the Netherlands or the German-speaking countries. In these countries, the government and statute law have mainly put forward a framework of institutions, rights and obligations

which leaves employers, unions and other actors to work out material
outcomes such as wages, equipment and health safety. In France, however,
determination of such material standards involves the government more
than in other countries. This is due, on the one hand to the power of the
state, and on the other to the kind of enterprise individualism and internal
organizational fragmentation mentioned earlier. For a long time, employees' associations have had no place to go. The employers kept them
out of workplaces until 1969, and they could not take root because the
construction of organizations and human resources did not work in their
favour. At the industrial level, the collective bargaining which developed
did not become significant. Only one major union confederation out of the
three large ones (*Force ouvrière*) considered it its main purpose, and this
confederation has been strongest in the public services. Furthermore,
enterprise individualism has restricted the importance of industrial
bargaining.

What was left was the political level, which has traditionally had greater
importance, though recently the political power of unions has dwindled
substantially (Segrestin 1990). In a way, the country has come full circle
with regard to the last century, when it had unimportant unions but a very
important political party which then called itself *radical–social*. This is
another characteristic of France which flies in the face of North European
conceptions—the assumption that leftism in politics and trade union power
go together. However, if one analyzes the workings of French organizations, human relations, industrial relations and politics, it becomes clear
why it is possible for power balances to be the other way round there, for
substantial periods.

Thus, low union membership in France in no way precludes intense
conflict. The country's characteristic is precisely that both go together, and
that conflict breaks out in an unpredictable fashion. This phenomenon is
part and parcel of the to-and-fro between Cartesian orderliness and spon-
taneous change, discussed earlier. Therefore, it can only be said that the
best moment to expect industrial unrest in France is when things have been
relatively calm for a while. No one can predict precisely where it is going to
happen and on which occasion, but when it comes, it will be quite different
in type from both the miners' strike in Britain—less orchestration by union
machinery, although possibly as violent—, and from the national strikes in
the German metal industry for a 35-hour work week—less planned and
carefully mobilized. At the time of revising this text, a marvellous example
has just occurred: a gigantic blockage of the major motorways in France,
by lorry drivers disgruntled with the government rather than with the
employers, bringing traffic to a halt at the beginning of the summer holiday season more effectively than a snowstorm at the beginning of the
winter.

Summary

Much of what we find in France can be explained on the basis of a societal mechanism of nation-building and social integration which is highly distinctive. The central government became more important much earlier and more pervasively than in other parts of Europe, constituting a larger interior market, promoting standardization and improving public infrastructure. This had important consequences for government–enterprise relations and the type of markets that were constituted. Organization and management practice are a mixture of feudalistic–paternalist elements and the full rational–legal bureaucracy, conforming with the types of markets created and the general habitus of nation-building elites. Human resources fit into this pattern, with a very streamed and selective education system, an emphasis on career-building based on getting to the highest entry position at the earliest moment, and a finely differentiated hierarchy of vertically and laterally segmented jobs. Industrial relations, likewise, feature a dominance of the government and of political considerations, a high amount of segmentation, and a low attractiveness of formal union and representation activity, because the motivation to react collectively conflicts with individual career-building and mobility.

The emphasis on large interior markets, full bureaucracy, elitist education structures, sophisticated hierarchies, organizational rationalism and low union membership appears to follow a North American pattern, but it is marked by a governmental centralization and feudal–paternalist history which coexists with, and continues to fuel, more recent traits. France has also achieved the most striking synthesis of individualism and hierarchical organization in Europe.

What we know would lead us to believe that, whenever the problem is how to
– produce a fairly homogeneous product or service on a large scale,
– pool efforts in a technologically sophisticated venture,
– or produce synergy between private and public actors,
it will be the French patterns that people will be looking to as models. The organizational and human resources patterns attached to such challenges will be France's source of strength in the future, as they have been in the past, and they will remain her unique contribution to European management and organization.

References

Barsoux, Jean-Louis, and Peter Lawrence (1990): *Management in France*. London: Cassell.

Boltanski, Luc (1982): *Les cadres: la formation d'un groupe social*. Paris: Editions de Minuit.

Crozier, Michel (1963): *Le phénomène bureaucratique*. Paris: Seuil.

Crozier, Michel (1970): *La société bloquée*. Paris: Seuil.

Hofstede, Geert (1980): *Culture's consequences*. Beverly Hills, CA: Sage.

d'Iribarne, Philippe (1989): *La logique de l'honneur. Gestion des entreprises et traditions nationales*. Paris: Seuil.

Lévy-Leboyer, Maurice (1979): "Le patronat français, 1912–1973" in *Le patronat de la seconde industrialisation*, M. Lévy-Leboyer (ed.), 137–188. Paris: Les éditions ouvrières.

Maurice, Marc, Francois Sellier and Jean-Jacques Silvestre (1982): *Politique d'éducation et organisation industrielle en France et en Allemagne. Essai d'analyse sociétale*. Paris: Presses Universitaires de France.

Maurice, Marc, Arndt Sorge and Malcolm Warner (1980): "Societal differences in organizing manufacturing units. A comparison of France, West Germany and Great Britain". *Organization Studies* 1/1: 59–86.

Pugh, Derek S. (1984): "The measurement of organization structures: Does context determine form?" in *Organization Theory*, D.S. Pugh (ed.), 67–86. Harmondsworth: Penguin.

Segrestin, Denis (1990): "Le syndicalisme français et l'entreprise (1968–1988)" in *L'entreprise une affaire de société*, R. Sainsaulieu (ed.), 46–68. Paris: Presses de la fondation nationale des sciences politiques.

Chapter 6: Germany

German Management

Malcolm Warner and Adrian Campbell

Introduction

Germany occupies a central, if ambiguous role, in Europe. Although one of the largest states (covering 356,900 square kilometres with a population, in 1990, of 79,070,000) it is a relative newcomer to statehood (1870). Its history, and therefore its image of itself, diverges sharply from the longer-established nation states of Western Europe. In this respect, it more closely resembles the nation states of Eastern Europe (with the possible exception of Russia), its borders being drawn partly from ethnic and linguistic allegiance, and partly from the outcomes of complex military and diplomatic processes. As C.M. Bowra remarked of the ancient Greeks: "A people lives by its geography" (1985: 3). Almost landlocked and with few natural frontiers, Germany increasingly dominates Europe (in practice, if not in recent years by intention) both East and West. Whilst the superpower *status quo* in Europe between 1945 and 1989/90 cancelled Germany's power in political and military terms, the economic advances of West Germany in the post-war period laid the basis for a strengthened role in the 1990s and beyond, following the collapse of the Soviet Union and the gradual diminution of direct U.S. influence on the continent.

Germany has presented extremes of stability and instability as compared to other European States. From the perspective of the 1990s, it may be said that defeat in two world wars and the physical and psychological damage incurred by militarism, economic disasters in the 1920s and 30s and, of course, Nazism (1933–45), and the subsequent division of the country by the Iron Curtain (1945–89/90) have not altered the long-term momentum of German advance relative to the rest of Europe (see James 1991).

Despite the fundamental uncertainties which underly German identity and destiny ("*die Deutsche frage*"), an uncertainty sometimes expressed by violent xenophobia in some quarters, Germany has also demonstrated a high degree of political stability over several decades. Prior to the end of the Cold War, the two German States presented particularly stable versions of their different economic systems. The Federal Republic has been characterized (largely) by consensus-oriented government based around corporatist "social partnership" in the economic sphere, and a highly decentralized system of government—both of these foundations having been built up with the active participation of Allied occupying forces concerned with eliminating from the system any sources of dangerous instability (see Malzahn 1991). The system's success drew on that side of German culture which values consensus and a joint, professional approach in all matters.

East Germany, meanwhile, provided the most stable and efficient of the Stalinist satellites of Eastern Europe. As late as 1989, the German Democratic Republic was being held up by hard-liners in Moscow as an example of how Communism could work if people were sufficiently disciplined. Although, with hindsight, the GDR's economic "success" was largely a sham, and depended on Western subsidy, it nonetheless demonstrated another side of German culture—bureaucratic, disciplined and oriented towards control. The regimented orderliness of the GDR contrasted with the position of other Soviet-style economies, and drew on indigenous traditions which dated back to the military bureaucracy of Frederick the Great in 18th century Prussia (of which the Soviet system was itself a direct descendant).

The Role of German Culture

How far do these historical and cultural factors influence the practice of German management. Does the national context determine variations of style in any coherent way? Although it is dangerous to generalize, Hofstede (1991) is surely right to recognize a degree of truth in the intuitive perception that nationality matters:

> In research on cultural differences, nationality, the passport that one holds should . . . be used with care. Yet it is the only feasible criterion for clarification. Rightly or wrongly, collective properties are ascribed to the citizens of certain countries; people refer to "typically American", "typically German", or "typically Japanese". (1991: 12)

In industrial and economic terms, the traditions referred to above can still be perceived in Germany. On the one hand, there is the *Handwerk* tradition of the autonomous craft worker, which was successfully defended against US-imported Taylorism; on the other hand, there is the tradition of the stratified bureaucracy which found earlier expression in the military factories of Prussia and may still be perceived in the German public sector. What is remarkable is the way in which the Germans have achieved flexibility from the fusion of the two, particularly in the area of training. An emphasis on protracted training and education, and formal qualifications, has been used in such a way as to provide flexibility and autonomy on the shop-floor.

In later sections, we will be looking in more detail at the culture and principles of German management. However, perhaps the over-riding cultural characteristic of German society and management does not so much lie in the details of these beliefs, but in the strength with which they are held. Germans appear to want to belong to a tradition, to ascribe to a set of values. These values are likely to be explicit and non-negotiable. It may be said that, paradoxically, the success of German post-war consensus has been due to the strictness with which Germans have disciplined themselves not to follow divergent paths. Principles are stated and accepted. A system such as that of the traditional British mode of industrial relations, with its curious, pragmatic interplay of the formal and the informal, conflict and co-operation, would be quite alien to the German understanding of how things should be done.

This desire to be grounded in clear and unambiguous principles may be seen as a cultural response to the uncertainties which have characterized German history; the lack of that long-standing sense of security that characterizes Britain (or rather England) and France, a security which allows for irony, pragmatism and understatement. German philosophy has reflected this search for metaphysical certainty and for belonging. As Sir Isaiah Berlin has argued:

> Herder virtually invented the idea of belonging. He believed that just as people need to eat and drink, to have security and movement, so too they need to belong to a group. Deprived of this, they felt cut off, lonely, diminished, unhappy ... To be human meant to be able to feel at home somewhere with your own kind (cited in Gardels 1991).

German culture is thus characterized by a striving for collectivism that clearly separates it from Anglo-Saxon culture, whatever the superficial resemblance between the two. As Canetti has argued, the difference may be expressed in terms of national symbols, the one individualistic, the other relatively collectivist:

> The Englishman likes to imagine himself at sea, the German in a forest. It is impossible to express the difference of their national feeling more succinctly. (Canetti 1973: 203)

German Industrial Performance

Whatever the question marks that still surround Germany's future political role, its economic dominance in Europe is unquestionable. On the eve of unification, in July 1990, the then West Germany was producing 40 per cent of the European Community's manufactured output, with little more than a sixth of its population. One third of this output was exported annually, and Germany maintained positive trade balances with ten out of its eleven EC partners. In cars, mechanical engineering, chemicals, textiles, and electronics, it maintains a powerful competitive industrial base.

It is too early to say how this solid performance will be affected by reunification with the former GDR (whose industries have been devastated as a result) or by the revolutions that have occurred in Eastern Europe and the Soviet Union. These developments may either consolidate or overstretch Germany's role as the engine-room of the European economy. In this chapter, we will not attempt to answer this question, but rather to look back at the management traditions which shaped the success of West Germany up until the end of the 1980s.

Here, another note of caution is required. German management has acquired something of a symbolic status as the antithesis of Anglo-Saxon management, the *laissez-faire* traditions of the United Kingdom and the United States, which Germans themselves have been known to disparage as "*Manchesterismus*", the capitalism of the nineteenth century. In setting up such a contrast, it becomes easy to forget that Germany's post-war growth has not been substantially different from that of most West European nations. France, Sweden, Austria, Italy and Spain and the rest could all claim to have experienced economic miracles—it is the British case rather than the German that has been puzzling (Pollard 1981).

However, the scale of the German economy has meant that its management approach has attracted outside interest to a degree only surpassed by Japan. Just as the United States' economic success fuelled interest in what is now termed "Fordism" and the approach to management embodied in the Master of Business Administration or MBA degree, so the German post-war economic miracle or *Wirtschaftswunder* has led to a search for a German "model", at least as far as manufacturing industry is concerned.

This interest, however, has usually focused around the German vocational training system, since German management itself has proved less amenable than Japanese management to broad stereotyping and characterization (whatever the accuracy of the latter in Japan's case). Despite a number of thorough analyses, including landmark studies such as that of Lawrence (1980), and the comparative work by Granick (1962), Maurice *et al.* (1980) and Sorge and Warner (1986), German management presents a picture that is difficult to categorize. Whilst it may be said that, in general terms, German companies have tended to be more product-led than market-led, bank-funded rather than stock-financed, managerial rather than entrepreneurial (Randlesome 1990: 1), the reality is somewhat more contradictory, as will become clear below.

A German Model of Management?

Any view of German management must be coloured by the post-war recovery, which was assisted by the "Marshall plan". Here, we find the first paradox. American "Marshall aid", so often vaunted as the single most important reason for Germany's subsequent prosperity is ranked by commentators such as Lawrence (1980) as merely one of a number of factors, and very likely less important than the mixing of population (the ten million refugees from the East), the experience of starting from starvation-point (*"Die Stunde Null"*), the diversion of national self-expression away from diplomatic and military symbols towards business, and the associated clarity with which exporting was seen from the start of reconstruction as the *sine qua non* of growth rather than as a means of balancing the books. Divided from its hinterland in East Germany and the former Prussian lands (re-)ceded to Poland, and cut off from traditional markets by the then Iron Curtain, West German industry turned its attention westwards, taking an early lead in the growing market of the EC.

Henceforth:- "High value-added products, high technology and technical innovation" (Randlesome *op. cit.*: 8) became the order of the day for manufacturing managers. These imperatives led to Research and Development expenditure rising to as high as 10 per cent in some companies. The share of exports in output rose from 22 per cent in the mid-1960s to over 32 per cent by the late 1980s. With manufactured goods accounting for more than three quarters of exports, there were few doubts as to the central role of the sector in guaranteeing national survival.

There was a clear emphasis on quality and product design, although criticisms regarding "over-engineering" remained. The strength of the Deutschmark did not deter sales, and the demand for German goods tended to be price-inelastic. German firms made reliability and after-sales service (*Kundedienst*) into decisive sources of competitive advantage well before the Japanese. Opinions may differ over the extent to which the punctuality and punctiliousness of such managerial practices reflected national cultural attributes, but it seems likely that the training of managers and workers, and the principles by which they were organized, played a large part (as we shall see below).

Economics and Regulation

Although the social market philosophy of West Germany consistently emphasized the need for free markets and competition, the way in which this market has been designed and regulated differs from any standard neoclassical approach. The German emphasis on economic regulation tends to be practical and based around what will support industrial success, rather than ideological, which might damage competitiveness (although this was allowed to take a heavy toll in East Germany after reunification).

In particular, German industry has tended to be highly resistant to the idea of hostile takeovers on the Anglo-Saxon model, and its stand is broadly in line with the rest of Western Europe, excluding the U.K. However, rather than a strong regulatory approach, such as that which characterizes France and Italy, Germany typically operates on a basis of cultural values backed up by a regulatory framework—hostile takeovers do not occur (although some slight movement has occurred in this direction over the last two years) because German managers basically do not think they add much to the efficiency of firms or to the economy as a whole. As Woolcock et al. (1991: 14) put it:

> the whole environment is one that tends to foster commitment to the company rather than provide incentives to sell up. All major stakeholders— including the major banks and insurance companies, which hold about 20% of all shares in the large joint-stock companies—and their employees, through their participation on the supervisory board, are directly involved in the future of the company.

The structure, itself, of board-level management in large German companies (AG) works against short-term restructuring. The supervisory board or *Aufsichstrat*, which supervises the performance of the executive board or *Vorstand* is elected for five-years and can only be changed if there is support for such a move from 75 per cent of the voting shares. Takeover activity is low and is regulated by the Federal Cartel Office (*Bundeskartellamt*), set up in 1973 in order to separate merger policy from politics— although ministerial intervention in favour of the MBB–Daimler–Benz merger belied this arms' length arrangement (Woolcock et al. op. cit.: 12).

Though German companies such as Siemens have been expanding by cross-national acquisition in recent years, the general tendency has been very much in favour of organic growth, from which takeovers are seen by many as a distraction.

In 1988, Britain accounted for 73 per cent of all takeovers in Europe, Germany for only 4 per cent (of which 40 per cent were cross-national). This approach limits *de facto*, although not explicitly, the degree to which German industry is likely to fall into foreign hands.

Some divergence has begun to occur between the strategies of service companies, such as banks, and manufacturing in this regard. The service companies are increasingly building up their presence through acquisition elsewhere in the EC, whereas in manufacturing, the market position of the big companies has tended to confirm them in their preference for organic growth, the assumption being that market deregulation will consolidate their leading role in Europe, rather than fragment it (op. cit.: 106).

While in favour of competition in general, German management tends to oppose de-regulation, particularly if carried out for ideological rather than practical reasons. German management, after all, emphasizes continuity, with change occurring only insofar as it is necessary and will add to efficiency. The partnership with the trade unions via the works council system, and the system of worker directorships, has tended to reinforce this. The long view taken with regard to product development and manufacture is matched by an unwillingness to risk long-term relationships and carefully negotiated consensus for the sake of short-term gains.

Technology and Management

Technology in Germany is assimilated by the industrial and managerial logics that have characterized its management over the long-term. The "conception and practice of technical work and training, organisation and industrial relations" (Sorge et al. 1983: 40) follows a distinctly German path. Companies train skilled workers for production, as well as for maintenance work, for example. Apprenticeships are pervasive, with examination and certification of skills at all levels. The line management hierarchy is more technical than in many other countries, with closer liaison between line managers and technical experts (Maurice et al. 1980; Sorge and Warner 1986; Campbell and Warner 1992). The German organization is distinguished by its tightly-knit technical staff superstructure, closely linked to supervisory and managerial tasks, which, when combined with a highly-trained workforce, produce high levels of performance. Compared with French or British industry, German enterprises have "a lower centre of gravity", that is they have less proliferation of administrative and technical staff support functions—skills are rooted to the shop-floor or around line management as far as possible (Sorge and Warner 1986: 125). Whereas in some other countries, the trend has been for manufacturing to look more and more like service industry—to the extent that production becomes a poor relation from which those employees with ability will try to escape—in Germany manufacturing follows an unmistakably manufacturing logic, with production centre stage rather than falling behind areas such as marketing and R & D.

The technical emphasis of German management is not a new creation. The mid-nineteenth century saw the development of a specifically German industrial–technical capitalist tradition, which emphasized long-term aims rather than short-term profit maximization (Landes 1960). This concern with the product rather than the bottom line combined with bank-led financing to provide German management with its characteristic long-term perspective.

Product Focus or Marketing Focus?

This inclination to see profit as a secondary objective appears to have left a strong imprint. Up to one fifth of smaller independent German firms (according to one study) have been found not to measure the profitability of their business or its component units on any routine or continuous basis (Reid and Schlegelmilch 1988: 17). Indeed, the same study found that, contrary to received views of the punctilious, analytical German manager, it was in fact British firms who exercised more comprehensive control over finance and marketing than the Germans, rather than *vice-versa*.

To this must be added the qualification that Germans, while largely unconcerned with the type of detailed management accounting information required by Anglo-Saxon firms, do tend to know their costs in detail, even if profitability as such often remains a matter of trust as a result. The authors implied that success in marketing on the part of German firms might be linked to the primacy of production—improving the cost, quality and reliability of the product, and then allowing price flexibility in marketing, in which they were less interested, as a focus of managerial policy and control.

Somehow or other, the Germans appear to have avoided the negative aspects of being producer-driven. Granick (1962: 160) cites German senior managers complaining about the "short-sightedness of 'technicians' who measure the company's success by its tonnage". Of course, sales and marketing have been given considerable emphasis, since this was required to boost the export-drive on which the country's continuing growth depended. However, this was merely relative to a pre-war past in which exporting had been much less of a priority, and had in any case been co-ordinated through State institutions rather than through specific functions at the enterprise level.

Post-war up-grading of the sales and marketing functions should not therefore be taken as achieving the thoroughgoing "Americanization" it was purported to mean. The product-oriented approach to management was adapted, but not fundamentally altered. The emphasis on marketing was in any case focused towards quasi-technical areas such as after-sales service and the meeting of deadlines. Granick's account also refers to senior management concern over high wages, and the danger that the latter might lose Germany's cost advantage and therefore its open access to export markets (Granick *op. cit.*: 161). In practice, as is well known, German industry was able to position itself as competitive on quality rather than price (although the industrial partnership with the unions allowed productivity to rise along with wages).

The Manager as Specialist

Many of the characteristics of German management and organizations may be traced back to national training patterns. In Germany, a person's occupation (*Beruf*) is especially important as the basis of social identity, reflecting the strength of craft and technical training traditions.

The tendency not to separate technical expertise and management should not be seen as applying only to the preserve of the professional, hired manager. On the contrary, it is well established in small family firms as well as in giant concerns (still in some cases family-owned). Product engineering is not unusually the special responsibility of the owner in such small firms.

Larger firms are more formally structured, but organization charts and similar outward symbols of status differences tend to be applied less than in U.S. or U.K. companies. Hierarchies are flat, with technical expertise as close to the shop-floor, and as close to the production/line hierarchy, as possible.

The longer time-horizon of German management referred to above, applies not only to capital investment decisions, but also to human resources management. There is a high degree of educational attainment in engineering at all levels of the hierarchy, and career paths tend to remain within the internal labour market in the larger firms. These factors, together with the industrial union system, reinforce the stability of manufacturing and the close links between industrial and financial capital (Lane 1990: 250–251).

Most German managers are trained as engineers, and more than a few have passed through craft apprenticeship training as well. Where engineering training is concerned, there is little formal detachment of academic from practical aspects of training, nor is engineering practice regarded as intrinsically separate from "pure" scientific work. This fact may help account for the high rate of R & D spending, 2.9 per cent of GDP in the late 1980s, compared to 2.3 per cent in the UK.

Education of Senior Managers

Many directors of the larger German companies have doctorates (Handy *et al.* 1988: 136). In the case of Siemens, no less than 14 out of 20 main board members have such titles, although lawyers are increasingly taking top positions from scientists (*Financial Times* 15 April, 1991). The larger the company the more likely are board members to have doctorates. The highest density of technically-qualified managers is in the chemical industry. Over 1370 managers in this sector have doctorates, mostly in scientific areas. Regarding first degrees, two in three German managers have such qualifications, a similar level as in France, twice as high as in the U.K., but far lower than the 90 per cent recorded in Japan and the U.S.A. (see Handy 1988: 3).

Two further points are worth noting: first, that in Germany first degrees in subjects such as engineering contain management education as an integral part of the course, part of a more general tendency for technical courses to be broader-based than in many competitor countries. The broad-based nature of training occurs at all levels—chemical industry workers above a certain level will know both chemical and mechanical engineering disciplines almost as a matter of course. Second, German degrees take longer than in Britain, usually between three and six years. If we then take into account study for the second or third degrees which so many managers in Germany have, not to mention the fact that many will have preceded university with vocational training qualifications as craft workers (not seen to be irrelevant to a career in management), then it becomes clear that German managers enter employment at a much later age than their counterparts in Anglo-Saxon business culture, where there is an implicit trade-off between education and the "real world".

This late entry into the managerial job market limits the extent to which "fast track" careers for young graduates can be the staple of human resource planners that they are in some other European companies. Indeed, German management tends overall to be less concerned with advancement for its own sake—there is less pressure to "get into management" in order to be taken seriously, and, accordingly, less pressure to leave one's professional discipline behind. In this connection, we may also note the broad bands of discretion that divide one level in the hierarchy from another. Fewer levels is widely seen to have improved job satisfaction among skilled workers, and to have provided sufficiently broad roles for managers that advancement is less of an imperative than in more centralized, multi-level organizations elsewhere. In general, qualifications and status attributes vary much less between levels in Germany than in comparable U.S. or U.K. firms.

Remuneration

Where salaries are concerned, if we apply the "buying power" measures of salary developed by the ECA (Employment Conditions Abroad) consultancy (see *Financial Times* 22 November 1991) we find that in Germany and France, junior management pay represents 38–39 per cent of senior management pay, whereas the comparable figure for the U.K. and U.S. is 44 per cent—so that despite status differentials, "Anglo-Saxon" pay, within management, is slightly less differentiated between levels. In terms of absolute pay levels, if we take U.S. pay as 100, German managers receive 82–94 per cent, French managers 73–78 per cent, and U.K. managers 65–69 per cent, these differences being broadly in line with productivity variations between the countries concerned.

We may note that since 1985, there has been a much closer alignment of relative pay with relative output between the U.K., France, Italy and Germany, so that unit labour costs in the three countries were virtually level in 1990. The main changes were a relative decrease in French and British labour costs, and an increase in German labour costs, partly due to the increased strength of the Deutschmark. Further devaluation of the other currencies would have undermined German price competitiveness, although the Exchange Rate Mechanism was designed to prevent this (*Financial Times*, 11 November 1991).

Expert Knowledge and Managerial Authority

Professional status is thus more important than purely organizational or managerial status. As Lawrence (1980) describes it, German industry provides an example of what Chester Barnard termed the "sapiental" as opposed to the "structural" basis of authority. Thus from the first-line supervisor or *Meister* upwards, supervisors and managers are respected for what they know rather than who they are. The *Meister*'s formal training reflects this emphasis. In West Germany, 52,000 first-line supervisors are formally qualified every year, compared to 15,000 in the U.K. (*Financial Times* letters, 16 November 1991).

This professionalization of all levels reflects a culture that involves a considerable degree of self-discipline and self-programming. German managers, at least in the major manufacturing sectors, are not as likely as their U.S. counterparts to play the "macho" role of leader. Instead, it is assumed that workers and supervisors will meet deadlines, guarantee quality and service, and since these matters are not negotiable, they do not need to be followed up and enforced so regularly. Independence within agreed parameters characterizes the preferred mode of working or managing. The idea of manager as administrator seems relatively weak in Germany, holders of such posts frequently preferring the more entrepreneurial connotations of *"Unternehmer"*. Although less inclined than Anglo-Saxon counterparts to improvise, German managers are more likely to idealize the independent family firm (Granick 1962; Lawrence 1980).

However, working reliably to rules and instructions is not the same as decentralization of the significant decisions. Child and Kieser (1979) found that more decisions were made higher up the hierarchy in Germany than in the U.K. (although some key decisions were taken at higher levels in the latter). This is supported by Heller *et al.* (1976) who found that older German managers centralized more than older British managers.

Hofstede (1980: 158) has argued that setting and abiding by clear rules is a way of avoiding uncertainty in a culture which is inclined to seek to do so. Similarly, Horowitz (1978), comparing French, German and British managers found that the French and Germans relied more on short-term feedback than the British, and were more prone to "uncertainty avoidance". In general, roles and rules are more defined in German organizations either in formal documentation or personally. The search for rules and unambiguous directions leads to greater emphasis on planning. If in Britain it may be said that "the more difficult it is to plan, the less you need full-time professional planners", the opposite may be true in Germany (*op. cit.*: 161). The flat hierarchy in German firms is qualified by management's technical orientation and associated love of detail. Horowitz (*op. cit.*) found that whereas U.K. top managers tended to engage more exclusively on strategy, German (as well as French) managers tended to concern themselves with details as well, which, as Hofstede (*op. cit.*: 188) points out, is another sign of "uncertainty avoidance".

The paradox of German management lies in the fact that Germans (according to Burnett 1977) score high on anxiety and assertiveness but (according to Hofstede *op. cit.*: 232) low on individualism. Like the Japanese, Germans project the image of purposive, collective effort towards agreed goals.

German Management and "Post-Fordism"

Despite a leaning towards the pedantic, and the application of formal rules, German management nonetheless emerges as quite distinct from the Taylorist/Fordist model, with its sharp separation of concept and execution, of strategy from operations, and ruthless division of labour. It is therefore not surprising that Germany (in particular Baden–Württemburg) should, along with the "third Italy", become the focus of attention in the debate over "flexible specialization" (Piore and Sabel 1984), which sees the survival of non-Fordist approaches to products and markets as the key to future prosperity. This debate was given a specific German focus with the work of Kern and Schumann (1987) on "new production concepts". Kern and Schumann's research in the car, machine tools and chemical industries in Germany led them to the view that a major change had occurred in terms of management of labour. The trends included greater integration of tasks, re-skilling and professionalization of production work, and management perception of skilled labour as a "positive planning concept rather than a necessary evil" (*op. cit.*: 161). Whilst these changes did not uniquely occur in Germany, they found fertile ground there in that these views were implicit in the management approach of many German firms, even when such thinking ran counter to the conventional wisdom.

"Organizational Shamelessness"

As Lawrence (1980: 92) has noted, German management is self-sufficient, pragmatic (regarding theory as opposed to principles) and less open to external influence. Lawrence describes the episode of the (1973) Booz Allen Hamilton Report on German Management, which castigated the Germans for their lack of business-school training, their ignorance of techniques such as PERT and financial planning, and conservatism about moving between sectors (see Lawrence 1980: 89–92). The lack of concern that German management has shown faced with these and similar criticisms testifies to a down to earth distrust of "secondary" disciplines, those which may distract from the matter in hand, or the product itself. Lawrence terms this attitude "organizational shamelessness", an unwillingness to conform with conventional wisdom on economics or business administration just for the sake of doing so. German conformism is expressed quite differently, through the wish to maintain specific operational standards, and the relationships involved in meeting those standards.

"Technik"

Behind these educational and organizational patterns stands a particular notion of technical competence. Lawrence (1989: 154), uses the phrase *"Technik über alles"* to stress the three-fold distinction made by Germans between:

Wissenschaft—formal knowledge (arts or sciences),
Kunst—art, but specifically artistic output or practice,
and
Technik—knowledge and skills related to work.
This division diverges from the Anglo-Saxon dichotomies between arts and
science, and between "pure" and "applied" sciences. As Randlesome
(*op. cit.*: 51) puts it:

> The concept of *Technik*, the art and science of manufacturing useful artefacts
> is so widespread in the country, that West Germany can be regarded as a
> manufacturing-friendly society.

Over 40 per cent of Gross Domestic Product is derived from manufacturing
and construction. Not only was West Germany in 1990 responsible for half
the exports within the EC, but it exported more per head than any other
country.

The persistence of *Technik* as a strength in German management might
have been thought by some to be a potential Achilles' heel. Critics might
point to the post-industrial service-oriented society as the wave of the
present and future. Could it be that the continuing German emphasis on
the traditional industries of vehicles and machine-tools, the massive *Mas-
chinenbau* sector is a potential time-bomb, a "sunset" or "smokestack"
industrial strategy?

This view would be in line with the "information society" or "post-
industrial" theory which gained ground in the United States and the U.K.,
in particular during the 1979–83 recession. This theory assumes that old
industries can be expected to disappear as a result of an evolutionary
process. Whilst it is undoubtedly true that employment is steadily being
transferred away from manufacturing, this does not mean that an absolute
cut in production levels in that traditional sector represents progress. The
maintenance of production levels, and even of employment levels in many
"traditional" sectors in Germany and Japan, let alone in the Newly
Industrializing Countries, calls the simplified logic of this theory into
question.

However, the increase in manufacturing efficiency has now reached a
point where some might rightly call into question the German strategy of
mass craft training for industry, although this approach would still seem to
be erring on the right side. Critics such as Spies (1985) highlight mis-
matches between supply and demand which result from the mass training
of the dual system, and argues that the British tripartite system was less
employer-dominated and more flexible. There was a view, during the early
1980s, that German vocational training for 16–19 year-olds merely
camouflaged unemployment, and led to the "best-trained dole queue in

the world" (Spies *op. cit.*: 24). Recession and rising labour costs are now major concerns (*Financial Times*, 3 March 1993).

Innovation in Traditional Sectors

Whereas mechanical engineering has been allowed to waste away as "cash cow" or "dog" in some competitor countries, in Germany it has been kept in the mainstream and provided with leading-edge technology. Thus, we find that the German mechanical engineering sector has distinguished itself by its rapid adoption of microelectronics into both products and processes. Furthermore, German mechanical engineering companies have not simply replaced electro-mechanical components with microelectronics, but have proved adept at integrating the design and assembly of microelectronic components into their own enterprises, in contrast to similar companies investigated in the U.K. (Campbell *et al.* 1989).

This achievement is an example of the German preoccupation with the product as a whole (and the need to maintain control of the whole product) serving as the impetus to rapid innovation and adaptation, even in the most traditional sectors. Rather than promote a distinct "sunrise" sector, at the expense of older sectors, German industry has redefined and up-dated these sectors to accommodate new technical developments. Its ability to do this has been closely linked to the maintenance of a particularly strong base of intermediate skills, with workers being trained well beyond the demands of any one job (Campbell 1991). This success in traditional areas has not yet been matched by expansion into new sectors such as biotechnology, lasers, IT systems and optamatronics. Here, there have been attempts to fill the gaps through federally-funded R & D institutes. The direct benefits to industry have thus far been disappointing and funding has been cut back in order to encourage firms to carry out their own R & D in these newer areas (*Financial Times*, 24 September 1991). Although such sectors have not seen aggressive or even effective competition from the Germans, the experience of microelectronics product applications suggests that product design and assembly can be integrated relatively quickly, once firms have become sufficiently aware of how to apply the technology.

The flexibility of German industry as a whole in achieving such shifts lies not only in the depth and breadth of non-graduate training, but also in the use of graduate science and engineering recruits. These have not been concentrated into semi-protected areas such as defence. Instead they have been spread wider across the range of middle-of-the-market sectors in which practical application of science holds sway, rather than the "back-room" isolation of R & D common elsewhere.

Simplicity and Narrowness of Focus

It would be wrong, however, to see German management as sentimentally tied to traditional holistic methods of manufacturing. A recent study of the German machinery manufacturing sector (Rommel 1991) found that successful German manufacturers followed a set of rigorous, commercially-driven principles, several of which call into question attempts to explain German success in terms of "flexible specialization".

It was found that the more successful companies in Germany were those which narrowed their product range, concentrated R & D on that narrower product range and produced the product at a dedicated factory, thus avoiding the complexity of mixed production sites. This narrowness of focus simplified manufacturing such as to enable a more genuine and far-reaching decentralization of authority to middle and junior management. It also allowed successful companies to economize through more effective targeting of R & D, and enabled new products to be launched more rapidly. Products were modularized so as to postpone customization to as late a point in the manufacturing process as possible.

Shop-Floor Training

Not only are German managers well-educated; the human capital of German industry is supported by what may be regarded as the best vocational training system in Europe. The training tradition, combined with the model industrial relations practice facilitates efficient production of goods and services—this despite periodic speculation that both training and industrial relations systems are too inflexible and expensive to adapt. Although the European Single Market may place a question mark over long-term competitiveness of the German labour market, the strength and quality of labour market and industry did seem likely to postpone the day of reckoning. Germany was able to absorb more than 2.5 million migrant workers in less than two years without any significant impact on unemployment—the difficulties of absorbing labour from abroad appeared to be mainly political not economic (*Financial Times*, 28 October 1991). By 1993, however, unemployment in the western *Länder* reached 8% (and 15% in the east).

German industry is also noteworthy in that the gap between large firms and small and medium-sized firms (*Mittelstand*) is not so wide as might be expected. The "dual system" of financing training ensures that all firms pay for training, and therefore share the benefits without the problems of "free-riders" and "poaching" that beset the training systems of certain other countries. In addition, the bank-led finance system for industry provides significant backing for smaller firms, who are therefore not the "poor relations" that they are elsewhere when recession occurs.

The dual system implies a degree of interested co-operation between large and small firms. The large firms over-train and then choose the people they want, whilst the smaller firms who do not have the facilities for training (although they pay for it) then hire the others. There is some evidence that the dual system is under strain, particularly following reunification—it is seen as too inflexible and too centred around qualifications. However unwieldy its output, it is nevertheless impressive—120,000 workers gained engineering qualifications in 1990 (*Financial Times*, 3 June 1991). However, training too has been hit by the post unification squeeze. In early 1993, the Federal Office of Labour ran out of money altogether (*Financial Times*, 23 February 1993).

Conclusion

To sum up, the image of "German management" appears as less of an abstract force, divorced from production, than its Anglo-Saxon counterparts. It is specialist rather than generalist, and product-led rather than market-led—although it could be argued that the German style of management avoids the need for such clear-cut choices.

Most senior managers are trained as engineers with practically-oriented *Technik* rather than academic science as their starting point. Thus, German managers do not manage as a general activity, they manage *something*. Management is linked to objects rather than concepts, to specialist knowledge rather than status. It is no coincidence that business schools in the North American sense scarcely exist in Germany, and appear not to be missed.

The management system is characterized by tightly-knit technical staff superstructures, backed up by a highly-trained workforce. High levels of competence allow management to operate through flat structures and large spans of control, with discretion pushed down the hierarchy. Initiatives of the "total quality management" type, aimed at re-activating craft-type pride in performance in bureaucratic structures, would appear less than necessary in the average German manufacturing company.

Although promoting self-supervision of skilled workers, German managers are not averse, however, to getting involved in the details of the tasks concerned. The distinctions that have characterized traditional Western hierarchical management thinking—strategy/operations, of conception/execution would appear not to operate in such a clear-cut fashion in German industry. Although German management is averse to uncertainty, this potential weakness is compensated for by the thoroughness and consistency of its training and co-determination arrangements, which allow flexibility to be built into the system.

However, German managers may, because of the very specific cultural context of their country's success, be less geared to operating as multinational executives, indeed too few of their top managers have worked or studied abroad. The very strengths of *Technik*-based training may paradoxically lead to a certain "parochialism" (Randlesome 1988: 160). Managers' skills are based on function- or area-linked specialisms, and their development is often company-specific. The challenge, therefore, as in the Japanese case (although much less so), is to develop a truly international set of repertoires and outlook.

All in all, managers in Germany benefit from (and help to maintain) a high level of investment, due to a very positive savings ratio and consistently low inflation. This boon results in highly-developed human capital at all levels, which in turn facilitates enterprise efficiency and effectiveness. The upshot is likely to be that just as the Deutchmark has come to dominate European finance, so too will the West German (and perhaps soon the all-German) business culture influence managerial practice within the European Single Market. It seems that German "parochialism" will know fewer and fewer boundaries. This at least is the theory.

References

Bowra, C.M. (1985): *The Greek experience*, Pbk. ed. London: Weidenfeld and Nicolson.

Burnett, L. (1977): *Die Bundesdeutschen*. Frankfurt a-M: Leo Burnett Werbeagentur.

Campbell, A. (1991): "Issues of training strategy in British manufacturing" in J. Stevens and R. Mackay (eds.), *Training and competitiveness*, 25–35. London: Kogan Page/National Economic Development Office.

Campbell, A., A. Sorge and M. Warner (1989): *Microelectronic product applications in Britain and West Germany*. Aldershot: Gower.

Campbell, A. and M. Warner (1992): *New technology, skills and management*. London: Routledge.

Canetti, E. (1973): *Crowds and power*. London: Penguin.

Child, J. and A. Kieser (1979): "Organization and managerial roles in British and West German companies: an examination of a culture-free thesis" in C.J. Lammers and D.J. Hickson (eds.), *Organizations alike and unalike*, 251–271. London: Routledge.

Gardels, N. (1991): "Two concepts of nationalism: an interview with Sir Isaiah Berlin". *New York Review of Books* 32: 19.

Granick, D. (1962): *The European executive*. London: Weidenfeld and Nicholson.

Handy, C., F. Gordon, I. Gow and C. Randlesome (1988): *The making of managers: a report on management education, training and development in the USA, West Germany, France, Japan and the UK*. London: Manpower Services Commission, National Economic Development Office, British Institute of Management.

Heller, F., R. Mays and B. Wilpert (1976): "Methodology for multi-national study of managerial behaviour. The use of Contingency Theory" . Paper presented at Third Congress of Cross-cultural Psychology, Tilburg, Netherlands, July.

Hofstede, G. (1980): *Culture's consequences*. Beverly Hills, CA: Sage.

Hofstede, G. (1991): *Cultures and organizations: software of the mind*. London: McGraw-Hill.

Horowitz, J. (1978): "Management control in France, Great Britain and Germany". *Columbia Journal of World Business* 13/2: 16–22.

James, H. (1991): *A German identity, 1770–1990*. London: Routledge.

Kern, H. and M. Schumann (1987): "Limits of the division of labour: new production and employment concepts in West German industry". *Economic and Industrial Democracy* 8: 151–170.

Landes, D. (1960): "The structure of enterprise in the nineteenth century; the cases of Britain and Germany". Berkeley California Institute of Industrial Relations, Reprint No. 152.

Lane, C. (1990): "Vocational training and new production concepts in Germany: some lessons for Britain". *Industrial Relations Journal* 21: 247–259.

Lawrence, P. (1980): *Managers and management in West Germany*. London: Croom Helm.

Lawrence, P. (1989): "Management education in West Germany" in W. Byrt (ed.), *Management education: an international survey*, 151–171. London: Routledge.

Malzahn, M. (1991): *Germany 1945–1949: A sourcebook*. London: Routledge.

Maurice, M., A. Sorge and M. Warner (1980): "Societal differences in organizing manufacturing units: a comparison of France, West Germany and Great Britain". *Organization Studies* 1/1: 59–86.

Piore, M. and C. Sabel (1984): *The second industrial divide: possibilities for prosperity*. New York: Basic Books.

Pollard, S. (1981): *The wasting of the British economy*. London: Croom Helm.

Randlesome, C. (1988): "West Germany" in C. Handy, F. Gordon, I. Gow and C. Randlesome, *Making managers*, 125–162. London: Pitman.

Randlesome, C., W. Brierley, K. Bruton, C. Gordon and P. King (1990): *Business cultures in Europe*. London: Heinemann.

Reid, D. and B. Schlegelmilch (1988): "Planning and control in the U.K. and West Germany: a cross-cultural comparison within the mechanical engineering industry". University of Edinburgh Department of Business Studies Working Paper 88/20.

Rommel, G. (1991): *The secret of German competitiveness*. London: McKinsey.

Sorge, A., G. Hartmann, M. Warner and I. Nicholas (1983): *Microelectronics and manpower in manufacturing: applications of computer numerical control in Great Britain and West Germany*. Aldershot: Gower.

Sorge, A. and M. Warner (1986): *Comparative factory organisation*. Aldershot: Gower.

Spies, B. (1985): "Does myth blur the facts of West German training?" *BACIE Journal* (September): 22–24.
Woolcock, S., M. Hodges and K. Schreiber (1991): *Britain, Germany and 1992: the limits of deregulation*. London: Pinter/Royal Institute of International Affairs.

Chapter 7: Greece

Management in Greece

James Georgas

Introduction

The current status of management and organization in Greek private enterprises and in the public sector has been described by most knowledgeable observers as relatively underdeveloped, in comparison with most nations in northern Europe. With the exception of a few large industries, the banks, and the multinational corporations, which are organized on the basis of modern management methods, the overwhelming number of organizations in Greece operate essentially as an extended family, in which the owner–manager makes all the decisions, is reluctant to delegate authority, controls all aspects, and is involved in all the day-to-day details of the employees.

There are many criticisms of the characteristics of the typical Greek owner–manager. Kostoulas (1984) states that the Greek manager is condemned to be restricted to, and to be exhausted by, unproductive efforts. The stultifying bureaucratic procedures in the public sector has led to its being called the "seriously ill patient". Kontogiorgis (1976) describes the typical Greek manager as involving himself in attempting to control all the daily details and problems of the enterprise, with the result that there is not enough time or energy to devote himself to organization and planning. The result is improvization, and "instinct" necessarily takes the place of long-term planning.

In order to understand the current situation of management in Greece, one must begin with some statistics regarding the types of business organizations. According to Pilavios (1989), at the present time, 99.5 per cent of the businesses in Greece employ less than 100 personnel. More revealing of the organization of these businesses, 97.2 per cent employ less than 20 personnel, and 45 per cent are one-man enterprises. These statistics indicate that Greece has by far the highest percentage of small businesses in comparison to the other members of the European Community. Viewed from the other end of the scale, ICAP (1991) statistics reveal that only 2 per cent of Greek manufacturing firms employ more than

500 personnel, 14 per cent employ 100–499, 69 per cent employ 10–99, and 14 per cent employ 1–9.

The next characteristic of these businesses, both small and large, is critical in understanding the problems of establishing modern management techniques in Greece. As already stated, these enterprises are if not all, then almost all, family owned and run. The major question raised by informed observers is, when such an overwhelming percentage of enterprises have fewer than 20 employees, how many and what types of managers are required. Even more relevant is the issue that since the enterprises are family owned there is a reluctance to permit anyone to run them except family members. The owner, the head of the family, is also the manager, and thus the other members of the family—brothers, sons, wives and daughters, sons-in-law, other relatives and close friends—according to their hierarchical role in the family structure, claim, by blood or by friendship, the important roles in the enterprise. The only exception at the management level is the accountant, who may be hired because of his specific knowledge and, in most small businesses, is not a full-time employee. On the other hand, other employees may not necessarily be family members. We shall return to a detailed analysis of the family-owned business and the economic–historical reasons for its development.

Pilavios (1989) describes what he considers to be the chief characteristics, and problems, of small businesses in Greece. He confirms that there is no separation between ownership and management. As pointed out above, the owner is also, by definition, the manager. Cultural values dictate that the owner cannot even consider the possibility of someone outside the family running the business.

The second characteristic is that these small businesses have to restrict themselves to a single activity, usually in areas of low technology. A third characteristic is that bank loans to small family-owned businesses carry a low level of interest, guaranteed by the state. The interest is eight points below that of industrial loans. The historical reasons for this will be explained later. A fourth characteristic is the very limited number of consumers—often restricted to the local neighbourhood or village—upon which these businesses can base their activities. A fifth is the extremely low level of exports. A sixth characteristic is the lack of motivation for growth, since if the gross of the business exceeds 350 million drachmas, the enterprise is not classified by law as a small business, and is then no longer eligible for low-interest bank loans. The last is the low level of taxes, and the high level of tax evasion.

From the above, it will be clear that the thrust of this paper cannot be a description of current modern management practices in Greece but rather the reasons why these have not developed. However, it must also be emphasized at this point that modern management techniques are known; they are taught at the business schools; they are taught at special seminars directed toward management; there are translations of non-Greek books and there are books written by Greek authors. The problem is that attempts to interject modern management techniques into Greek enterprises encounter obstinate resistance, primarily on the part of the older generation.

Understanding the current status of management in Greece, or rather, the reluctance to establish modern techniques of organization, requires an understanding of its ecological, social and historical development (Georgas 1988; and in press).

History

At the beginning of the 19th century, the Hellenes were but one of many ethnic groups with a distinct language and culture within the Ottoman Empire which, during the 15th century, had captured Byzantium or New Rome, the seat of the Orthodox church and the antipod to the capital of Catholicism in Rome. The dissolution of the Byzantine Empire and subsequent Ottoman control had the effect of isolating the Hellenes from the profound cultural, religious, and economic changes that took place in Southern and Northern Europe during the Renaissance. However, the survival of both the Greek language and the Orthodox church was due, among other things, to the Ottoman rulers, who were essentially warriors, needing the knowledge and skills of the administrators of the former Byzantine Empire to undertake the bureaucratic tasks of running their empire. Because the Orthodox church was administered by the Hellenes, the Hellenic language became the predominant means of communication within the Ottoman Empire. Therefore, even though there was no nation state of Hellas or Greece, the continuity of the identity of Hellenism was maintained.

The profound social and economic evolution taking place in Europe during this period did not leave the Hellenes completely untouched. The Renaissance in Italy during the 16th and 17th century led to the renewal of interest in the ancient Greek classics, and Hellenes from Venice reintroduced the written language and culture to compatriots within the Ottoman Empire through secret schools. The withdrawal of Venice from the Eastern Mediterranean during the latter part of the 18th century, together with the opportunities afforded to enterprising sailors and merchantmen during the Napoleonic wars allowed Hellenes to engage in trading and merchant shipping throughout the Mediterranean, an historic means of subsistence which continues to the present day.

At the end of the 18th century, the Ottoman Empire was in a period of decline. Aided by the interest of Philhellenes such as Lord Byron, and because England, Russia and France were at odds with the Ottoman Empire, the Hellenes revolted in 1821, and within a decade had established an independent nation, which was under the influence of both the German States and the British Empire for the next 100 years.

During the first 20 or so years of this century, Greece was enmeshed in a series of conflicts such as the Balkan war, World War I, and at its conclusion, the attempt to regain Constantinople and other parts of the Ottoman Empire. What are today the island of Crete and all of northern Greece were not given up by the Ottomans until the early part of this century.

During the 20s and 30s Greek political life was characterized by coups against the royal family, counter coups and dictatorships. Greece entered World War II after being invaded by Italy, but after beating back the Italians, was defeated by Hitler in the spring of 1941. At the end of World War II, a civil war between the communists and the nationalists lasted until 1950, with the effect of delaying development.

During the 1950s, Greece at last began to industrialize, albeit tardily in relation to other European nations devastated by war. The rapid industrialization led to demographic changes, as young people left their agricultural pursuits in the small villages to go to urban centres such as Athens. During the 1960s clashes between the royal family and the political parties led to a military coup, which in turn led to the Papadopoulos dictatorship from 1967 to 1974. After the return of Caramanlis from exile, Greece became a member of the European Community in 1980.

Geographical Features

The characteristic natural features of Greece are its mountains, the hundreds of islands scattered throughout the Ionian, Aegean, and Cretan seas, and its few fertile plains.

In the past, the characteristic environmental and demographic features were small, isolated communities in the mountains and on the many islands, and relatively large cities on the plains, and at natural ports on the mainland and on a few islands. Because communication or travel between isolated communities in the mountains was very difficult, it resulted in their becoming autonomous and self-sufficient. Even in present-day Greece, it is only possible to travel between some islands once a week, or even less frequently. Another geographical feature which explains the delayed development of management is the relative isolation of the country from the rest of Europe, which became even more difficult after the Second

World War when Greece became separated from Europe by the Balkan states.

However, although small communities still exist in Greece, they are populated mainly by the elderly, and are no longer as autonomous as they used to be. Migration from the small communities to the large urban centres began in the 1950s and reached its peak in the 1970s. By 1981, almost 40 per cent of the population was concentrated in the two large urban areas of Athens and Thessaloniki.

Organization and Institutions of the Society

Economic Organization

The geographical features of Greece shaped specific types of subsistence patterns, which remained unchanged for hundreds of years. The plains, essentially broad valleys between mountains, permitted the cultivation of crops. Cities on the plains and mainland or island ports became trading and mercantile centres. In the mountains, the natural environment was only amenable to the herding of goats and sheep, and also to vine and olive oil cultivation, whereas, for maritime communities, fishing was the standard mode of subsistence, together with merchant shipping. Compared with northern Europe, industrial development in Greece remained limited until the 1930s, geared mainly to domestic needs. Greece was primarily a nation of peasant farmers, fishermen, herders, and merchants.

It was only after 10 years of German occupation and civil war that, in the 1950s, reconstruction and industrialization began in Greece. In the attempt to develop industries, new laws were passed allowing high import taxes and other favourable taxation, in order to protect fledgling industries from foreign competition (Editor 1987). Both this economic climate and political decisions favoured the creation of a few large industries which were granted monopolies in their spheres, together with a large number of small businesses. It is important to note that both large industries and the small ones were family owned and run. Although protecting markets from foreign competition is a common practice among industrialized nations, such measures are only usually taken for specific periods of time, until the industries become competitive. In Greece, this protectionism and state dependence remained until entry into the European Community in the 1980s, by which time Greek industry had gained control of the internal market, was protected from foreign competition by the state, and thus had not been stimulated to modernize its management techniques.

A second point regarding the development of monopolies in Greece

(Editor 1987), something which, at an early stage, may be necessary to the creation of an industrial base, was that their protection for long periods meant that competitive industries could not develop. In addition, as the banking system was almost completely nationalized, the small number of private banks had very little influence over financial policy-making. Governmental decisions inevitably led to supporting unproductive industries in order to avoid the political costs of unemployment and other effects of bankruptcy. In the 1980s the government went further and nationalized industries which were essentially bankrupt.

Under such a protectionist system, when either private industries or nationalized industries are subsidized by the government, there is little motivation for drastic and necessary changes in management techniques, since there are few consequences to pay for low productivity and poor management.

The above analysis refers mainly to the few large industries in Greece. However, as pointed out at the beginning of this chapter, Greece is characterized by an overwhelming number of businesses which employ less than 20 people. As indicated above, this too is a result of governmental policy which began during the 1950s, and which successive governments have supported because of the political cost of forcing such firms to become competitive. Low interest bank loans, available only below a ceiling of gross sales, discourage growth. In addition, as we shall see further on, the small family-owned business and a desire for autonomy, together with the low social status of being an "employee", has been part of the Greek culture for many generations.

Overall, in 1983, 30 per cent of the working population—a comparatively high figure—was engaged in either agriculture, forestry or fishing; 28.6 per cent were in industry, and 41.4 per cent in services.

Political Institutions and the Legal System

The geographical features of Greece, as discussed previously, are functionally related to the establishment of many small, isolated, and economically self-sufficient communities. The history of Greece has shown that effective political control of such communities, where communication was extremely difficult, was almost impossible. Thus, geographical features played a significant role in the development of self-government and a considerable degree of autonomy within these isolated communities. It must have been clear to the Ottoman rulers that effective political control of each of the thousands of small communities would have required a military presence well beyond their manpower capacities. The situation was different, though, with respect to the coastal cities and those on the accessible plains. It was here that the Ottomans concentrated their forces.

In the more remote communities, the Ottomans allowed partial self-government, providing they paid their taxes. The system of taxation, which originated in the Byzantine Empire, consisted of taxing the community as a whole, rather than individuals or the heads of households. Each community had an elected president and board of councillors, who were responsible for administration and for assigning to each family its share of the community tax burden. As will be discussed later, this relative local autonomy and self-government under which each community essentially set its own traditions, customs and the right to judge its own members according to local "laws", encouraged a critical approach to the social perception of law, fairness, and government, and a suspicion of central government. This has continued until the present time.

Yet despite this, and even because of it, governments from the post-war period to the present, have exercised strong control over all aspects of the economy (Pilavios 1989). As over 90 per cent of the banks are governmental, and thus dependent on political policies, price controls are traditionally very strict.

In addition, the state bureaucracy, which has members of each political party at every level, is very antiquated, slow, rigid and not conducive to flexible and quick decisions. At the present time, the government is trying to reform the bureaucratic system by evaluating and retraining civil servants; by introducing a promotion system based on merit rather than on years of experience; by installing information technology; and by reducing the number of signatures on applications, etc.

An illustration of the stultifying effects of bureaucracy is an experience of the author in obtaining a personal computer through the university. In July, a written request for buying a personal computer and a printer for the department was sent to the Rector's council. Three weeks later the Rector's Council approved the request and the price. The approval was typed and received by the author another three weeks later. The author then had to prepare an application regarding the specifications for the PC and the printer which was sent to the administrative offices of the university. The administrative offices then passed on this application to the Ministry of Education which also had to approve the request. In October, after approving the application, the Ministry of Education sent the request to the Ministry of Coordination which informed the author that he had to send a further application justifying the need and the uses of the PC. The author sent this application to the Ministry of Coordination in November. The relevant committee then had to prepare an evaluation of the request which was discussed in committee, approved and sent to the Minister of Coordination for his signature. The Minister approved the request in December and the request was passed back to the committee for action, which then informed the Ministry of Education, which informed the

University, which then sent the written approval to the author, who then ordered the PC in March of the following year, that is, eight months later. The supplier of the PC, in order to seek and extract payment, had to go through a similar procedure!

The Educational System

Management has been taught in four-year undergraduate programmes at Schools of Business Administration in Athens, Piraeus and Thessaloniki since the 1950s. The University of Piraeus offers a programme in management within the Department of Business Administration, as do the Economic University of Athens and the Macedonian University. The University of Patras has a Department of Management and the Panteios University in Athens a Department of Public Administration. The University of Athens has a Department of Political Science and Public Administration. In addition to the universities, the Technological Educational Institutes throughout Greece, with 3-year programmes similar in structure to those of the Polytechnics in the United Kingdom, offer courses in management and economics, and the Ministry of the Presidency has organized a National School of Public Administration, independent of the universities. Short business courses for graduates have also been established in the above schools during the past few years.

The Greek Productivity Centre (ELKEPA) is the oldest and the most active educational and research centre with a programme directed toward middle and upper managers, personnel directors and administrators in both the private and public sectors. Approximately 300 seminars, from 18 to 700 hours in duration, are presented every year, to approximately 10,000 recipients. The programme covers management and the development of human abilities, marketing, finance, and production. Close ties have been established with organizations, institutes and universities within Europe, such as the London Business School, the Irish Institute of Management and Le Institut Superieur des Affaires in France. The Hellenic Society of Enterprise Management (EEDE) has a systematic educational programme consisting of seminars, special courses, and conferences directed towards managers, and there is a similar course at The Institute for the Development of Human Potential (IEKA). In addition to graduates from Greek schools of business administration, a large number of Greeks have been trained in management techniques in Western Europe and North America.

Indeed, the number of books and articles on management theory (Kanellopoulos 1986; Kontogiorgis 1976; Kostoulas 1984), management techniques (Zevgarides 1978; Varlas 1981), and even on topics related to organizational psychology (Gedeon 1966) written by Greek authors, or translations of books and articles by internationally known management experts, is very impressive. Though all of these publications present current management theory as developed internationally, with little or no reference to the Greek context, there are, however, an increasing number of reflections and comments on the state of management in Greece (Pilavios 1989; Editor 1987).

Thus, Greek managers are fully aware of, and conversant with, modern management theory and practice. The intriguing question, which this chapter tries to address, is why—with few exceptions—the theory is not applied, and why there is such resistance to its application.

Religion

Perhaps the most important single influence during the Ottoman rule in maintaining the language and the identity of the Hellene was the Orthodox church. The clergy acted as teachers of the language and the culture to the young, were arbitrators within the small communities, were sometimes elected to the board of councillors, and were often the only literate members of the community. In addition, the church and the clergy were often the leaders of insurgencies against the Turks, and thus martyrs and symbols of opposition. The church played a major role in the revolution against the Ottomans. At the present time, 98 per cent of the population is Greek Orthodox.

Communications

The physical features of Greece had the important dual effect of limiting the amount of contact with the outside world, and restricting the amount of information available to the inhabitants of the small, isolated communities. Those living on the plains, at the large ports and trading centres, and those islands which had their own merchant fleets, were exposed to more sources of information and to foreign influences, than the inhabitants in the mountains. On the other hand, the lack of communication with the outside world helped to preserve the Greek language and culture.

The full effect of the mass media, and its most important medium, television, has reached the isolated villages only within the past 10 to 15 years. Construction of the nationwide road network began during the 1950s, with the result that nowadays virtually all areas are accessible. The recent increase in tourism has exposed people in isolated villages to foreign influences, and has played a strong role in the acculturation of Greece.

Bonds with Groups in the Immediate Community

The understanding of personal relationships in the community has to be based on concepts and data from social psychology. People belong to different ingroups, which vary according to the structure of the society, and the more complex the society the greater are the number of ingroups. Hofstede (1980) has studied the individualist–collectivist dimension in society and its relationship to organizations. Individualism is related to nuclear families, to self-orientation, to the emotional independence of the individual from organizations, to autonomy, to individual decision-making, and other social and individual variables. Collectivism is related to close ties with extended families, to collectivity-orientation, where duty and security is provided by the organization or the clan, and where group decisions are made, etc. Collectivistic societies also have fewer ingroups than do individualistic societies (Triandis et al. 1986). Triandis further elaborates the types of relationships characteristic of ingroups in collectivistic societies, such as, unquestioned attachment, distrust of outgroups, perception that ingroup norms are universally valid, automatic obedience to ingroup authorities, distrust and unwillingness to cooperate with outgroups. These concepts can be ultimately used to classify cultures along this dimension (Triandis et al. 1986).

In his study of work-related values, Hofstede found that Greece is placed nearer to the collectivist end of the dimension, in comparison with other nations. The collectivist Greek community was described by Giannopoulos (1975) in this way:

> The community was closed and highly suspicious of any outsider who might attempt to involve himself and possibly influence changes in civic affairs. Any violation of traditional ethical standards or religious customs, as well as local prohibitions, provoked the reaction and sanctions of the entire community. The members of the community were judge, jury and punishers of those who violated their customs, whatever was the law of the central government. The collective responsibility of the community members, the respect for life, the respect of one's honour and one's property, institutions collectively supported by the community, were carefully protected. The fair distribution of the tax burden among the community members, the right to elect their own leaders, the right to choose their teachers, their right to reject their priest, were rights carefully nurtured and guarded.

On the other hand, inter-group relationships, between factions composed of different families, were often hostile and destructive. As Giannopoulos (1975) describes it,

> The same community system which nurtured collective responsibility as a protection against outside intervention by the Ottomans, enclosed within itself the causes of complaints, disputes, fractionalism, and the division of the community into factions. The assignment of the amount of taxes by the

elected councillors was often unfair, which led to complaints and disputes. Thus, self-interest, ambitions and animosity divided the leaders and many of the families into factions.

Yet even in large urban centres such as Athens, where bonds within the neighbourhood are quite different from those in the small traditional community, families originating from the same rural community maintain their links and often have celebrations and dinners together. Moreover, families from the provinces return to their villages during Christmas, Easter and the summer months.

The Family System

The characteristic collectivist Greek family was an extended family, as is typical in many agricultural societies. The father was the *pater familias*, who controlled all aspects of the family, particularly economic and financial, and whose word was law. Within this strict hierarchy, the father made all the decisions, even with regard to the married children, but was also responsible for the welfare of the family members. Obedience and tradition were important values. Married sons or even cousins lived either in the same home, or nearby, and worked together cooperatively on the farm or in the small family business.

Although in Athens, and the other urban areas, nuclear families predominate, relationships even there are not as individualistic as elsewhere in Western Europe or in North America. The nuclear families maintain daily contact with their relatives. In many cases, brothers or sisters live in the same apartment building, or nearby, and the grand-mother or grandfather live either with the family, or nearby. An interesting statistic which illustrates the continuing close dependence on relatives is that approximately 90 per cent of young mothers report using a relative as a baby-sitter.

The extended family system was probably functional in agricultural societies because many hands are needed for the cultivation of the land. However, in traditional Greece, such an extended family was also characteristic of fishermen, merchants, and indeed occurred throughout the society. Perhaps the most cogent description of the functional relationship between social factors and the structure of the Greek family was given by a traveller through Greece, Thiersch, in 1833:

> Because there never was a central government which was able to control or protect the people, one had to search elsewhere for protection and support. The most natural and secure support was found in the family, whose members, including second cousins, are nowhere so united and so willing to help

each other as in Greece. The isolated individual has to ally himself with some group. He becomes a follower, or a leader of a group. In this case, a prominent person has a group of followers dependent on him, who call on him, who ask his advice, who execute his wishes, who protect their common interests, always being careful to be worthy of his esteem and his trust. This is the nature of the many groups in Greece. . . Rather than being astonished regarding this, one must recognize in this system, the course and the natural and necessary organization of a political society which was left to its own devices for survival.

Thiersch's description more than a century ago is remarkably similar to the analysis by Triandis and Vassiliou (1972). They show that the Greek ingroup is composed of more than the extended family, and includes such people as, for example, the best man at a wedding, the godfather, in-laws, and friends, with the basic criterion that they show concern and support during times of need. The appropriate forms of behaviour towards members of the ingroup are cooperation, protection and help, while appropriate forms of behaviour towards members of the outgroup are competition and hostility (Triandis et al. 1968).

Thus it is clear why businesses in Greece, both small and large, are family owned and run. The only people you can trust are members of your extended family. One would not trust a stranger to run the business, but only to handle the accounting for the purpose of fulfilling one's tax obligations. The recent call for modern management in Greece is typically answered by the small family business sending a son or a nephew to business school, not with the idea that he will venture into wider realms, but for him to return to help run the business.

Even in larger industries or middle-sized corporations, the members by law of the board of trustees are inevitably members of the family or close friends and the stock is 100 per cent family owned. The reaction of the average business owner towards professional management is typically that of the person who has built his business from rags to riches. He dismisses the outsider as not having the experience. It is interesting that even in shipping, in which Greeks have been successful, the business in London or New York is still run by the head of the family (Melissinos 1991).

Because of the large number of small enterprises in Greece with a relatively small number of employees, and due to the primarily internal market, the owner–manager can effectively control everything. Even if the business grows and he is forced to hire more employees, so that the firm has to be more impersonally organized, he is still reluctant to delegate authority to professional managers.

Conclusions and Prospects for the Future

This chapter has attempted to explain the current situation of management in Greece in terms of an historical analysis of social and economic forces and in terms of socio-psychological concepts. These forces have led to the creation of a very large number of small businesses and manufacturing firms, almost all of them family owned and run. In addition, the nature of the Greek extended family, in which immediate family members and relatives work in the business, has played a special role. Because of the closed family system, there is a reluctance to employ non-family members as managers. The family ingroup mistrusts outsiders, and because the owner–manager operates in a paternalistic manner, he is used to making all the decisions, and controls all aspects of the business.

If one analyzes the problem of the Greek family owner–manager whose small business begins to expand, in terms of the open system theory of Katz and Kahn (1978), it is the problem of how one person can effectively maintain control over an increasing number of input variables. As the business expands, and the number of employees increases, the owner–manager who attempts to personally control all the details of the enterprise soon becomes overwhelmed by the volume and increasing complexity of the managerial tasks. Whereas the next typical step in other nations is to delegate some responsibilities to other levels of management, the Greek owner–manager still operates as if the enterprise were an extended family system. Just as the paternalistic, but autocratic, father of the traditional extended family is highly reluctant to delegate, so is the Greek owner–manager. The emphasis on control of all details and the maintainance of total authority results in an inability to deal with information, and a low level of organization and productivity.

On the other hand, the paternalism, and the fact that many of the employees are either family members or have close personal ties with the owner sustains close emotional ties with employees. Theodoratos' (1989) study of 180 upper and middle level managers from 42 manufacturing firms situated in small cities in Greece, excluding Athens, using Fiedler's contingency model of effective leadership (Fiedler 1967; Fiedler and Garcia 1987), is pertinent. Theodoratos found that the degree of power in the manager's role was greater than in American findings, and the rating of the "least preferred co-worker" (attitude to fellow employees) was more positive. Theodoratos interprets the latter finding as indicative of the attempt of the Greek manager to maintain positive and close emotional relationships with personnel, in order to eliminate antagonistic behaviour. This suggests that in small cities and towns, the relationships between managers and personnel are an extension of social ties within the community.

Within a closed internal market, as Greece has been for generations, this system of organization was functional. The current problem is that the system of family management is ill-equipped to deal with the entry of Greece into the European Community, and with the growth of many of these small businesses into larger firms.

In addition, the protection of internal markets from foreign competition and laws which regulated small businesses did not offer the motivation to create larger units or to improve efficiency through modern management techniques (Nicolaou-Smokoviti and Stavroulakis 1991).

This can largely explain why, although there has been a plethora of information about management theory in Greece for many years—it has been taught in the schools of business administration, there have been many seminars and conferences, and books and articles on the topic—, Greek owner–managers have strongly resisted its application.

On the other hand, Greece's entry into the European Community has resulted in imperative pressures to integrate its economy into that of the international market (Nicolaou-Smokoviti and Stavroulakis 1990). Multinational firms, particularly banks, have led the way by attracting top personnel. The large Greek firms have begun to adapt by employing modern management methods. It is clear that there is a large pool of local talent which, given the right inducements, could be successfully mustered. However, the need for managerial talent is not restricted to the private sector. Bearing in mind that more than half of the activity in the economy is run by the public sector through a multitude of state-owned corporations, which the government is attempting to privatize, the necessity for applying management techniques is obvious.

Although it is difficult to believe that the behaviour patterns of Greek businesses will change overnight, processes of change can already be seen. The ultimate factor is time. It is inevitable that the resistance of the older generation to management techniques will wither away as the younger generation takes over, and that management will experiment with more effective organizational methods in order to enhance productivity. However, management is more than the efficient organization of the manager's job and of the structure of the enterprise. At its heart are harmonious relationships with people. It may well be that the emphasis on family bonds and close emotional links within the workplace, which are so central to Greek culture, will be a future asset in maintaining good manager–employee communications and relationships.

References

Editor (1987): "Organosi ton epichiriseon. I1 Helleniki 25eti empiria" [Organiza-
tion of enterprises: 25 years of Greek experience]. *Deltio Dioikisis Epichiriseon*
239: 23–25.

Fiedler, F. (1967): *A theory of leadership effectiveness*. New York; McGraw-Hill.

Fiedler, G. and J.E. Garcia (1987): *New approaches to effective leadership*. New
York: Wiley.

Gedeon, S. (1966): *Psychologica themata gia dioikitika stelechi* [Psychological
themes for administrative personnel]. Athens: Industrial School of Piraeus.

Georgas, J. (1988): "An ecological social model: The case of Greece" in J.W.
Berry, S.H. Irvine and E.B. Hunt (eds.), *Indigenous cognition: Functioning in
cultural context*, 106–123. Dordrecht, The Netherlands: Nijhoff.

Georgas, J. (in press): "An ecological–social model for indigenous psychology: The
example of Greece" in U. Kim and J.W. Berry (eds.), *Indigenous psychologies:
Theory, method and experience in cultural context*. Beverly Hills, CA: Sage.

Giannopoulos, I. (1975): "Koinotites" [Communities] in *History of the Greek
nation*, Vol. II, 134–143. Athens: Ekdotiki Athenon.

Hellenic Society for Business Administration (1972): *Helleniko management*
[Greek Management]. Athens: EEDE.

Hofstede, G. (1980): *Culture's consequences*. Beverly Hills, CA: Sage.

ICAP (1971): *To Helleniko management* [Greek management]. Athens: ICAP.

ICAP (1991): *ICAP Directory*. Athens: ICAP.

Kanellopoulos, C.K. (1986): *Apotelesmatiki dioikisi anthropinon poron* [Effective
management of human resources]. Athens: Industrial School of Piraeus.

Katz, D. and R.L. Kahn (1978): *The social psychology of organizations*, 2nd ed.
New York: Wiley.

Kontogiorgis, D. (1976): "Ta epichirisiaka stelechi kai e koinoniki empiria"
[Administrative personnel and the social experience]. *Spoydai* 3: 13–20.

Kostoulas, G.I. (1984): *Management*. Athens: Hellenic Euroekdotiki.

Melissinos, G. (1991): "Greek management today". (personal communication)

Nicolaou-Smokoviti, L. and D. Stavroulakis (1990): "Trends toward the change of
organizational structure and the decision-making process in Greece". Paper
presented at the conference "Man and Work on the Threshold of the Third
Millenium". Bratislava, Czechoslovakia.

Nicolaou-Smokoviti, L. and D. Stavroulakis (1991): "Small and medium-sized
firms in Greece". Paper presented at the conference "Small Business, Market
and Society". Tbilisi, Republic of Georgia.

Pilavios, A. (1989): "Hellenic management: Poso kostizi e elleipsi hellenikou
management" [Greek management: The cost of the lack of Greek management].
Management Newsletter 4: 9–11.

Theodoratos, E.F. (1989): "Hegesia: To syntelestiko protypo tis apotelesmatikis
mathisis" [Leadership: The contingent model of effective leadership]. Ph.D.
Dissertation, The University of Athens.

Thiersch, F. (1833): *De l'état actuel de la Grèce*. Leipzig.

Triandis, H.C., V. Vassiliou and M. Nassiakou (1968): "Three cross-cultural
studies of subjective culture". *Journal of Personality and Social Psychology*
(Monograph Supplement 8) 4: 1–42.

Triandis, H.C. and V. Vassiliou (1972): "An analysis of subjective culture" in H.C. Triandis (ed.), *The analysis of subjective culture*, 299–335. New York: Wiley.

Triandis, H.C., R. Bontempo, H. Betancourt, M. Bond, K. Leung, A. Brenes, J. Georgas, C.H. Hui, G. Marin, B. Setiadi, J.B.P. Sinha, J. Verma, J. Spangenberg, H. Tousard and G. Montmollin (1986): "The measurement of the etic aspects of individualism and collectivism across cultures". *Australian Journal of Psychology* 30: 257–267.

Varlas, P. (1981): "Axiologisi ton epichirisiakon stelexon stis hellenikes biomixanikes epichiriseis" [Evaluation of the managing personnel in Greek manufacturing firms]. Ph.D. dissertation, Industrial School of Piraeus.

Zevgarides, S. (1978): *Organosi kai dioikisi: Theoria kai helleniki praktiki* [Organization and management: Theory and Greek practice]. Athens: Papazisi.

Chapter 8: Ireland

Managing the Economy of a Newly Independent State

Brian Leavy

Introduction

The Republic of Ireland acceded to the European Community in 1972, along with the United Kingdom and Denmark, and has a current population of around 3.5 million. It has effectively enjoyed sovereign government since 1921 when the Irish Free State was established. Prior to that it was an integral part of the United Kingdom and was governed directly from London. Ireland is an island economy with a small domestic market and a location which is on the western periphery of Europe. Its peripherality is, however, often exaggerated. It is in fact geographically closer to the community's largest and richest population concentration, the London–Paris–Bonn triangle, than many other countries or regions of the EC.

The Irish economy has been characterized as small, open and mixed. Private enterprise, cooperatives and state-owned enterprise all play major roles in the economic activity of the country. Ireland imports much of its raw materials and capital goods and exports much of its production. As such it is always very exposed to the prevailing economic conditions of its major trading partners. However one notable feature since independence has been the degree to which the country has diversified its trading relationships and activities. In 1922 nearly 98 per cent of Irish exports, almost all of which were agricultural goods, went to the United Kingdom. Now the UK accounts for just 29 per cent of total exports, France, Germany and the United States for almost 30 per cent and Italy, the Netherlands and the Benelux countries for a further 15 per cent. These are now the country's seven largest trading partners.

The economy is small in international terms. The total market capitalization of the Irish top 500 is less than 2 per cent of that of the top 500 in the United Kingdom. However, it is an economy which has been substantially modernized in terms of technology, management and organization. Ireland is now one of the Community's largest manufacturers of high technology computer equipment using all of the latest developments in advanced manufacturing techniques. The computer–electronics sector, with a turnover of £4.2B, now accounts for almost 30 per cent of Irish exports and rivals agri-business as the country's main export activity. While the computer–electronics sector is dominated by foreign-based multinational companies, the last decade has seen the emergence of some indigenous companies of world-class standing and multinational scope in such diverse industries as printing/packaging, building aggregates, electric heating appliances, and aircraft leasing.

The central underlying theme of this chapter is that Irish management and organization is quite a recent creation. Its current character has been forged, and its particular ecology fashioned, through the process of national economic, social and cultural development since the country became independent in 1921. Though "the traditions of the Irish are the oldest of any race in Europe north and west of the Alps" and though "Ireland is today the only Celtic nation state left in the world" (Curtis 1961:1) it is the distinct nature of the historical evolution of Irish management and organization under national self-government, as much as any generic Celtic quality, that gives it its unique niche within the broader category of English-speaking, Western management. The rest of the chapter, therefore, sets out to examine how the current nature of Irish management and organization has evolved since independence. It begins by reviewing briefly the major phases in the country's development. It then goes on to examine the major forms of organization that now dominate the nation's economic life and assesses their historical importance in the shaping of modern Irish management. The chapter ends with a brief review of the current position of Irish management and organization in relation to greater European integration.

The Modern Irish State since 1922

Since the first millennium, the history of Ireland has been dominated by its relationship with Britain. Nature had placed the two islands in such close proximity that it was "inevitable that their destinies should be interwoven in various ways" (Curtis 1961:v). The British influence in the country began with the Norman invasion in 1169. The Norman colonization of Gaelic Ireland was not fully successful, however, and the 15th century was marked by a Gaelic recovery and a return to effective Irish aristocratic home rule. Ireland was "reconquered" and "resettled" by the Tudor monarchy in the late 16th and early 17th centuries and from this time until independence in 1921 the political State had "seldom been representative of the majority who believed themselves to be the true and historic Irish nation" (Curtis 1961:vi). Ireland continued to be administered as a separate kingdom under British rule until, in the revolutionary ferment of the late 18th century, William Pitt tried to finally pacify the country and quell her long-running separatist tendency through the establishment of the full political union of Great Britain and Ireland. The United Kingdom of Great Britain and Ireland lasted for just over a century until Britain finally accepted that nothing short of granting a substantial measure of self-government to Ireland would ever satisfy the vast majority of her people.

The modern Irish State was founded in 1921 when British administration in southern Ireland finally came to an end under the terms of the Anglo-Irish Treaty. Northern Unionists, many of them direct descendants of the Tudor settlers, were strongly opposed to the break up of the union with Britain and Ireland was partitioned under the new arrangement. This still left a large number of nationalists under Northern Irish jurisdiction, which in time proved to be a poor basis for the development of a stable polity in that part of the island. As a result the question of Northern Ireland has remained the central political issue in Anglo–Irish relations to the present day. The 1921 settlement was contentious and split the nationalist movement. This split was the origin of the two main parties that have dominated southern Irish politics ever since. Both Fianna Fail (anti-Treaty) and Fine Gael (pro-Treaty) parties are essentially parties of the centre with a broad spectrum of appeal. Changes of government in Ireland since the foundation of the State, have tended to be viewed by the electorate as changes of management rather than ideology.

The partitioning of the country left the new Irish Free State with a polity that was over 90 per cent Catholic in practice, tradition and conviction. Nationalism and Catholicism were very central cultural forces in the first 40 years of the new state's existence. Since the 1960s the influence of each has been on the wane (Fennell 1983).

Self-sufficient, Inward-looking and Traditional — The First 40 Years

Economic development was slow during the first forty years of the new state's independent existence and was overshadowed by political concerns. The first Free State administration inherited an agrarian economy, a functioning state apparatus and political instability. The country's main industries in the 20s were brewing, distilling, biscuit-making and agriculture, with agriculture being far and away the predominant economic activity. The inheritance of a functioning civil service was a major advantage. Irish public administration was, from the outset, firmly rooted in the traditions of the British civil service. The main contribution of this first administration was to establish and secure a system of parliamentary democracy for the future government of the country. Its economic approach was "cautious and experimental" (O'Brien 1962:15).

A new administration came to power in 1932 with a very definite vision of the kind of Irish society that it wanted to create. This was the vision of its charismatic leader Eamonn de Valera. De Valera was a very able politician and statesman who readily inspired the political pride of his followers in their newly acquired status as an independent people. He was obsessed with sovereignty. He wanted to make the country as economically self-sufficient as possible and to recover as much of the country's cultural distinctiveness as was salvageable after many centuries of British dominance. Economic efficiency and comparative living standards were of secondary importance. The society that he wanted to create was to be essentially rural, Gaelic, Catholic in ethos, and secure from unwanted outside influences (Lee and O'Tuathaigh 1982). De Valera was the architect of the Irish constitution.

Sean Lemass, de Valera's most able minister, supported the policy of self-sufficiency but was determined to advance the country's industrialization. When private capital was slow to invest in industrial projects, in spite of the incentives offered by the new policy's protectionist measures, Lemass had had little hesitation in using the resources of the State. During the 1932–48 period the number of state-owned enterprises (SOE's) quadrupled from 6 to 24 and the SOE became a firmly established part of the country's economic structure in such diverse areas as transportation, life assurance, peat processing and sugar processing. The setting up of such SOE's, as Lemass later explained, was always based on pragmatism and expediency and not as "part of a deliberate policy of state socialism" (Chubb and Lynch 1969:177). The very pragmatism and expediency of the approach helped to avoid potential Church–State conflict. Catholic social thinking on the proper organization of society was at its most influential in Ireland at this time and was generally wary of any extension of the state apparatus (Whyte 1980).

In spite of the best efforts of Lemass and his colleagues, the economy of the country was still grossly under-developed by the 1950s. The new enterprises which were fostered under the protectionist self-sufficiency policy were not providing enough industrial employment to cope with the flight from the land. Many had simply remained small scale, inefficient, and complacent behind the tariff barriers. Emigration was running at a rate of 50,000 per year. The Irish people were clearly not to be satisfied with the de Valera rural idyll of frugal comfort and traditional values. The prevailing mood throughout the country was one of despondency. The attempt to close off the society, and to keep as many people as possible on the land, had led to economic and cultural stagnation. The people had lost confidence in the ability of their leaders to control the economic destiny of the country.

Change and Modernity — Ireland in the 1960s

This despondency was quickly reversed in the following decade. The 1960s brought with them some major changes right across the whole spectrum of Irish life as Irish society swung "on its axis to face a new direction" (Lee 1979a:166).

The first major change was the economic sphere. In 1958 Lemass embarked on a dramatic new economic strategy. He officially abandoned the isolationist policy of self-sufficiency and determined to open out the Irish economy, and with it Irish social and economic life in general, to new investments, new ideas and new markets. In line with this fresh approach it was decided to seek entry into the European Economic Community at the earliest possible opportunity. He further embarked on a deliberate programme for economic expansion, based on the French model of national indicative planning, in order to bring out a resurgence of will and confidence throughout the country. Lemass recognized that this new approach to economic development demanded "a very high degree of national solidarity and cooperation" (*Irish Press* 6–7–61). It heralded the beginning of a new level of cooperation between future governments and their "social partners", the employers, unions and farming organizations, in the process of national economic management and development.

This fundamental change in national economic strategy allowed the country to take full advantage of the general improvement in economic conditions that were then prevailing in international trade and the Irish economy expanded at an unprecedented rate throughout the decade. Fiscal policy shifted from protectionism which had tended to encourage complacency and inefficiency to tax incentives for exporting activity which were designed to encourage initiative, expansion and efficiency. This policy was extended to the active encouragement of foreign investment in the Irish economy in order to help accelerate the modernization and industrialization of the country. The foreign-owned projects were targeted at areas that tended to complement indigenous capital rather than displace it and so helped to create a more diversified export-oriented economy. It was from this initiative that the computer–electronic and pharmaceutical sectors of the present economy were to eventually evolve.

Ireland's transition during the 60s was not purely economic. It extended into all aspects of the social fabric. Irish society became everywhere more empirical and less traditional throughout the decade, with "a new emphasis on information" (Lee 1979a:171) and the "increasing tendency for Irishmen to measure their achievements by the standards of Western Europe" (Lyons 1973:652). Television brought mass access to new ideas and new influences and was increasingly used to subject traditional authority figures and their religious, political and economic dogmas to mass scrutiny. Vatican II played its part by encouraging the development of a more involved, more questioning, and more empirical laity in religious matters, which in itself was culturally very significant in a predominantly Catholic country.

The new openness to other societies and other ideas also led to a greater appreciation of the importance of education in general, and of science and technology in particular, for the development of a modern industrial economy (Coolahan 1984). In the most radical reform of the educational system since the foundation of the State both the second and third level systems were greatly expanded in this period to make it possible for all young people of whatever means to progress to their highest level of capability (Sheehan 1979). Finally, as the decade progressed, the influence of the revolutionary generation in Irish society was everywhere receding and the mantle of leadership was being handed over to a younger, more pragmatic generation of career professionals. Lemass tapped into the nationalism of this new generation, which was still a potent motive force at that time, and harnessed it to help him with the "historic task" of reviving and modernizing the economy.

The Lemass-led strategy for economic expansion led to the expansion of the state sector of the economy in a concentrated effort to mobilize national resources in the economic development effort. Again, this was done for pragmatic rather than ideological reasons. Many state-funded development agencies were initiated or expanded during this period in such areas as agricultural, industrial, economic and social research and in industrial and management training and development. The leading agency in the whole economic development drive was the Industrial Development Authority (IDA). The IDA spearheaded the effort to attract direct foreign investment to Ireland and became a model of its kind in the international arena.

Living standards in the country rose by over 50 per cent during the 1960s and Ireland became "a net gainer from migration for the first time in recorded history" (Walsh 1979:35). However, economic expansion also brought with it a new set of problems and tensions. As the 1960s progressed, and the economy expanded, the attention of many interests turned to the question of the fair distribution of the benefits. Progressive urbanization and industrialization brought with them new tensions between town and country, between farmers and industrial wage-earners. The economy became more diversified as it grew and old relativities were challenged by the emergence of new classes of workers and salaried professionals. The existing machinery was unable to handle these newly emergent tensions in the economic and social structure and the decade was one of unprecedented "upheaval" in industrial relations (McCarthy 1973).

Industrial relations in Ireland had been based, since the start, on voluntarism and collective bargaining (Hillery 1980) and had largely followed the British pattern in terms of traditions and organization (Fogarty 1980). The 1970s witnessed a number of industrial relations initiatives to cope with the newly emergent tensions. The responsibilities of the Labour Court, in existence since 1946, were redefined in 1969 to bring them more up to date. The employer–labour conference was reconstituted in 1970 and played a major role throughout the inflationary 1970s in the centralized development of a series of National Wage Agreements over the 1970–78 period.

Ireland in Europe—1972 to the Present

Ireland's decision to join the EC had already been anticipated in the programme for economic expansion that was initiated in 1958. For this reason, when accession finally came it was undramatic, though it was potentially the most far-reaching choice that the country had made since it gained its independence. Indeed by giving the country a seat, in its own right, at the European table, EC entry was seen by most Irish people as a positive expression of their sovereignty rather than as a diminution. From an economic standpoint Ireland had already tried the isolationist approach and had abandoned it as a dismal failure. EC entry then became the logical extension of the new, more outward-looking, approach. Ireland expected EC entry to help accelerate the process of economic development and modernization. From a political point of view, EC entry appeared to many Irish people, north and south, to offer a more positive context within which the age-old problem of Northern Ireland might be eventually resolved.

By the 1980s, the underlying structure of Irish economic and social life had undergone substantial transformation after over two decades of unprecedented economic expansion. The economy, as a whole, had become more diversified internally and more integrated internationally. Agriculture's share of GDP dropped from 22 per cent to 15 per cent over the 1960–79 period; industry's share rose from 28 per cent to 38 per cent over the same period. Over the 1961–78 period employment in agriculture fell from 397,500 to 229,000, employment in industry rose from 257,000 to 319,000 and employment in services grew from 416,000 to 500,000. Over the same period, the proportion of those at work classified as employees rose overall from 56 per cent to 69 per cent. The proportion of those classified as professionals or managers rose from 7.6 per cent to 13.3 per cent and the class profile of all of those in the employee category had changed from 36 per cent middle class, 20 per cent skilled manual workers and 44 per cent unskilled manual workers to 50 per cent, 29 per cent and 22 per cent respectively. As Rothman and O'Connell (1982:63) concluded from these data "by 1979, Ireland had clearly ceased to be characterised as petit bourgeois: the predominant categories were of large scale employers and of well-qualified employees".

The public service had also become enlarged and more diversified in line with the general expansion in the rest of the economy. Public authority spending had increased from 24 per cent of GNP to 42 per cent over the 1958–78 period, while over the same two decades the numbers employed in the public sector had risen from 182,000 to 295,000. By the early 1980s, Ireland had been transformed into "one of the most socialised countries outside of the centrally planned economies" (Walsh 1986:62), though not as a result of any conscious strategy or ideology. This increase in the public sector reflected the growing importance of the government as an employer in the economy. In the late 70s the government became directly involved in negotiations with employers and unions as National Wage Agreements evolved into National Understandings. These national understandings widened the agenda to include issues of taxation, social welfare, job-creation and health education in the overall negotiations around wage demands and inflation containment objectives. On the trading front, the economy had become more open and more integrated in line with the overall strategy for export-led development. Irish exports as a percentage of GNP rose from 25 per cent in 1960 to over 60 per cent by 1985 and international trading became more extensive as the UK's share of the export pattern fell from 75 per cent to 34 per cent over the 1960–84 period (McAleese 1986).

The general recession in international economic activity in the early 1980s brought with it a new set of problems for Irish economic development. Indeed, as was the case in many other Western economies, the decade of the 1980s proved to be one of low growth and retrenchment and brought radical changes throughout the whole economy. No sector was left untouched. Leading private sector companies went through major transformation on an unprecedented scale. The whole thrust of industrial policy was redirected, in the light of the Telesis Report (1982), to put renewed emphasis on the indigenous sector. The leading dairy cooperatives were forced to redefine their business missions and capital structures under pressure from the quotas and cutbacks imposed under the Common Agricultural Policy. Direct state involvement in the economy came under fresh scrutiny. It had grown to a level that the economy could no longer support. Reform and rationalization of the public sector became an urgent priority. Yet this was resisted at every turn by powerful sectional interests, vocational and organizational, that sought to defend their traditional preserves (Farrell 1986). With the progressive weakening of nationalism and Catholicism as traditional bonding agents it had become more difficult for national leaders to "mobilize the national will" than in previous times. The situation reached critical proportions before concerted action was taken, as the spiralling public debt, at over 70 per cent of GNP and rising, became the biggest impediment to any return to economic growth.

In 1987 the Government was able to persuade the employers and the unions to enter with it into an agreed programme for national economic recovery. This was a return to the kind of corporatist approach which had operated during the 1970s but had been abandoned in 1981. The first phase of the programme for national recovery was effective in helping to create the conditions for a return to economic growth, including the rationalization of the public sector, the stabilization of the public debt and the control of inflation through a general agreement on wages and personal taxation. This framework has been sustained for a further phase to carry the country into the first half of the 1990s. In contrast to the indicative programming of the 1960s, however, there has been no expansion in the state sector to lead the recovery. National policy in the 1990s is now firmly banking on the private sector to lead the process of future economic expansion, with public policy playing a supporting role.

Profiles of Irish Organizations

In the last section, we examined how the modern Irish state has evolved and modernized since independence in 1922 and how the economic and social fabric of Irish life has developed and diversified. We now turn to examine each of the main forms of organization that have come to play prominent roles in the nation's economic structure during that period and to assess their importance in the development of Irish management. These are co-operatives, state-owned enterprises, private capitalist concerns and state agencies.

Co-operatives

The co-operative form of organization was introduced into Irish economic life in the 1890s. While it has since ramified into many sectors of the nation's economic activity its main success as an organizational form has been in the dairy industry.

The foundation of the co-operative movement in Ireland represented a unique triumph of economic reason and pragmatism over political passion.

Sir Horace Plunkett persuaded nationalist and unionist parliamentarians alike to put aside their deep political differences over the Home Rule question to try to find a better way to organize Irish agriculture in the interests of the producers and their communities. Farmers, and their rural communities, were being kept at subsistence level by their lack of economic power over the value of their produce. This failure by the mass of Irish farmers to rise above subsistence level was, in Plunkett's view, the major impediment to the development of the whole economy at that time. He introduced the co-operative form of organization into Irish agriculture in the 1890s in tandem with the mechanical cream separator so that organizational and technical innovation together helped to transform the dairy industry from farm-based processing to a creamery-based system. His early success in the dairy industry led him to establish the co-operative movement on a national footing in 1894. Plunkett and his fellow co-operators fully intended to promote the co-operative form of organization into all forms of economic activity but the dominance of the form in the dairy industry completely overshadowed any contribution that it was ever destined to make elsewhere in the economy.

The co-operative form of organization is very significant in Irish life not only for its current role in the organization of the dairy industry but also for its historical role in the development of Irish management and organization. By the early 1920s, when the Irish state had gained its independence, there were already over 400 co-operative creameries established throughout the country. Creamery managers had emerged as one of the first major classes of professional manager in Irish economic life. As time went on, this class of manager began to take on more and more of the characteristics now associated with professional management. Training and qualification, first in dairy science and later to include business methods, became over time an integral part of their professional development. In pre-1960s Ireland they were pivotal, not only to the economic development of their creameries but also to the social and economic fabric of the rural communities that they served. They were part of a close-knit parish structure and were people of status and influence on a par with the other two main community leaders, the local teacher and the parish priest. The Irish Creamery Managers Association, founded in 1902, was also one of the earliest professional management associations to be established in the country.

Irish governments, led by either of the major political parties, have tended to be supportive of the co-operative movement's position in Irish economic life, if at times not always patient with it. For example, in 1927 the dairy industry was suffering from severe over-capacity and a shake-out was inevitable. While there were over twice as many co-operative creameries as proprietary creameries in existence at the time, the co-operative units were the most vulnerable. The direct intervention of the government of the day was crucial in preserving and enhancing the pivotal position of the co-operative movement in the future organization and management of the industry. All of the proprietary creameries were bought out by the State for transfer over time to the movement. As a further example, in 1958 a survey team was set up by the Lemass Government to examine the readiness of the dairy industry for EC entry. The team highlighted the need for greater consolidation in the industry's structure. It questioned the capacity of the co-operative movement to lead the industry through the process and suggested by-passing it if necessary because the need for structural change in the national interest was so urgent (Survey Team 1963). The government's response was to commission an international expert to help the movement to reform itself (Knapp 1964). Then it publicly chartered the movement, in its indicative programming process, with the national role of leading the industry through major structural rationalization.

The rationalization process was slow and painful. It effectively meant the break-up of the parish-based structure and the creation of new larger-scale, regionally-based, dairy processing centres with more complex organizational structures. Many of the older creamery managers resisted the change because it meant the passing of a tightly-knit economic system and way of life within which they had position and status. Many of the younger managers welcomed the transition to larger, more complex, organizations because it offered better career prospects and more varied professional challenges. The transformation in the management of Irish dairying that happened during the 1958–74 rationalization of the industry was a direct microcosm of the larger transformation in the wider social and economic structure that took place during this transitionary period in Irish national life.

The current structure of the industry has been largely determined by the outcome of this rationalization process which was virtually complete by 1974. Six major processing centres emerged from this process to lead the industry in its further development. These six organizations are now among the largest enterprises in the national economy, accounting for almost £2b in turnover between them. During the 1970s they were production-oriented and commodity focused and grew easily with this strategy within the context of the Common Agricultural Policy. Then conditions in the dairy industry changed dramatically during the 1980s. In the face of zero-growth in national milk production, under CAP restraints, all of these processing centres have turned to formal strategic planning processes to manage their further development. This has led to greater elaboration in internal organization as marketing and product development functions were strengthened. It has also led to the redefinition of business missions, business domains and corporate structures. The Kerry Group has led the way. It has redefined itself from a leading Irish dairy processor to a major international food business and has led the sector in diversification and overseas acquisition activities. The Group has also led the sector in securing fresh capital through the stock exchange and in transforming itself into a private limited company at corporate level. Other major processors are already following this lead.

The influence of the co-operative form of organization on the future development of Irish agri-business now seems to be on the decline. This is a reflection of some of the endemic problems and features of the Irish experience with this organizational form. One major problem with the movement in Ireland was that it was ideologically weak from the beginning. The co-operative form of organization was embraced by many "less as a social creed and more a business device" and education in co-operative philosophy and principles was too often "glossed over as an academic consideration" by industry leaders (Bolger 1977:121, 127). This weakness in basic ideological commitment was manifest in destructive competition between co-operatives, in the failure of individual societies to combine effectively for marketing purposes and in the inadequate financial support forthcoming from these societies for the further development of the movement as a whole. As a result it now seems that the co-operative form is beginning to be discarded or transformed as pragmatically as it was adopted in the first place.

State-owned Enterprises

State-owned enterprises have been a major element of Irish economic activity since the 1930s. Currently there are ten such organizations in the top seventy Irish companies with a combined turnover of over £3.5B. The activities of the top ten range from electricity generation through energy, telecommunications and transport, to the running of the national lottery.

As noted earlier in the chapter, the emergence of state-owned enterprise as a major organizational form in the Irish economic structure owed more to pragmatism than to ideology. Many of these enterprises were set up to help accelerate the process of economic development at times, or in economic activities, where private capital was not forthcoming. In some of these cases, in such areas as energy and transportation, the state would have wanted to have some controlling interest for reasons of national security, but then found itself having to fund the entire enterprise. In other instances the state intervened to rescue and revitalize an industry of strategic importance to the economy only after private enterprise had tried and failed; this was what happened in the case of the sugar industry. State-owned enterprise was used to rationalize the dairy industry in 1927 in order to buy out the proprietary interests that were threatening the whole future of the co-operative movement in that industry. In the 1950s there was even a suggestion in the Dail that state enterprise should be used to develop the export market for Irish whiskey (Magee 1980). In more recent times, the state has intervened to take over certain concerns in the financial services industry that were in imminent danger of collapse, with ramifications that would have had disastrous effects throughout the country at large.

Over the years, state-owned enterprises have been subjected to all kinds of criticism. It has been said that they competed too much with the private sector, that they took too large a share of the managerial talent available to the country, and that they have held the consumer to ransom. Some or all of these criticisms have been true to some extent at certain times in the history of these bodies. It is also true that a number of these organizations have witnessed some of the most protracted and bitter industrial relations difficulties in the history of Irish enterprise since independence, particularly in the years since 1960 (McCarthy 1973; Kelly and Brannick 1986). However, it is also true that many of these bodies have been subjected to political interference over their histories with ambiguous, mixed or often no messages coming from the "shareholder" about what the political, social and economic priorities of these enterprises should be, or how they should be balanced. If these organizations have not always been effective and efficient as enterprises, it has not always been because of poor internal management and organization. It has often been because overall direction and control from the super-structure has been poor or non-existent, and because the organizations have been under-capitalized or over-burdened with debt.

State-owned enterprises, whatever their faults and shortcomings, have played a major role in the development of the Irish economy and of modern Irish management. They were the primary engine of early industrialization in the 1930s and 1940s and played a formative role in the emergence and early development of a modern techno-managerial class in Irish society. The full nature and significance of this contribution, particularly in the first four decades of the country's development after independence, was graphically described by C.S. (Todd) Andrews when he said that these companies had "given to the administrators and technologists in Ireland opportunities for advancement which would never have been available to them in an economy where the family-owned firm was dominant and the crown prince blocked promotion to the top posts", that they had "introduced into Ireland modernity in mechanization and in management methods, in industrial environment and in the training of staff" and that without them the country would have been "little better than a cattle ranch" (quoted in Chubb and Lynch 1969:194–198). Andrews was one of the early chief executives in the state sector. He gave a lifetime of service to Ireland's state-owned enterprises at the highest level.

Some of the earliest leaders of the state-owned sector, men like Andrews and General Costello of the Sugar company, were more than company leaders. They saw themselves as nation-builders. Both had fought in the War of Independence and Costello had risen to the highest ranks in the new Free State army at a very tender age. Men of this type were committed to the development of the State in a very fundamental way. They became the transitional figures that led the economy through its early industrialization and helped to pull it up by its own bootstraps. They were handpicked to lead state enterprises in this crucial formative period because of Lemass's conviction that "in a small society with no inherent momentum of its own . . . the initiative or lack of it of a handful of individuals could make or mar important institutions for a generation" (Lee 1979b:24). General Costello, for example, during his tenure at the sugar company, played a national role in revitalizing and reorganizing the whole sugar-beet industry when it emerged in a state of exhaustion after the war. He brought the mechanical and chemical revolution into Irish sugar beet production and fresh hope to the communities that depended on it (Leavy 1992).

State-owned enterprises have seen their roles and relative importance to the economy change dramatically over the years. All were imaginative initiatives when first taken and were crucial in the early modernization of the economy. All provided important scope for the development of technical and managerial skills at a time when the private sector was underdeveloped. For example, Tony O'Reilly, the Heinz Corporation chief and Tony Ryan the entrepreneurial leader of Guinness Peat Aviation are among the many talented managers whose early career development took place within such enterprises. Later, as the emphasis in government economic strategy turned elsewhere, many of these organizations lost their sense of mission and their pride of place in national economic affairs. This led in many cases to internal hubris, government neglect and declining public confidence.

The 1980s saw the beginning of major transformation in the entire sector. The rising crisis in the public finances helped to re-focus public interest on the importance of these national resources and on the need to ensure that what they had achieved over the years should not be allowed to wither on the vine. The issue of their ownership has now become of secondary importance in many cases to the historical fact that they are still leading commercial institutions in Irish economic life. The national economy now needs them to succeed as enterprises in their own right. Political interference is on the decline and commercial viability is to the fore. The current transformation in the sector involves the transition to new customer-oriented and commercial approaches. This involves the development of new management skills and priorities and of leaner, fitter organization structures.

As an organizational form, the state-owned enterprise is now an historical heritage in the structure of Irish economic life which is unlikely to be added to in the foreseeable future. Indeed, with a number of prospective privatizations already in view, it is more likely to decline in influence as an organizational form in the country's future development.

Public Limited Companies

In the years from independence up to the onset of the 1960s the role of public limited companies in the economy, and their influence on the development of modern Irish management, were largely outshone by those of the cooperatives and the state-owned enterprises. Now, in the 1990s, public limited companies, both indigenous and foreign, are the leading institutions in the country's economic structure and in the development of Irish management and organization. Most innovations in organizational structures and processes, and in management practices, now tend to diffuse out from this sector to the rest of the economy.

Private capital was slow to support the economy's early industrialization, and it was left to state-owned enterprises and cooperatives to help convince people with capital that post-colonial Ireland was able to develop the managerial and technical expertise, and the work ethic necessary to build an industrial economy. The policy of economic self-sufficiency that guided national economic strategy up to the end of the 1950s did succeed in attracting private capital to help widen the country's industrial base under its protectionist measures. However, many of the new industries developed under this policy remained small scale, inefficient and production-oriented. Most remained focused on the small home market and showed little appetite or ambition to grow beyond it. Even those with a history of exporting prior to the protectionism of the 1930s, such as brewing, distilling, and biscuit-making, retreated into the safety of their newly-favoured positions on the home market and lost their competitive edge. Many were still family-owned enterprises and, in the absence of much competition, were slow to modernize in management, structure and technology.

The change in national economic strategy at the end of the 1950s transformed this situation in a very fundamental way. By dramatically reversing the self-sufficiency policy, it opened the way for future industrial development to be accelerated by direct foreign investment, and it offered to those indigenous companies with the ability and the ambition to respond to it the opportunity to grow more rapidly through unrestricted access to much larger markets. The price for doing this was to progressively dismantle the protective wall around the indigenous sector, and it was accepted that many in the sector were not going to survive the transition at all, and others only through major reform. The profile of the private sector of the economy has changed dramatically in the three decades since this dramatic

shift in national economic strategy. Very few of the industrials that dominated the Irish stock market in the early 1950s have remained in the top
hundred Irish businesses. Some have lost their former pre-eminence in
Irish economic life. Others have ceased to exist as independent entities and
many are no longer in business.

The role played by the foreign sector in Irish economic life, and in the
development of Irish management and organizations, has been very significant since the late 60s. By 1985 there were nearly 900 foreign-based firms
operating in Ireland employing 78,000 people or 42 per cent of total
manufacturing employment. Their significance for Irish management and
organization is even greater, because these foreign-based operations are
proportionately larger, and organizationally more complex, than has been
the case in the indigenous sector. The foreign sector has brought a rich mix
of management cultures and influences to Irish management. U.S. firms
have dominated this sector up to now, accounting for around 50 per cent of
it in terms of employment, with the U.K. and Germany—the other major
interests—accounting for around 20 per cent and 12 per cent of the sector,
respectively. Since the mid-80s there have been a growing number of
projects from Japan and the Far East which have been adding to the
richness and heterogeneity of the mix.

This foreign sector, particularly the dominant U.S. segment, has been at
the fore of the diffusion of modern management and organizational
principles and practices throughout Irish management. This has ranged
from the MBO and matrix management innovations of the early 1970s to
the most recent organizational innovations in the areas of autonomous
work group structures and cellular manufacturing. This transfer of the
social technology of modern management has arguably been as important
as the transfer of advanced physical technologies in the contribution that
these firms have made to the modernization of Irish industrial and economic life (Leavy 1989). This contribution has also been amplified by the
"demonstration effect" which it has had in first showing what is leading-
edge "best practice" in many aspects of organization and management to
much of the rest of the economy (Boylan and Cuddy 1988).

Since the mid-1980s, there has been a renewed emphasis of national
industrial policy on the development of the indigenous sector. This has
since taken two major directions. The first has been to try to widen the
indigenous supply base for the foreign sector and to make the country as
vertically integrated in the manufacture of high technology products as
possible. As late as 1983 the foreign sector was still sourcing over 60 per
cent of its raw material requirements outside the country, as compared
with less than 25 per cent in the case of indigenous firms. The second major
thrust has been to try to build up the scale of indigenous companies in
those traditional sectors where they have already taken root. In 1990 this
sector had only 150 companies with an annual turnover of over £5M and as

an *Irish Times* editorial described it (22 June 1990) was "composed of a lot of minnows and very few big fish". National industrial strategy now aims to have at least ten £1B Irish multi-nationals by the year 2000. There are just three at present.

The relative lack of dynamism in the indigenous sector has been one of the main disappointments in Ireland's industrialization since the early 1960s. However, in spite of its overall sluggishness, the indigenous sector has had a number of very significant successes and the leading companies in this sector have made their own unique and valuable contributions to the development of modern Irish management and organization. One of the structural problems that has faced most indigenous companies has been the small size of the domestic market. The two indigenous industrials that have led the sector to the £1B plus level, and have set a pattern for others to follow, outgrew the domestic market in their core businesses during the 1970s. Both operate in non-traded areas, one in paper/packaging and the other in cement/aggregates. Both have expanded aggressively by strategies of direct investment in foreign markets, mainly in the U.S. and Europe. Both have developed particular expertise in the targeting and management of acquisitions. Between them, they now account for over 30,000 employees across their international operations with more than two thirds of their total turnover generated overseas.

This pattern is now being followed by other large indigenous organizations in both the non-traded and traded sectors. While Irish managers in the foreign sector have been learning how to manage cost-effective, high-tech operations and subsidiaries within complex multinational corporate structures their fellow countrymen in the leading indigenous companies are increasingly learning how to develop and manage Irish-based complex, multi-national organizations. The total Irish management experience is now being advanced, enriched, diversified by the concurrence of both of these processes in the further development of the economy.

The Public Bureaucracy

Public administration in Ireland comprises the central administration, the local authorities and the state-funded agencies, both commercial and non-commercial. The commercial agencies, or state-owned enterprises, have already been dealt with in a previous section. In 1981, at the height of the public sector's expansion, there were over 300,000 public servants in all, or roughly 30 per cent of the total workforce. Of this number around 85,000 (27 per cent) were in state-owned enterprises or soon to be SOE's with the then impending restructuring of the postal and telecommunications services. Of the remainder, around 32,000 (10 per cent) were civil servants in central administration; 10,000 (3 per cent) in non-commercial state agencies; 35,000 (11 per cent) in local authority administration; 64,000 (20 per cent) in the health service; 47,000 (15 per cent) in education at all levels and 27,000 (9 per cent) in the police and army, with the balance in miscellaneous categories (Gaffey 1982). The rest of this section concentrates on the development of modern management and organization in the areas of central administration and the non-commercial state agencies, which have tended to have a major influence on the sector as a whole.

In the early 1920s the newly established Irish Free State inherited a functioning state apparatus manned by 21,000 civil servants, most of whom made the transition from British to Irish administration with little difficulty. Open competition for future recruitment was introduced soon afterwards and, in 1924, the service was organized into government departments within which the responsible minister was the only executive empowered to make decisions. This centralization of all authority in the person of the Minister was to become a growing encumbrance in the later expansion of the service.

The emphasis in the central administration throughout the first 30 years was on efficiency in the "unimaginative role of carrying into effect ideas that were formulated elsewhere" (Barrington 1967:84). However, this was an under-utilization of some of the nation's brightest and best talent, particularly in a situation where the country urgently needed economic and social development. In the 1950s, senior civil servants began to take a more active role in policy formulation, in the analysis of the workings of government and in the importation of ideas from other systems. The Institute of Public Administration was set up to help to professionalize the service; the model was the *L'Ecole Nationale D'Administration*. Lemass's First Programme for Economic Expansion, which was so crucial in reviving national confidence in the early 1960s, was based firmly on the policy analysis, "Economic Development", carried out by the senior civil servant in the Department of Finance, Whitaker (1958).

The State's direct role in the development of the economy was raised to a new level in the early 1960s. The dramatic turnaround in the country's fortunes had come directly from some bold and imaginative thinking that had emanated from the public sector. Lemass wanted to build on this new dynamism and make every department of government into a "development corporation" as economic and social development became the national priority. However, the Devlin Study (1969) of the period, highlighted the kind of radical reform in the organization and management of the sector that would be needed if its full potential for the planning and coordination of the country's economic and social development was to be realized. Reform, however, came slowly during the 1970s and early 1980s as the public service expanded and became more complex. The whole momentum for development planning and structural reform was weakened by new pre-occupations, most notably the administrative challenge posed by EC accession and the major uncertainties posed by the Northern troubles, the energy crises, rampant inflation and eventually world recession (Barrington 1982).

Instead of overall structural reform, the primary development activities of the public sector were set up as non-commercial state-agencies which were accountable to their own boards rather than directly to parliament through the responsible minister. In all, about forty of these agencies were set up over the 1960–1980 period. Many of these agencies, by the nature of their charter, came to develop a dynamism that was uncharacteristic of the service in general and became catalysts in the diffusion of modern management and organization throughout the public sector. Some, like the Irish Management Institute and the Institute for Public Administration, were deliberately set up for such a role. Others, like the Industrial Development Authority came to mirror the kind of management outlook and skills that typified their main client base of high-tech, multinational corporations. However, the extension of the central administration in this way, through the proliferation of semi-autonomous agencies, eventually made the task of rationalizing and restructuring the public sector as a whole all the more difficult, when that became the urgent priority in the low growth of the 1980s (Walsh 1986).

Since the early 1980s, the whole concept of the role of the public sector in economic and social development has undergone radical change. The burden of the enlarged sector had become the major impediment to economic growth and further efforts at internal reform were overshadowed by the need for major cutbacks and rationalization. The country is now looking to the private sector to take the lead in the process of further economic development.

Irish Distinctiveness?

The current character of Irish organization and management has been largely formed since the country became independent in 1921. Co-operatives, state-owned enterprises, public limited companies and state agencies are all important elements in the overall ecology of Irish organizational life. This in itself is not unique. What is most characteristic of the Irish experience is the way in which all of these organizational forms have come to the fore in the overall process of national development, and how their roles have changed over time.

Modern Irish management and organization is the product of a newly independent society trying to come to terms with its independence. The co-

operative form of organization came to prominence when the business of
the country was almost entirely agriculture. From the early 1930s to the
late 1950s the national outlook was isolationist as the country's leaders
tried to recreate as far as possible the kind of distinct Irish culture and way
of life that had been undermined by centuries of foreign administration.
This was the period in which state-owned enterprise rose to prominence in
the country's commercial life. These enterprises were the first to undertake
large-scale projects and to develop large, elaborated managerial hierarchies. They had a greater need for depth and diversity in technical and
managerial skills than the creameries or the private companies of the time
and provided the richest base for the early development of a modern Irish
managerial and technical class.

A prominent feature of the Irish experience to date has been the major
role that public policy and leadership have played in the overall process of
economic development in general, and in the evolution of Irish management and organization in particular. This extensive involvement by the
state, which has been matched in capitalist societies only by Japan, has
been a product of nationalism and pragmatism rather than of any socialist
or statist ideology. The State's leadership in the area of economic development reached its nadir in the early 1960s with the bold and imaginative
programmes to open out the economy to new investment, new ideas and
new influences. The growth of the foreign sector and the extension of the
state apparatus into non-commercial "development corporations" have
been the prominent features in the ecological evolution of Irish organizations since the early 1960s.

The early 1990s is now characterized by the full emergence of the private
sector into the leading role in the process of further economic growth. Not
only is the State's direct role now diminishing, but a number of the larger
co-operatives and state-owned enterprises are transforming themselves or
being transformed into leading capitalist concerns, as what Chandler
(1977) has called the "managerial revolution" reaches an advanced state in
Irish economic life. This is perhaps most manifest in the way in which the
provision of management education has greatly expanded since the mid-
1960s and the newer foreign sector has been an important catalyst in this
process. Managerialism and modern management education have also
since extended into the public sector and into the trade union movement
and are now pervasive influences throughout Irish economic and social life.

It is probably still too early in the evolution of modern Irish management
to be able to identify how the uniqueness of the Irish experience will
ultimately come to be reflected in a distinctive Irish management style or
approach. This is partly because the evolution of a management tradition
in Ireland is such a recent phenomenon. Equally, however, it is because
the very processes of modern managerialism and industrialization have
themselves contributed greatly to the breakdown of the old Irish identity

which served the new state for the first forty years of its existence and on which, unfortunately, many of the dearly held stereotypes of the overseas view of Ireland and the Irish are still based, even those held by many of our own emigrants. The very notions of the "Irish manager", the "Irish engineer" or the "Irish multinational corporation" seem to challenge this traditional stereotype to its very foundation. However, the replacement of the traditional identity with a national identity more relevant to the Ireland of the post-1960 era is still not complete. The question of what are the distinguishing features of the modern Irish manager is inextricably bound up with the broader question of what it is to be Irish in general and, as we approach the new millenium, this, in itself, is still being actively debated by modern Irish social commentators with, as yet, little sign of significant convergence (Lennon 1986).

What we can say is that the country has come through some kind of national adolescence since the 1960s which is reflected in the national character. The old identity was fed on, and led to, a combination of national narcissism and a carefully cultivated sense of national grievance at centuries of English domination. This had allowed many Irish to accept, with fatalistic resignation and with little loss of national self-esteem, many decades of sluggish economic development and cultural stagnation. Since the 1960s there has been a kind of transition to national maturity where the Irish have been more willing to take the destiny of the country into their own hands and to accept responsibility for it (Bestic 1969). We are also now more willing to confront and to recognize both the positive and negative elements in the national character and in our evaluation of national performance.

Lennon (1986:360) suggests that "perhaps the positive element has something to do with the gift of imagination, with our sense of history, our openess to religious experience, our willingness to speak of death, our experience of being a relatively small island community". In business relationships this seems to translate into the Irish being relatively informal, flexible, resilient, friendly, interested in people, easy to deal with and very obliging, provided that you remember to say "please"! Irish informality, however, becomes a problem when it sometimes runs to being over-cavalier with bureaucratic procedures and with other people's time (Bestic 1969). The Irish are generally known as great talkers and this reflects the strong oral tradition in Irish culture which has always held the poet and storyteller in special esteem since the era of the early Celtic settlements. However, our loquaciousness can often be used to conceal as much as to communicate. "The peasant residue in the Irish psyche confuses the distinction between necessary confidentiality and furtive concealment", a confusion which is reinforced by "suspicions grounded in the face to face nature" of Irish society (Lee 1982:4). Indeed this residue may explain, in part, the finding of a recent joint Cranfield/Irish Management Institute study that Irish general managers remain comparatively more "uncomfortable with the dynamics within the top team" than many of their European counterparts (Kakabadse et al. 1991:26).

The values of the small island community have little time for pomposity, pretentiousness or undue concern with titles and status in commercial or political life. Perhaps the biggest single vice of traditional Ireland has been a debilitating tendency to begrudge the success of others—to see life and life chances as a sort of zero-sum game within the community as a whole (Bestic 1969; Lee 1989). The forces of modernity are still fighting off the remnants of this traditional begrudgery in their efforts to foster a success culture in Irish social and commercial life. A further remnant of traditional Ireland is that the country's leadership elite remains too small a group, and the cult of personality remains too strong a feature of Irish organizational life. This is an indicator of the gap that still needs to be bridged between the ambitions and abilities of this elite and those of the rest of the management population, though this gap is now narrowing.

The evolution of a new national identity is still in flux, and how it will ultimately be reflected in the character of modern Irish management and organization remains to be seen. What we do know is that Irish management and organization has, since the 1960s, been fashioned by a plurality of influences. It is now modern, empirical, outward-looking and relatively classless in the ideological sense. Indeed Ireland's top managers, according to Kakabadse et al. (1991), are currently among the most educated, energetic, strategically perceptive and goal-oriented business leaders in Europe. If higher levels of integration are going to mean more cross-national organizational forms and alliances, then Irish management and organization seems to be reasonably well positioned to adapt to this process. The isolationism and insularity of the 1930s and 1940s were very much against the grain of Irish historical experience which has always had extensive links with a broader European canvass. Long before the first millenium, the Irish monastic community was active in spreading the Christian faith far beyond Irish shores; a missionary tradition that has been a prominent feature of the Irish experience ever since. Modern Irish republicanism had its birth directly in the ideas and ideals of the American and French revolutions and modern Irish nationalism was directly influenced by the Risorgimento in 19th century Italy. The long and close historical links between Ireland and Catholic Spain were a constant security worry to successive British administrations in Ireland for centuries following the Reformation. Ireland and Britain, whatever their political problems, remain closely tied by the bonds of history, geography, language, common traditions and migration.

The Irish experience since independence has shown Irish people the value of cultural diversity and the dangers of cultural isolation and insularity. Irish management poses little threat to the national chauvinism of any other Community member and can indeed be a positive force for closer integration. It can also be a positive force for the development of closer links between the Community and newly emergent nations of the Third World for many of whom Irish management and organization, fashioned as it has been through the experience of post-colonial self-government, may well present the most acceptable face of the modern Western genre.

References

Barrington, Thomas J. (1967): "Public administration 1927–1936" in Francis Mac Manus (ed.), *The years of the great test 1926–39*, 80–91. Cork: Mercier.

Barrington, Thomas J. (1982): "Whatever happened to Irish government?" in Frank Litton (ed.), *Unequal achievement—the Irish experience 1957–1982*, 89–112. Dublin: IPA.

Bestic, Alan (1969): *The importance of being Irish*. London: Cassell.

Bolger, Patrick (1977): *The Irish Co-operative Movement*. Dublin: IPA.

Boylan, Thomas and Michael Cuddy (1988): "Multinational companies and economic development: aspects of the Irish experience". *Irish Business and Administrative Research* 9:76–86.

Chandler, Alfred D. (1977): *The visible hand: the managerial revolution in American business*. Cambridge Mass.: Harvard University Press.

Chubb, Basil and J. Lynch (1969): *Economic development and planning*. Dublin: IPA.

Coolahan, John (1984): "Science and technology as elements of educational and socio-economic change in Ireland, 1958–83". *Administration* 32/1:89–99.

Curtis, Edmund (1961): *A history of Ireland*, 6th ed. London: Methuen.

Devlin, Liam St. John (1969): "The Devlin Report—an overview". *Administration* 17/4:340–353.

Farrell, Brian (1986): "Politics and change" in Kieran A. Kennedy (ed.), *Ireland in transition*, 143–151. Cork: Mercier.

Fennell, Desmond (1983): *The state of the nation*. Dublin: Ward River Press.

Fogarty, Michael P. (1980): "Trade unions and the future" in Donal Nevin (ed.), *Trade unions and change in Irish society*, 142–152. Cork: Mercier.

Gaffey, Peter (1982): "The central administration" in Frank Litton (ed.), *Unequal achievement—the Irish experience 1957–1982*, 115–132. Dublin: IPA.

Hillery, Brian (1980): "Industrial relations: compromise and conflict" in Donal Nevin (ed.), *Trade unions and change in Irish society*, 39–52. Cork: Mercier.

Kakabadse, Andrew, Siobhan Alderson and Liam Gorman (1991): "Cream of Irish management". Working paper, Cranfield School of Management/Irish Management Institute.

Kelly, Aidan and Teresa Brannick (1986): "The changing contours of Irish strike patterns 1960–1984". *Irish Business and Administrative Research* 8/1:77–88.

Kennedy, Kieran A. (1986): "Industry: the revolution unfinished" in Kieran A. Kennedy (ed.), *Ireland in transition*, 40–49. Cork: Mercier.

Knapp, Joseph G. (1964): *An appraisement of agricultural cooperation in Ireland.* Dublin: Stationery Office.

Leavy, Brian (1989): "The quiet industrial revolution". *Technology Ireland* 21/ 7:36–38.

Leavy, Brian (1991): "A process study of strategic change and industry evolution— the case of the Irish Dairy Industry 1958–74". *British Journal of Management* 2/4:187–204.

Leavy, Brian (1992): "Strategic vision and inspirational leadership: two case studies" in H.E. Glass and M.A. Hovde (eds.), *Handbook of business strategy* (1992/93 Yearbook), chapt. 21. Boston: Warren Gorham Lamont.

Lee, Joseph (1979a): "Continuity and change in Ireland 1945–70" in Joseph Lee (ed.), *Ireland 1945–70*, 16–26. Dublin: Gill and Macmillan.

Lee, Joseph (1979b): "Sean Lemass" in Joseph Lee (ed.), *Ireland 1945–70*, 166– 177. Dublin: Gill and Macmillan.

Lee, Joseph (1982): "Society and culture" in Frank Litton (ed.), *Unequal achievement—the Irish experience 1957–1982*, 1–18. Dublin: IPA.

Lee, Joseph and Gearoid O'Tuathaigh (1982): *The age of de Valera*. Dublin: Ward River Press.

Lee, Joseph (1989): *Ireland 1912–1985*. Cambridge: Cambridge University Press.

Lennon, B. (1986): "Towards a new Irish identity". *Studies* 75/300:357–360.

Lyons, F.S.L. (1973): *Ireland since the famine*. London: Fontana.

Magee, Malachy (1980): *1000 years of Irish whiskey*. Dublin: O'Brien Press.

McAleese, Dermot (1986): "Ireland in the world economy" in Kieran A. Kennedy (ed.), *Ireland in transition*, 19–30. Cork: Mercier.

McCarthy, Charles (1973): *The decade of upheaval—Irish trade unions in the nineteen sixties*. Dublin: IPA.

O'Brien, George (1962): "The economic progress of Ireland". *Studies* 1/i:9–26.

Rothman, David and P. O'Connell (1982): "The changing social structure of Ireland" in Frank Litton (ed.), *Unequal achievement—the Irish experience 1957– 1982*, 63–88. Dublin: IPA.

Sheehan, J. (1979): "Education and society in Ireland, 1945–70" in Joseph Lee (ed.), *Ireland 1945–70*, 61–72. Dublin: Gill and Macmillan.

Survey Team (1963): *Report of the survey team on the dairy products industry*. Dublin: Stationery Office.

Telesis Consultancy Report (1982): *A review of industrial policy*. Dublin: NESC.

Walsh, Brendan (1979): "Economic growth and development 1945–70" in Joseph Lee (ed.), *Ireland 1945–70*, 27–37. Dublin: Gill and Macmillan.

Walsh, Brendan (1986): "The growth of government" in Kieran A. Kennedy (ed.), *Ireland in transition*, 62–70. Cork: Mercier.

Whitaker, T.K. (1958): *"Economic development"*. Dublin: Stationery Office.

Whyte, James H. (1980): *Church and state in modern Ireland 1923–79*, 2nd ed. Dublin: Gill and Macmillan.

Chapter 9: Italy

Aspects of Italian Management*

Pasquale Gagliardi and Barry A. Turner

The Broad-based Pyramid of Italian Industry

The economy of Italy has a distinctive and an idiosyncratic structure which strongly influences the options and opportunities open to Italian managers. Since the types of companies which make up this structure provide the environment within which Italian managers have to operate, we shall have to look at the features of these organizations and their interrelationships if we are to find out about the nature of Italian management. Italy has a primary sector made up of a handful of very large companies, many with very strong governmental involvement; these rest on the broad base of a secondary sector which contains a myriad of small and very small enterprises. Compared with other West European countries, Italy has a distinct lack of medium-sized companies between these two extremes (Istituto Centrale di Statistica 1981). This slightly anomalous structure—sometimes referred to as the "flattened pyramid" of the Italian industrial system (Fondazione Agnelli 1974)—has been seen as an indication that Italian industry has a great deal of *imprenditorialità* or entrepreneurship amongst the multiplicity of small firms at the bottom, but a distinct lack of organizational skills (Fuà 1980). This picture of the context of Italian management, however, is unduly oversimplified and in the following pages we will elaborate on it further.

Even as it stands, the picture shows contrasting qualities. A productive economic ferment has been generated by the multitude of small enterprises and, in the nineteen-seventies and eighties, they provided a new and characteristic industrial pattern. "Flexible specialization" is seen as a distinctively Italian contribution to contemporary economic organization. This pattern also represents an Italian variant of the exploitative "dual economy" with which we are more familiar in less developed countries. In the classic model of a dual economy, the primary sector of large, well-established organizations is typically a high status one, offering higher paid, more secure employment in positions which promise careers for life. By contrast, the secondary sector is more fragmented and more exploited. Its organizations are less permanent and they operate closer to the margins, drawing upon a different labour market, paying their employees significantly less and offering short-term, temporary or part-time employment with little or no security. Later on we shall look in a little more detail at the debate about this issue of *dualismo* or the dual economy in Italy.

Some Background

Italian industry has grown up against a backcloth of national diversity and major regional differences. Italy was established as a unitary state only in 1861. Before that time, the peninsula was made up of many small states, each with their own distinctive traditions which were endorsed and amplified by their various geographic and climatic contexts, their differing economic emphases and their different experiences of external domination by Austrian, French and Spanish invaders. These very strong cultural and linguistic traditions still persist in the deeply felt regional identities which are encountered across Italy. They are seen in their most extreme form in the *questione meridionale*, the economic and cultural split between the north and the south. This split is one which is always at the centre of Italian political debate, a division which persists in spite of the very large investments made by the government in attempts to eliminate it.

Superimposed upon such regional differences, we also find a rather different degree of diversity. This arises from the kind of differentiation of life-styles produced in all contemporary industrial societies by variations in social and demographic factors. Recent market research, for example, has identified 14 different types of Italian life-styles which depend upon age, census and class elements as well as having some cultural, geographic and historical variation (Eurisko 1986). In trying to sketch a view of Italian management, then, we are looking at arrangements in a country which shows diversity arising from a strong pattern of regional identity, regional economies and regional government.

Italy is one of the most densely settled West European countries, with the second largest population in the European Community. Its per capita income is amongst the highest in the world and while both its production and occupational structures are those of an economically advanced country, its agricultural sector also continues to be very prominent. In the public sector, Italy runs a high budget deficit and its national debt has recently exceeded its Gross Domestic Product, although it has to be said that, at least up until the final removal of barriers to capital flows in 1992, much of the public debt was funded by Italy's traditionally high rate of domestic savings. Many public services are notoriously inefficient and also offer opportunities for corruption. Functionaries from all of the major political parties are involved, at every level, in issues which affect the management of public services, and this practice does little to improve efficiency or to reduce the possibilities for corruption. It is no secret that there is much organized crime in Italy, and difficulties and complications from this source are now spreading further into areas of public administration. This, then is the Italian context: the variety of organizations which operate within this context provide the arena for Italian management.

The Family and the Enterprise

Italian life attaches high significance to the family, both as a basis for much social life and as a factor in Italian industrial development and Italian management (Haycraft 1987: 116-178). The family is important in Italian life as reality, as structure and as metaphor. The *reality* of Italian family life is clearly evident in the patterns of housing, of social support and obligation, of inheritance and of socialization. The family provides an example for other *structures*, allowing the development of industrial patterns which either follow the ramifications of the family or which mimic them. The idea of the family is then available as a *metaphor* for the specification of obligations, for the setting of expectations about cohesion and loyalty and as a justification for regarding those who find themselves outside the boundaries of the family with a degree of wariness. The relevance of the familial pattern is often raised by Italian managers and consultants when they are interviewed about the organizations which they manage, study or confront. Aspects of family-related behaviour interpenetrate industrial enterprises at all levels, sometimes taking the form of *clientelismo*, a pattern of obligations and exchanges which uses linkages set by particularistic relationships and personal contacts.

The family enterprise is a fundamental of Italian capitalism, and it has a major contribution to make to its vitality, adaptability and competitiveness. The family enterprise develops when the family has the capacity to define economic objectives and to cooperate to mobilize human and financial resources to pursue those objectives (Boldizzoni 1988). Of course, family companies are important in all major, industrial countries, especially among the smaller enterprises, but in Italy, family and business links are much more widespread, most of the major private companies being family based. The family in Italy constitutes the main motivational basis for investment and for work and it also provides a way of handling the risks of economic activity, by offering protection and support in difficult situations. At the same time, of course, the need to use the members of an extended family network to handle complex industrial issues may inhibit decision-making, and often this limitation is not helped by the pressures on a paternalist system to favour family members systematically over outsiders, pushing the organization over the fine line which separates family cooperation from nepotism.

A particular difficulty which has been observed in family enterprises in many countries is the problem of the succession of leadership. This issue causes stress in both large and small family-owned Italian organizations. Succession is a problem for top companies outside the state sector which are family owned. The Gardini family in Ferruzzi Finanziaria, the Agnelli family of Fiat and the Pirelli family have all recently had to make hard decisions about the choice of family members to succeed to key executive positions. Other major Italian industrial families which may share similar problems are the de Benedetti, Benetton, and Pininfarina families. There is evidence, too, that some offspring who cannot be absorbed directly into such family firms are showing a preference for moving into senior positions in banking and finance, a development which shifts them into positions where they are likely to be able to continue to assist the family.

Boldizzoni (1988) suggests that whether succession proceeds smoothly or not depends upon the age and the life-cycle of the company, on the personal characteristics of the key executive to be replaced, on the availability of suitable candidates from amongst the family and their collaborators, and upon the nature and type of any succession plan they might have. The problem is most difficult with first generation entrepreneurs who identify strongly with the company. Such men, for men they usually are, will often have exceptional personal qualities, but they may nonetheless be reluctant to prepare for their own replacement. There is a strong preference for keeping the company in the family, and a corresponding reluctance to bring in from the outside professional managers who might counter the lack of innovation which many small family companies display. Within this family setting it would be typical to find a reluctance to become involved in strongly expressed conflicts and a willing acceptance that power should be concentrated in the hands of the founder or his successor. Moreover, these family-influenced views of the way in which corporate power and conflict should be handled spill over into other, non-family and state-owned companies in Italy.

In the small family-run companies, there is no separation between ownership and control, and they tend to employ only a limited range of specialized professionals. The entrepreneur and the company tend to learn at the same time, usually reacting to problems rather than anticipating them. The particular types of enterprise-related behaviour within the company (cost reduction, diversification, exporting) and the policies of development are strongly determined by the size of the company (Gibbs and Scott 1983).

The entrepreneurs in the family enterprises which Boldizzoni studied were strongly individualistic, strongly motivated and well educated, nearly half of them having attended university. A majority were influenced by the presence of other entrepreneurs within their family network. The companies had a strong sense of the reputation of the family and there was significant involvement of the family in management.

The Large Enterprises

The major Italian enterprises are either state owned or family owned. This means that, effectively, Italy has neither "public" companies, nor the associated debate about the separation between ownership and control of such enterprises which has been heard in other regions of modern capitalism, particularly the Anglo-Saxon ones. The Italian state is also more deeply involved in the economy than is the case in any other capitalist country, the size of the public sector making the private sector the smallest of any Western European state.

The large state-owned, state-controlled or state-associated enterprises exert a major influence. Apart from their size and their dominance, they have also been important in the past in that they provided, at least at a more formal level, some models for Italian management. Their high level of influence has been traced both to the Italian totalitarian corporatism of the twenties and thirties, (Heckscher 1946: cited in Anheier and Seibel 1990) and to a pattern which characterizes those civil law countries where the church played a dominant role in social reforms following the industrial revolution, and where absolutism was slowly or incompletely abolished. The power of these church and state-influenced models continued to be quite persuasive in the post-war period, and it still means that those organizations operating between the private, for-profit sector and the government (what is sometimes called the "third sector") tend to look more like state agencies than for-profit firms (Anheier and Seibel 1990). However, in the past twenty years, this influence has waned as the smaller companies started to make the running in the Italian economy.

After the major oil companies, IRI, the principal Italian state holding company, is the largest firm in Europe (Ward 1990). Companies such as Fiat, ENI, Ferruzzi, Olivetti, Pirelli and Esso-Italia are included in the list of the top 500 non-American companies, but there are fewer of them than might be expected for a nation of Italy's size, the great majority of Italian companies having less than 100 workers. IRI itself, set up originally in 1933 by Mussolini as a measure to counter the effects of the Depression, has some 600 subsidiaries, including RAI—the national broadcasting corporation; the state tourism company, CIT; engineering companies and most of the steel industry; maritime insurance; the shipyards; telecommunications and four major banks. The state also has direct ownership of ENI, the State Agency for Hydrocarbons, and the two major financial agencies EFIM and GEPI, together with six other national banks, thirty-one lending banks and a group of regional savings banks, not to mention the Istituto Mobiliare Italiano (IMI) which funds the majority of Italy's public works. "IRI, ENI, EFIM and GEPI together are responsible for almost 30 per cent of sales and almost 50 per cent of fixed investment in Italy" (Ward 1990: 238).

Within the state-owned enterprises, the stability which one might expect from the continuity of state control under the direction of the *Ministero delle partecipazioni statali* is only partially evident, for, in practice, this form of direction means that with every change of government the stockholder changes. Even though the *Democrazia Cristiana*, or Christian Democrat, regime has provided long-term continuity of government since the Second World War, individual governments in Italy have been of very short duration. Moreover, while it is reasonable to assume that the board of a "normal" company would be primarily interested in the profitabiliy and development of the business, the state-owned enterprises are given additional, more political goals relating, for example, to employment, to the state presence in strategic, non-profitable sectors neglected by private entrepreneurs and to regional development. These goals, which may well at times be mutually contradictory, are very often expressions of the *lottizzazione*—the system by which there is an agreed attribution of particular areas of influence and managerial posts to each political party.

In addition, the state-owned enterprises have a multiplicity of stakeholders pushing each company in different directions: the unions, the employees, consumers, public opinion and the political parties all have a view, and the managers of the enterprise itself will add to the debate with their own interpretations of the "social responsibilities" of the enterprise. These claims intrude not only into strategic decision-making, but are heard at all operational levels, so that state-owned enterprises exhibit a high degree of dependency upon many other groups, a condition which has been labelled "allodependency" (Ferrario 1978). Political goals and pressures of this kind cut across the patterns of management and organization which we might otherwise expect to be pursued by professional managers working largely according to criteria of economic rationality and efficiency.

The Small Enterprises

At the opposite end of the industrial scale, in contrast to the large, state-dominated enterprises which have been perceived over the past quarter of a century to be rather static and conservative, there has developed a distinctively new and lively form of industrial development, a form novel enough to have been called at times, "post-industrial". Many small Italian companies seem to have jumped, somehow, beyond the constraints of the mass-production technology and the management practices of F.W. Taylor and Henry Ford to create a new form of small-scale, craft-based family enterprise. These enterprises offer a high degree of responsiveness to customers and, because of their small size and their propensity to demonstrate a high degree of "flexible specialization", are able to fit themselves into small adaptive niches. They also appear, from some points of view, to offer the benefits of a human-scale and a family-based pattern of relations in the workplace.

The small organizations of the secondary sector have been vigorously active since at least the 1960s. Already, at the start of this period, establishments with less than 100 employees produced 57 per cent of the value of manufactured goods in Italy, compared with around 40 per cent in Germany and France and 20 per cent in Great Britain and the United States (Barbetta 1989: 157). There has, though, been little evidence of a consequent growth in size of the enterprises at the base of the system. This may well be because there are quite specific constraints upon the growth of small companies in Italy: legal, trade-union based, fiscal, economic and administrative (Barbetta 1989: 184–189). As the Italian economy "matured", we might have expected small companies to undergo a progressive process of industrial concentration but these restraining factors seem to have served to check such changes. In addition, there are other, specific constraints which relate to the nature of small, family-based companies which we shall look at in more detail below.

In the 1980s, however, a number of the pressures towards greater industrial concentration seem once more to have made their presence felt. After a decade of quite spectacular activity in the nineteen-seventies, the small enterprises are starting to cede some ground to larger corporations. The large enterprises in the primary sector turn out to have adopted strategies in this period which are very similar to those adopted by major companies elsewhere in Europe, and they have started to take on a similar look. The larger Italian enterprises during the 1980s have slimmed down workforces and increased both their turnover and their level of productivity. However, these strategies do also, in fact, contribute something to the growth of small enterprises in the secondary sector. As the larger companies move away from internal vertical integration and start to favour a decentralized form of production, the overall system accommodates its needs to adjust to variability of demand and increased costs of primary inputs by increasing the opportunities for small companies to join the system, but also to bear a significant proportion of the risks and the costs of possible downturns and reductions in business.

Over the past two decades, the development of the smaller enterprises has shown both continuity and a break with the past. Continuity from the sixties can be seen in the persistent growth of enterprises with between 10 and 100 employees, most of this growth occurring in the companies within the most "advanced" industrial sectors—machine tool, transport, electrical and electronic—although it can be seen also, to a lesser extent, in basic industries and in traditional industries such as textiles, clothing and engineering. The rather surprising break with the past is visible in the growth which has taken place among companies with less than 10 employees, for, compared with the 'sixties, these have increased both in number and in the aggregate number of people employed.

So far we have presented a sketch of some of the major features of contemporary Italian industry. However, this sketch must be taken with great caution. Quite apart from the high degree of regional variability, Italian industry has followed an intricate dynamic since the 1960s, with a series of complicated interchanges between the enterprises at the top and at the base of the industrial system. At some points, in the early sixties, for example, the bigger enterprises were placing emphasis upon larger and larger industrial units. The smaller enterprises grew by making use of opportunities which this policy overlooked. They were able to react more rapidly to market changes at times of high uncertainty, and this gave them benefits which carried them through the following decade. The search for advantage shifted from the large to the small enterprises and back again in a far from simple pattern, according to the period (Barbetta 1989: 198). Since, however, the growth in the number of very small companies, and thus the degree of fragmentation at the base of the system now seems to be increasing rather than decreasing (Lorenzoni 1990), we do need to raise here the question of how such a fragmented system can compete effectively.

The Constellation and Flexible Specialization

Although it is impossible to offer a simple understanding of the processes of development during the last twenty years in Italian industry because of their great complexity, it is clear that the smaller enterprises have been

responsible for many of the novel developments at the base of the structure. To gain a better understanding of these changes, it is useful to look at
some attempts to analyze just how these companies related to other parts
of the industrial sector.

Sabel (1982) characterizes the enterprises of Emilia Romagna, together
with those of the Marches, Tuscany and Umbria as small-scale, high-
technology cottage industries which employ craft labour to supply diversified consumer tastes on a changing world market (see also Brusco 1982;
Brusco and Sabel 1981). In what is perhaps a slightly Utopian view of the
small- to medium-sized engineering, clothing and textiles artisan firms of
these areas, he sees them as giving back to labour some of the creativity
removed by Fordist mass production, since such small enterprises avoid
both a minute fragmentation of work and a strict separation between
conception and execution. The regional diversity and the Utopian
appearance are both enhanced by the co-existence with industry of a mixture of both very rich and peasant subsistence agriculture. Sabel sees this
rather complex texture of craft and agricultural enterprises as one which is
being promoted positively by regional government, in collaboration with
the PCI—the Italian Communist Party—and the trade unions. By offering
support to innovative proprietors to strengthen their will to train appren-
tices for the future, regional government is encouraging the continuance of
this novel industrial pattern. Thus, in this region of Italy at least, Sabel
suggests that we find a system where the dominant Western mode of
multinational mass production is being replaced by a new, forward-looking
amalgam of work and politics on a more human scale.

A diametrically opposed interpretation has been offered by Murray
(1987) who argues that Italy has been dominated, and continues to be
dominated by large Fordist and neo-Fordist companies. He sees little
evidence of the direction of development by regional administration, and
points instead to the logic of international capital as the driving force of
development. The small firms, which are themselves not free of conflicts
between capital and labour, play their part in the system by making small
batch, customized investment goods which are difficult to mass produce.
Workers in these small firms are subdivided by race, gender and skill, and
Murray suggests that Sabel neglects both the wide variety of working
conditions to be found in the artisan sector, and the variation in the levels
of wages paid. Because he concentrates upon the companies employing
middle-aged, male, skilled, Emilian workers, he neglects those which
employ predominantly women, or low-skilled Southern Italians and North
Africans. For Murray, it is not only the small companies at the base of the
pyramid which are splintering and fragmenting but also the working class,
so that such solidarity as was developed in the seventies is now being
considerably undermined.

Murray offers as an example the engineering industry in Bologna, which has several segments. Larger firms subcontract into the artisan sector to offset their own rigidity and to cope with market fluctuations. There is an extensive subcontracting network, which includes some firms with "tragic" working conditions and very low unionization. The system provides an enormous degree of labour flexibility for the capital interests of the area. At the same time, the larger firms are investing heavily in information technology and new production technologies and developing their links with multinationals.

This stress upon the interlinkages of the system is echoed in a striking new analysis by Lorenzoni (1990) who has suggested that it is misleading to concentrate too much on trying to assess the capacity of individual small enterprises or wondering how it is possible for such weak units to survive in a rather tough economic climate. Rather than making reference to some unspecified qualities of entrepreneurship or to the benefits accruing from tax evasion or from the use of underpaid labour in order to explain the brilliant results which have been obtained, he suggests that we look at the enterprise system as a whole. A single enterprise, he says, is "like a table without legs". Instead of looking at a single component, we need to look at the properties of the complete pattern of linkages. Analyzing a number of case studies which he has carried out, again in the Emilia region, he advances a theory which is valuable in understanding this pattern of organization which is so widely diffused in northern, eastern and central Italy.

His basic hypothesis is that rather than trying to explain the success of small Italian companies by reference to some single company or management factor we should look at the wider innovative pattern of inter-organizational relations which has been developing. Small companies in the Italian setting turn away from the possibility of developing through internal growth (*crescita interna*), either by increasing direct investment or by expanding the number of staff employed. Rather they develop by increasing their connections and links with other small companies through a pattern of networking and external growth (*crescita esterna*).

We have already noted that there are a number of factors—legal, fiscal and economic—which help to persuade many Italian companies to sustain operations on a small scale. These inclinations are reinforced by the family network which typically forms the base of the small Italian enterprise. The series of studies of both small companies and family-based companies by Boldizzoni (1985, 1988), which we have already referred to, has demonstrated that family companies grow by progressively co-opting members of the family into the enterprise, and that this means that the potential for the development of companies is proportional to the potential of the families involved. Even when the potential base of recruitment is enlarged by marriage links, using precisely the mechanisms by which mediaeval Venetian merchants secured the expansion of their enterprises, there is still a constraint upon the size of the enterprise if it is to be kept within family boundaries. In market terms, if we look at their competitive, structural and financial profiles, such small companies are weak in themselves, especially given the tendency to undercapitalization which they display (Boldizzoni 1985). In aggregation, however, these companies can display strong competitive qualities.

Lorenzoni suggests that they achieve their strong competitive aggregate qualities by adopting a particular pattern of linkages based upon the development of complementary enterprise roles. One leading company becomes associated with a group of other small companies in an arrangement which Lorenzoni refers to as "the constellation"—*la costellazione*. The leading company, the *impresa guida*, is typically managed by a creative and innovative entrepreneur, while the other companies, looked at individually, could be said to be managed by what Lorenzoni calls a style of *imprenditorialità limitata* or limited entrepreneurship. Those working in this style are far from the Schumpeterian archetype and are concerned to maintain their autonomy within a limited but stable sphere of activity defined by the existing enterprise and its family connections in a way which is already familiar to us from Boldizzoni's study of family firms. Such limited entrepreneurship focuses upon the efficiency of internal activity, mainly in production. It takes little or no interest in the wider business environment and has no desire for growth.

The typical constellation is held together by integration devices of extreme simplicity. It is not driven by a sophisticated project but by negotiation between the members to obtain a consensus on the "facts" to be confronted and on the actions which then must follow the shared diagnosis of the situation. Business within the constellation is done with a degree of informality which presupposes a high degree of trust between members of the constellation. Like all such loosely connected networks (Gouldner 1959), if the interests of the member units and those of the constellation as a whole are to be optimized, an appropriate balance has to be found between the autonomy of the member units and the benefits which they derive from their place in the constellation.

Although the pattern of networking which Lorenzoni describes may be one which has distinctively Italian features, in a more general sense, many of its traits can be found in a variety of other locations in the early stages of industrial take-off: in the metal-working firms of the English Black Country in the Industrial Revolution, for example, or in the nearby Birmingham jewellery quarter in the late nineteenth century. The physical proximity of a number of small, related and overlapping enterprises makes it both sensible and possible for them to tackle the division of labour needed for larger industrial projects by adopting a collaborative network in one form or another, while at the same time preserving the formal autonomy of their individual units. These conditions, Williamson (1975) would suggest, are ones in which the costs of the transactions to be carried out between the various participants are cheaper if small individual producers enter into the transactions than if all of the participants were merged into a single large organization. If a point is reached at which the formation of a single organization would lower transaction costs significantly, then on a strict economic calculus, the "constellations" would disappear.

Against this economic view, however, we should set the quasi-familial pattern which is evident in the informal and consensus-based linkages of Lorenzoni's networks, an arrangement which is reminiscent of the clan pattern which Ouchi (1981) describes in his critique of Williamson's model. Japanese organizations, and some American ones which approximate to them, remain together rather than fragmenting in response to economic pressures, Ouchi suggests, because of the cultural commitment which their members share towards social cohesion. In an inversion of this relationship, the cultural commitment of Italian, family-based entrepreneurs to the autonomy of units of limited size within an informal, quasi-familial network of joint obligations may allow constellations to continue to operate even in situations where a pure transaction-cost analysis might suggest that there should be growth and aggregation into larger units. (For a complementary discussion of the ramifying symbolic benefits which may be gained when networks are specified, see Kreiner and Schultz' (1991) study of international networks in biotechnology.)

Management of the Organization

We can now finally turn to look at some of the features which characterize the way in which the complex and distinctive Italian industrial structure which we have so far been describing is managed. Although firmly based data is hard to come by, virtually everyone who has looked at the question has felt the need to try to relate Italian managerial characteristics to the patterns of Italian national culture. However, it is not easy to sketch in the characteristics of Italian culture, especially given the degree of diversity and difference which we have already noted. We can, though, make use of some survey evidence in attempting this task.

Very few studies have looked specifically at Italian managers. Instead we have to draw upon Latin and Italian characteristics identified in cross-national managerial studies. International surveys suggest that the Italian culture, and to some extent Latin cultures more generally, operate with a distinctive cluster of interrelated attitudes: specificity, familialism, a lack of trust in other people in general, combined with a general view that support and *favoritismo* rather than isolated individual effort are needed in order to succeed, (Eurisko 1991). The element of specificity reflects a preference for dealing with known individuals rather than with representatives of general categories or classes, a preference for the personal contact which can be regarded as an extension to the family. It then becomes more difficult to place trust in those who cannot be located socially in this fashion.

Laurent (1983), for example, characterized French and Italian managers as having a more personal and social concept of authority than American, Swiss or German managers; and as having a highly politicized rather than a structural view of their organizations. Italian managers in particular showed a preference for clarity and the control of uncertainty within their organizations, an arrangement which would minimize potential internal organizational conflicts. They were also suspicious of arrangements such as matrix organizations which blurred hierarchical relationships. These findings are echoed in other studies which suggest that Latin European managers prefer a strong hierarchy and that they display little autonomy, and gain little management satisfaction (Haire et al. 1966), or that they demonstrate individualism, autocracy, paternalism, a stress upon masculinity and a strong sense of hierarchy (Hofstede 1976, 1977, 1980; Bollinger and Hofstede 1987). These findings echo the preferences expressed among the members of family firms which we have already noted in the third section of this chapter.

In Italian family firms, Boldizzoni (1988) found that a characteristic pattern of management was a strong concentration by the chief executive or founding entrepreneur upon various key commercial, financial or productive activities. Those functions considered to be marginal or less important were delegated to members of the family or to collaborators. There was a strict relationship between the strong points of the company and the primary responsibilities of the entrepreneur. New managerial capacities were not well developed in such companies. They tended to improve and to consolidate the managerial competencies and strengths which they already possessed rather than developing additional ones. Planning tended to concentrate upon improving the quality of products and developing new ones rather than changing and improving other aspects of company activities.

Ciferri (1990) is preparing a comparative study of British and Italian management which will concentrate upon attitudes to actual management systems rather than the managerial preferences which Hofstede has examined in great detail. In spite of this difference in emphasis, however, he suggests that Hofstede's work offers an accurate compendium of findings to date, when he argues that, in Italy, subordinates at all levels of the hierarchy are heavily dependent on their superiors; that subordinates expect superiors to act autocratically; that the ideal superior to most managers is a benevolent autocrat or a paternalist; there is a wide expectation that superiors will enjoy privileges, laws and rules which are different from those of their subordinates; and that status symbols are very important in contributing to the authority of the superior manager. To these patterns can be added support for *"clientelismo"*, that highly specific and person-based relationship which occurs between people with mutual interests or between those who need and those who can offer various forms of patronage.

As with the Arabic pattern of *wasta*, *clientelismo* recognizes the wider network of obligations beyond the organization in which the manager is located. Someone in a superior position not only has obligations and responsibilities within the company, but also responsibilities to and mutual obligations with family members and with other individuals who may be tied into a quasi-familial, personal network. Family-specific or family-like contacts and relationships make sense when there is an absence of reassurance about the reliability of those who cannot be located on such personal networks.

Some interesting insights into management in the *middle* layers of the industrial structure are offered by one study which has looked at a small group of 25 private companies. These are quite an elite group of mainly medium to large companies sophisticated enough to respond to quite an extensive and complicated questionnaire study. Rugiadini (1985) sought to try to determine the "distance" which might exist between these Italian companies and a general "universal model" of advanced European management which he had devised. The study distinguished four different areas of management practice: control, organization, planning and personnel appraisal, and defined an "advanced" model for each of these. The criteria vary from one area to another, sometimes implying the adoption of increased levels of formalization or the use of specific methods, sometimes more substantial integration between levels and roles in management processes and sometimes the use of certain decision criteria.

He came up with the following findings. In general, in the first three areas of practice: control, organization and planning, the Italian companies studied were at or were close to the author's model. They diverged substantially from the model, however, in the fourth area, the field of personnel appraisal. In these companies, the managers did not organize or handle the merit-rating process systematically, and when they were carrying out appraisals, they did not attempt to refer to impersonal, objective criteria. The managers involved seemed either to resist or to refuse outright the acceptance of a clear definition of either individual responsibilities or objective appraisal criteria linked to company results. Instead they showed a response which is consistent with the general patterns of autocracy and paternalism which we have already noted.

To the general picture of the stance of Italian management which we have presented so far, we might add the common perception that there is a

high degree of aesthetic sensibility in Italian culture and a concern for a
widely construed notion of design which transmutes into the Italian flair for
style, even if some writers see this flair constituted as adaptability to the
tastes of others rather than a genuine design creativity (Ward 1990: 251–
257). There is, however, no doubt that the attribute most frequently associated with Italian organizations is a sense of *style*. The flair for design and
visual appeal which grows out of the public concern with dress and the
plastic and visual arts, is also associated with the special place of design and
designers in Italian culture and in Italian managerial life. The absence of a
clear dividing line between fashion, art, architecture and design, is
accompanied by a high degree of public recognition for leading designers.
This fits with the emphasis upon corporate image and styling in corporations such as Olivetti, Ferrari, Alfa-Romeo and Fiat. It also connects with
the variety of design options available in the Italian marketplace, as part of
the pattern of flexible specialization offered by the small, family-modelled
organizations of the constellations. In seeking their own distinctive niches
in the market, many of them are able to build upon or make use of the
cachet of "made in Italy", especially in the fields of textiles and fashion,
motor car and electrical and domestic product design, circumventing to
some degree the major standardizing demands of the process of mass
production.

Concluding Comments

A first level of understanding of Italian management has to commence with
a recognition of the diversity of the country and its enterprises, and of the
skewed distribution of size shown by Italian enterprises, with much state
involvement in the larger organizations. In addition to the formal factors
which often make it sensible for small companies to remain small in Italy,
the values, practices and structures associated with a strong emphasis upon
the family also push towards the same end.

It does not make sense, however, to try to understand individual small
enterprises without looking at the "constellations" of collaborating companies of which they form a part. These constellations permit the continuance of traditional Italian views of interpersonal relationships and
obligations and allow a concentration upon the quasi-domestic unit, even
as the combinations of such units form into novel industrial patterns. Their
knack of flexible specialization has boosted the Italian economy considerably over the past two decades, but, while elements of the small-scale
enterprises may have their Utopian appeal it would be short-sighted not to
recognize the ties which link all of these companies, admittedly sometimes

very ineffectively, into an interplay with the larger private and state-owned companies which form the other major element of the Italian managerial scene. It is an open question how far these larger forces, especially those arising in the context of a unified European economy, are likely to exert pressures for industrial concentration which will remove many of the specifically Italian features noted above and how far the industrial diversification and cooperation provided by the existing industrial districts and constellations will resist such inroads.

In companies at both ends of the industrial scale, there is a distinctively Italian outlook on management which stresses dependence and paternalism or autocracy; personal relationships and *clientelismo*; and a clarity of hierarchical relations which makes it easier to avoid overt conflict. If the moves towards the Single European Market do bring about significant structural change in Italian industry, it could be expected that cultural lags associated with the strongly embedded Italian cultural patterns will make key values and beliefs rather more difficult to change, so that Italian management will be likely to retain its distinctive features well into the twenty-first century.

Note

*The assistance of Marco Mariani is gratefully acknowledged in the preparation of this chapter.

References

Anheier, H.K. and W. Seibel (1990): *The third sector: comparative studies of non-profit organizations*. Berlin: de Gruyter.

Barbetta, G.P. (1989): "La evoluzione della struttura dimensionale dell'industria italiana" in G.P. Barbetta and F. Silva (eds.), *Trasformazioni strutturali delle impresse italiane*, 155–205. Bologna: Il Mulino.

Boldizzoni, Daniele (1985): *La Piccola Impresa: Gestione e sviluppo delle aziende minori*. Milano: Il Sole 24 ore.

Boldizzoni, Daniele (1988): *L'Impresa Familiare: caratteristiche distintive e modelli di evoluzione*. Milano: Il Sole 24 ore.

Bollinger, D. and G. Hofstede (1987): *Les differences culturelles dans le management*. Paris: Les Editions d'Organisation.

Brusco, S. (1982): "The Emilian model: productive decentralisation and social integration". *Cambridge Journal of Economics* 6/3: 167–184.

Brusco, S. and C. Sabel (1981): "Artisan production and economic growth" in F. Wilkinson (ed.), *The dynamics of labour market segmentation*, 99–113. London: Academic Press.

Istituto Centrale di Statistica (1981): *VI Censimento Generale dell'Industria, del*

Commercio, dei Servizi e dell'Artigiano. (Industrial Census). Roma: Istituto Centrale di Statistica

Ciferri, M. (1990): "Managerial attitudes, values and perceptions: an Anglo–Italian study". Unpublished Research Paper, May 1990.

Eurisko (1986): *Sinottica: Indagine Psicografica.* Unpublished market research report.

Eurisko (1991): Eurobarometro. *Social Trends* 54: 14.

Fondazione Agnelli (1974): "Il sistema imprenditoriale italiano". *Contributi di ricerca*, Vol. 3.

Ferrario, M. (1978):"Strategic management in state enterprises". Unpublished doctoral dissertation, Graduate School of Business Administration, Harvard University.

Fuà, G. (1980): *Problemi dello sviluppo tardivo in Europa.* Bologna: Il Mulino.

Gibbs, A.A. and M. Scott (1983): *Strategic awareness, personal commitment and the process of planning in small business.* Durham: Durham University Business School.

Gouldner, A.W. (1959): "Reciprocity and autonomy in functional theory" in L. Gross (ed.), *Symposium on sociological theory*, 241–270. New York: Harper and Row.

Haire, M., E.E. Ghiselli and L.W. Porter (1966): *Managerial thinking: an international study.* New York: Wiley.

Haycraft, John (1987): *Italian labyrinth: Italy in the 1980s.* Harmondsworth: Penguin.

Hofstede, G. (1976): "Nationality and espoused values of managers". *Journal of Applied Psychology* 61: 148–155.

Hofstede, G. (1977): *Cultural determinants of the exercise of power in a hierarchy.* European Institute for Advanced Studies in Management, Working Paper 77–8.

Hofstede, G. (1980): *Culture's consequences.* Beverly Hills, CA: Sage.

Kreiner, Kristian and Majken Schultz (1991): "Soft cultures: the symbolism of international R&D projects". Paper presented to the Eighth International SCOS Conference on Reconstructing Organizational Culture, Copenhagen, June 1991.

Laurent, André (1981). "Matrix organizations and Latin cultures". *International Studies of Management and Organization* 10/4: 15–41.

Laurent, André (1983): "The cultural diversity of Western conceptions of management". *International Studies of Management and Organization* 13/1–2: 75–96.

Lorenzoni, G. (1990): *L'architettura di sviluppo delle imprese minori.* Bologna: Il Mulino.

Murray, Winton (1987): "Flexible specialisation in the 'Third Italy'". *Class and Capital* 33: 84–95.

Ouchi, William G. (1981): *Theory Z: How American business can meet the Japanese challenge.* Reading, MA: Addison-Wesley.

Rugiadini, A. (ed.) (1985): *La managerialità nelle imprese italiane.* Bologna: Il Mulino.

Sabel, C. (1982): *Work and politics.* Cambridge: Cambridge University Press.

Ward, William (1990): *Getting it right in Italy: a manual for the 1990s.* London: Bloomsbury.

Williamson, Oliver E. (1975): *Markets and hierarchies: analysis and antitrust implications.* New York: Free Press.

Chapter 10: The Netherlands

Open Borders, Closed Circles: Management and Organization in the Netherlands

Nic van Dijk and Maurice Punch

Conflicting Images

National stereotypes are an insidious trap. There is usually sufficient evidence for the outsider to have stereotypes confirmed; but for the expatriate living in a foreign country the reality behind the stereotype is often complex if not elusive. One might feel, for instance, that a small, densely populated country such as the Netherlands must be relatively homogeneous: but nothing is further from the truth and regional identities are multiple and resilient. Furthermore, you might believe that a country with an open economy, a cosmopolitan reputation, and a history of tolerance, would be easy to understand and to penetrate for foreigners. Yet we would argue that the Netherlands remains something of a mysterious society—with a near impenetrable language—and with curious social codes that frustrate the outsider. Indeed, Lawrence (1986: 2), in his highly insightful paper on Dutch management, speaks of his "attempt to decode Europe's most complicated country".

Most Europeans, in fact, remain fundamentally ignorant of the Netherlands and base their stereotype on a few symbols such as tulips and cheese. The Dutch themselves continue to promote these products assiduously as if they were charming relics of an agrarian past; when, in reality, the rustic image is tinged with the mercenary mind of the trader, because both products are representative of two highly prospering areas of the economy. For example, a manager from the national airline, KLM, was interviewed before his departure for a position in the U.S.A.;

> What will be your strongest weapons in the competitive battle to be fought in America?
> "A rock-solid confidence in a number of very positive Dutch qualities: we are flexible, quick in improvising, client-oriented, and we also deliver an assortment of quality products . . . . . The Netherlands is a country of quality . . . .

And when we promote the Netherlands then we are not ashamed of our
tulips, cheese, butter, canals, dykes and cows. They are simply by definition
our strongest products" (*Flying Dutchman* 1: 1991: 16).

It is our contention, then, that most people are poorly informed about
the Netherlands and the Dutch and that their views are based on a few
misleading stereotypes. Our task is to delve behind those superficial symbols to explore the ambivalences and complexities of a society, and in
particular its economic system and managerial style.

Not much is known of the prehistoric peoples who eked out a living in
the marshy areas and who left few remains. The Romans found a mixture
of tribes—Gallo-Celtic in the south (Belgae), Germanic in the north
(Batavi), and Frisian along the coast—who spoke a variety of Frankish
dialects (some of which were influenced later by the Saxons). Those
dialects, which still retain their influence on the spoken language today,
developed into modern Dutch when the economically dominant
Amsterdam in the province of Holland gradually provided the standard
Dutch (a Germanic language) which was adopted all over the country by
the upper classes, the government, and in the literary high-point of the
"Golden Age" in the seventeenth century.

Hofstede (1987) sought to encapsulate the characteristics of the Dutch in
terms of eight social roles—"preacher, housewife, nurse, innkeeper,
traveller, tradesman, bourgeois and farmer"—which relate to both men
and women and which can be played simultaneously. In his earlier research
(1984), Hofstede classified Dutch culture as reflecting individualism,
"femininity", egalitarianism (low "power distance"), and relatively weak
"uncertainty avoidance". His data on these four dimensions, collected in a
world-wide survey of IBM personnel, revealed that the Netherlands forms
a "culture cluster with Norway (our closest cultural relative), Denmark,
Sweden, and Finland: countries of North-Western Europe with a maritime
and agrarian past, which, in spite of relatively small population sizes,
succeeded in defending their independence from much larger neighbour
states" (Hofstede 1987: 7).

In general, there seems to be a contradiction in the views about the
Dutch. On the one hand they are seen as sober, regulated, mercenary and
conformist (De Baene 1966); yet, on the other hand, they are viewed as
progressive, tolerant, avant-garde, and as challenging convention (in
ostensibly a democratic–liberal's paradise rampant with state-subsidized
abortion, euthanasia, drugs, generous welfare provisions, and unbridled
nudity on prime-time television). The clue to unscrambling these conflict-
ing themes is that both are partially true; but much more crucial is the fact
that they exist side by side without somehow threatening one another or
engaging in mutually abusive debate. There is no Mary Whitehouse, or
Jerry Falwell, in Dutch society, which perhaps makes life duller than

elsewhere, but which indicates the Dutch distaste for extremism and their preference for balance. Anything goes socially and culturally providing it is labelled, localized and subsidized. Dissent knows its place and can thrive providing it does not invade bourgeois enclaves; and does not interfere with business!

In the views that the Dutch have of themselves restraint, tolerance and bourgeois values—embodying "civility" (Goudsblom 1967)—figure prominently. Heerinkhuizen (1982: 108) summarized Dutch national characteristics as follows;

> The character traits that I came across repeatedly included: the love of freedom, individualism (particularism) with its counterparts of licentiousness (indiscipline), unemotionalism (not very romantic or imaginative), sobriety, domesticity (a great amount of interest in family life, very little interest in public social activities), reserve ("secondary functioning", phlegmatic), commercial spirit, bourgeois mentality, tendency to maintain a show of respectability, an aversion to violence (peace-loving, not cruel to animals), awkwardness (stiffness), seriousness, honesty, a critical attitude, tolerance, thriftiness (economical, stingy), cleanliness (but, as was often noted, not with respect to personal hygiene), interest in religious questions.

Huizinga (1960: 154–155), the historian, noted that the national character was bourgeois "in every sense of the word", that bourgeois values permeated the whole society ("from the baron to the common labourer"), and that this helped to explain the lack of rebelliousness among the lower classes and the "general tranquillity of the nation's life"; indeed, "our very spirit has sprouted forth from bourgeois seeds, not a military spirit but a commercial one".

However, in endeavouring to comprehend the nuances of Dutch social life we feel that the mechanism of pragmatic accommodation, which seems to permeate so many institutional arrangements, is crucial.

What are its roots? Let us focus on three possible explanations. First, Schama (1987) initiates us, in his fascinating study of Dutch society in the sixteenth and seventeenth centuries, into the primal Dutch contradiction, for the principled puritans were confronted with tempting prosperity that led them to a continual wrestling between God and mammon. Their accommodation was to combine surface obedience with private (and discreet) consumption. Erasmus competed with Calvin, restraint with excess, and the rigours of doctrine with the flexible opportunism of trade. Second, a tiny, trading nation that is surrounded by powerful neighbours (not only politically and militarily, but also intellectually and culturally) learns two basic skills; one is to adapt superficially and the other is to sustain cultural identity. The alternative is to become a cultural door-mat. Perhaps the third element is the most elemental, namely, the need historically to survive. A minuscule country, with few natural resources, an unpromising habitat, and especially with the ever threatening presence of water, produced a people who were tough, pragmatic, adaptable and resourceful, because those qualities were essential to *survive*. The comparison with the Japanese arises immediately, but it is a comparison that should not be pushed too far.

By a happy coincidence of history and geography that unpromising habitat became the territory of a major European power in the sixteenth and seventeenth centuries. The mighty Spanish Empire was defeated; abstemious protestantism helped to foster a flourishing mercantile capitalism; and the strategic position at the mouth of two great European waterways turned the threatening water into a valuable resource. A nation of traders was born; a great sea-borne empire emerged; and there was a rich explosion of cultural expression (Geyl 1958).

The only way this could be accomplished was, first, to sink one's differences in order to fight the common enemy and, second, to go on to make a profit from others. That even included the enemy and observers were amazed at "the Dutch practice of trading openly with Spain in wartime, even allowing money for the army of Flanders (the very troops who were trying to attack them!) to be sent from Spain through the banks of Amsterdam" (Parker 1979: 269). Survival spelt out the need to accommodate and to avoid injurious conflict; that civilizing influence (much admired by foreigners) then enabled a tiny country to become the shrewd, adaptable, mercenary tradesman of Europe.

Dutch Society

> The Law appeals to both the preacher and the tradesman in us: the first writes the laws, and the second finds ways to elude them (Hofstede 1987: 9).

Trade, we would argue, is a dominant leitmotiv in Dutch society. It makes the Dutch natural "networkers" and skilful negotiators who drive a hard but generally fair bargain. For this was a country of fishermen, farmers, and sea-farers who were typically tough, reticent, and level-headed; but there was always the preacher to remind them of the importance of principles. Greed was good, and godly, long before Boesky, Milken, and Gekko; and the church readily gave its blessing to the slave trade (Kousbroek 1987: 45). This historical background has left an indelible imprint on the Dutch character and on Dutch society.

As if by a curious conspiracy of principles and pragmatism the Dutch have evolved a social life characterized by the following dynamism. A lot of energy is invested in devising complex and impressive-looking rules, which everyone feels free to break. No one feels any conscience about not keeping to the rules, but what everyone enjoys is the lengthy bargaining and negotiating about their application. No one suggests that the rules are superfluous or not to be taken seriously; it's just that no individual seems to think they actually impinge on him or her personally. This is not a recipe for anarchy because the consensus produces a meta-rule spelling out the boundaries of flexibility beyond which it is prudent not to go. The worst fault an outsider can make is to point out to an individual that they are departing from a rule; first, this is an invasion of the individual's right to tolerance within the meta-rule and, second, it individualizes criticism which is resented as a shaming device to make the person feel uncomfortable. Normally there are subtle patterns of digression and tolerance that are widely understood, but not made explicit. This can be extremely frustrating for foreigners (particularly those from an Anglo-Saxon culture). The rules are essential, however, to promote the feeling of order and to avoid painful conflict; and the indulgence about applying them is to enable people to feel liberated from their tyranny. This embedded cultural ambivalence, or national schizophrenia, has to be understood in order to survive—and to do business—in the Netherlands.

In general, observers remark on the Netherlands as a small, orderly, peaceful society with a reputation for progressive social policies, political stability, and an open economy. Criminal and political violence, social unrest, organized crime, and ideological disharmony are comparatively rare; and the country exemplifies a bourgeois, social–democratic structure of wide-ranging affluence, low poverty, low inflation, and ostensibly highly regulated social and economic activity. Politicians, businessmen, and public figures exude an air of Calvinistic respectability and reliability, while their overt life-style is restrained and sober (colourful personalities and public displays of extravagance are generally frowned upon).

A number of commentators have argued that the Dutch approach to dealing with social and political issues has been deeply influenced by a historical tradition of tolerance, compromise, and pragmatism. This tradition emerges strongly in the reliance on delicate coalition politics which contributes to a political culture characterized by negotiation, a willingness to compromise, and secrecy (Lijphart 1968). Political life is not adversarial, histrionic, and flamboyant but rather people remind themselves that today's opposition could be tomorrow's coalition partner (Gladdish 1991). Debate in public life is restrained, business-like, unemotional, mostly humourless, and often plain boring. The subliminal message is "you can trust us"; yet everyone knows that a considerable amount of wheeling and dealing takes place behind closed doors and beyond public scrutiny.

This sometimes leaves the critical, curious outsider with a feeling that a lot goes undiscovered in Dutch society and that social and political life is regulated by closed circles who negotiate settlements secretively. It is not done to openly discuss the rules of the game but everyone understands them as taken-for-granted. Lijphart's analysis of the rules, according to Bagley (1973: 17–19), focused on proportionality, agreement to disagree, neutralization of sensitive issues, the government's right to govern, and that "politics is business" based on results (while the "apparent dullness of politics is functional for the system's survival"). Partly because of this shield of secrecy, the Dutch have often been called the "Chinese of Europe"; and they are often seen as portraying characteristics that are more typically "Asian" than European (Hofstede 1987).

The central mechanism for explaining much behaviour in public and institutional life was that of "pillarization" ("verzuiling"). Although its impact has been considerably watered down recently, its influence is still recognizable. In short, the argument is that modern Dutch society developed a structure of vertical divisions—rather than horizontal ones based primarily on class—which parcelled out institutions along religious/ideological lines in a way which minimized conflict between the "pillars". At the top, a relatively small elite bargained for the division of the spoils among the contending pillars and developed a model based on consensus, negotiation, paternalism from the top, and of "non-aggression treaties" to avoid disruptive conflict among, and open embarrassment of, elite members. Although there is a danger of being over-deterministic in explaining this phenomenon, it is almost as if the Dutch sought out a structure that minimized conflict between divergent groups while enabling each one to retain its own identity. Usually, analysts classify three main pillars—Protestant, Catholic and Socialist—and, while each pillar contained its own inner variations, they broadly helped to define social identity in politics, the media, sport, and even business.

Although a lot of discussion has taken place on "de-pillarization", it is still the case that politics, the trade-unions, education, employers' organizations, and particularly the media, continue to reflect the influence of the pillars. Its inheritance has left an indelible cultural imprint reflecting balance, reasonableness, bargaining, compromise, and accommodation.

To outsiders, these processes can appear to be incestuous and inflexible, as if decisions are being regulated by a mysterious and impenetrable code. At one level, it is as if people are more deferential and less critical—than say in America or Britain—whereas, at another level, they are highly critical of authority if it imposes on them directly (they are an orderly people who hate being ordered around).

Of course, all societies are highly complex entities that are shaped by history, geography, climate, culture, religion, and so on. Here it has only been possible to skate over a few features of Dutch society (for critical insights into some features of Dutch society, see Phillips 1985). We believe that it can only be analyzed, and understood, by focusing on the ambivalences and contradictions that lie concealed beneath the surface of an apparently comfortable consensus that functions to protect diversity. These ambivalences are all based on a number of fundamental factors—the avoidance of conflict, the need for adaptability and resourcefulness in order to survive, and the almost calculative application of rules to avoid the least burdensome application of authority to sub-groups and even individuals in the interests of consensus and harmony.

For some, these may raise the spectre of a Friedmanite capitalist's nightmare—an intrusive state, overly liberal welfare provisions, and mollycoddled workers who need to be consulted on everything and who report sick if you are not pleasant to them—but that only leads to another apparent contradiction. Namely, that this small society with few natural resources and an apparently unenviable competitive position (high taxation, high labour costs, inflexible social legislation, etc.), still manages to perform more than adequately on the economic front. Its post-war recovery from the devastating effects of the Nazi occupation was as much an economic "miracle" as that of its defeated enemies; and recent performances (since the recovery from the malaise of the early eighties) have been remarkable. Of central interest, then, is how does this tiny player in the global economy manage not only to survive, but also to notch up record export figures, despite being confronted by such powerful competitors? Can it really be the case that cheese competes with chips, and tulips with cars?

The Dutch Economy

To a certain extent, the answer to the last question is an emphatic "yes". For the Netherlands dominates the world market in cut-flowers and its agricultural productivity is a more than healthy contribution to the balance of payments (while the Dutch cow is legendary). This also helps to remind us that the Netherlands was slow to industrialize (much slower, for instance, than its neighbour Belgium) and was until after the Second World War largely an agricultural society. There are still people who bemoan the fact that industry is undervalued, *compared* to say Germany and France where it is pre-eminent (c.f. interview with senior civil servant at the Ministry of Economic Affairs "De industrie wordt in Nederland ondergewaardeerd [Industry in the Netherlands is undervalued]" *De Volkskrant*, 26 March 1991). What, then, are the strengths and weaknesses of the Dutch economy?

First, it is perhaps useful to provide a swift, thumb-nail sketch of the post-war development of Dutch society and its economy. The immediate post-war period was characterized by high consensus, low industrial conflict, and considerable wage restraint in order to re-establish the shattered economic infrastructure inherited from a cruelly devastating war. The sixties witnessed new levels of affluence, resistance to wage restraint, a challenging of traditional styles, and the bloom of progressivism (with Amsterdam, "the swinging city", forming the centre of an international, alternative youth culture). There had also been a substantial shake-out in some traditional industries—such as textiles, shoes, shipbuilding, and coal—and a wave of mergers.

The seventies was seen as the apotheosis of the welfare state where governments (of *all* persuasions) took a series of measures that subsidized ailing companies, expanded employment in the civil service, constructed an admirable but expensive network of social security provision, and (under the centre-left coalition led by the socialist Den Uyl) took—or threatened—a number of proposals that were seen as anti-business. There was a high level of regulation and of taxation; and businessmen complained that profit had become a dirty word and that their children were afraid to admit at school that their father was a manager (Lawrence 1986: 10). There was a general regrouping of industries in the Southern provinces—particularly paper, building, metal, machinery, electro-technical and chemical products—and the emergence of the "randstad" (the area linking the four cities of Amsterdam, Utrecht, Rotterdam and The Hague in the West of the country) as the hub for services, transport, high tech., information systems, and banking/insurance (De Smidt and Wever 1987).

The country had been shielded to a large extent from the first oil-crisis by its vast reserves of natural gas but following the second oil-crisis, and subsequent world depression, there was a definite down-swing in the economy. There was talk of "Hollanditis" and of the "Dutch Disease";

> During the 1970s the "Dutch Disease" became the standard expression to refer to countries that used the reserves from their natural resources to boost various forms of consumption, especially services and social security (Harvard Business School 1985: 11).

The Dutch economy had proved particularly vulnerable in the recession and suffered for the profligacy of the seventies. Some foreign commentators delighted in reporting that the "tolerance" had gone sour and that the down-side was dirt, drugs, and crime; e.g. "The Netherlands is dirty, unsafe, impoverished and has become intolerant, was the unanimous opinion of foreign newspapers this summer" (*Elsevier*, 19 December 1987). There were high taxes, high unemployment, uncharacteristically high inflation, a rash of bankruptcies, and a certain measure of pessimism.

In the early eighties a centre-right coalition came to power determined to lighten the fiscal load of business, to encourage competitiveness and entrepreneurial activity, to cut public spending, to foster deregulation, and above all to revitalize the economy. A new political partnership with business was formed (Van Schendelen 1987), and this was epitomized by the Wagner Report "Towards a New Industrial Elan" (1981) which was a clarion call for co ordination of government policy and industrial needs and especially for a revitalized fighting spirit in the business world. The second half of the eighties witnessed a new wave of mergers. In the late eighties record export figures were achieved but, in the face of another recession and of the repercussions of the Gulf Crisis, the same vulnerabilities as the early eighties are being echoed about the Dutch economy.

Let us take a closer look, then, at that economy and at its strengths and weaknesses. The first point must be that the Netherlands is an important economic player despite its relatively small size (Jacobs et al. 1990). The country is only 36,000 square kilometres (the longest distance is 350 kilometres), the population is 15 million and there are few natural resources. Yet it is one of the "large foreign traders in the world" van Oijen 1990; this section draws heavily on van Oijen's book which is a useful introduction for foreigners to the Dutch economy.

The Netherlands is, for instance, ranked ninth in the world in terms of value of imports and exports; it has the largest port in the world (Rotterdam handled 272,779,000 metric tons of goods in 1988); Schiphol Airport is tenth in the world for shipments of cargo; some 27 per cent of EC goods are transported in Dutch trucks; the Amsterdam stock exchange is twelfth in the world (and Amsterdam also houses the European Options Market); and it is the second largest investor in the United States (next to the U.K.). Furthermore, just two flower auctions claim over 60 per cent of the world trade in cut flowers; this is a business representing three billion guilders per annum and it attracts flowers from France, Israel, and even Thailand to be auctioned and retransported (while the proximity of Schiphol Airport, and purpose-built customs facilities on the premises, means that flowers can be auctioned in the morning and be on sale in North America on the same day). Royal Dutch Shell (an Anglo-Dutch concern like Unilever), is the largest industrial company outside the U.S.A., and the second largest oil company after Exxon. The Netherlands is also the world's largest exporter of potatoes, chocolate and beer (of which two thirds of beer exports go to the U.S.A.). It is also strong in cocoa, yacht-building, photo-copying machines, and records/c.d.'s. In an overview of products exported by all the major market economies, the Dutch could claim that they were first to third in 22 products and market leader in meat, butter, eggs, vegetables, margarine, and natural gas. Finally, in terms of gross domestic product, the Netherlands ranks sixteenth in the world.

The strong points in the economy are transport, tourism, banking and insurance, agricultural products, chemicals, and mineral fuels. *Diversity* is an important element here as the economy is not over-dependent on one or two branches. It is also an "open economy" that has long functioned as the "Gateway to Europe"; for a considerable number of foreign companies see the Netherlands as an important distribution, trading and processing centre. IBM uses Schiphol Airport as its distribution hub for Europe, the Middle East, and Africa. The benefits of Rotterdam, Schiphol, Dutch trucking companies and inland shipping have attracted ITT, Fuji, Digital, Canon, Nissan, Du Pont, Hewlett Packard, Ricoh, Honeywell, Mazda and the United States Line to set up companies in the country. Indeed the United States has 1400 companies employing some 110,000 people in the Netherlands (van Oijen 1990: 104); and this is followed by the U.K., Germany, France and Japan. The Netherlands ranks fifth in Europe in terms of the concentration of Japanese companies.

While 640,000 Dutch people live abroad some 550,000 foreigners live in the Netherlands (not to mention the many thousands of illegal immigrants who often play an important role in the hidden economy). Ironically for a country with notoriously high taxation, the Netherlands is something of an "off-shore" for foreign companies that can locate in the country on most favourable terms. There is also a considerable penetration of foreign capital that potentially nibbles away at the ownership of Dutch companies, but most are tightly sealed legally against unfriendly take-overs (although some of these constructions will doubtless be contested from 1993 onwards).

Generally the Netherlands offers a favourable environment for foreign firms in terms of a good distribution network, amenable fiscal incentives for newcomers, high levels of productivity, a well-trained work-force, and a working population skilled in languages, especially English. Indeed, Dutch productivity has been high for some six hundred years! (according to De Jong 1990); and currently productivity per person-hour is higher than in Germany, Sweden, and Japan.

Another crucial factor is that there are many small companies that do not suffer the weaknesses of the large Dutch corporations. Although the Dutch-based multinationals catch the eye—Philips, Akzo, Shell, and Unilever (with the latter two being Anglo-Dutch enterprises)—they are quite *unrepresentative* of Dutch corporations. There are roughly 500,000 registered companies of which half are one-person companies or "empty" companies; but of the other half 90 per cent have less than ten employees. The typical Dutch company is, then, quite *small*, but the multinationals, and the banks, do tend to dominate in many ways. There are webs of interlocking directorates with 18 men holding 156 influential positions with other companies; these top dogs generally come from the multinationals or the financial institutions.

The *"Vereniging van Effectenbezitters"* (Association of Shareholders) investigated managers with multiple corporate positions: the Netherlands has a two-tier system of company control with a board of management and then a supervisory board of experienced, and often pensioned, managers from other companies. There are clear concentrations of power; one man holds twelve positions, and the companies with potentially the most influence on other firms via interlocking directorates include Shell, Unilever, ABN–AMRO Bank, Nationale Nederlanden (insurance), and Hoogovens (*De Volkskrant*, 21 March 1991, "*Macht concentreert zich bij achttien ondernemers*": "Power is concentrated around eighteen business-men"). The Dutch business elite is frequently filled by lawyers from Leiden University, economists from the Erasmus University Rotterdam or engineers from Delft. It is characteristically small, intimate, intertwined and self-recruiting. Everyone knows everyone else and reputation is important because news travels fast through the network; it is reliability and industry that is rewarded and not flashiness or unnecessary risk-taking.

It has been precisely the larger Dutch companies that have run into rough water recently with Philips (electronics and white goods), Daf Trucks, Fokker (aeroplanes), Hoogovens (steel), Vendex (department stores) and KLM (Royal Dutch Airlines, the national carrier) being par-ticularly hard hit by increasing global competition, by high personnel costs, by the low dollar, by high interest rates and by the recession. In contrast, one company that is doing particularly well is Ahold (parent of the supermarket chain "Albert Heijn"); it is now the tenth largest supermarket owner in the U.S.A. with four substantial and shrewd acquisitions.

On the whole, though, large Dutch companies tend to be bureaucratic, comfortable, and somewhat inflexible. They attract considerable loyalty, offer excellent secondary labour conditions (and, until quite recently, virtually life-time employment), and managers generally spend their whole career within one company. Perhaps thirty years of social legislation and of security have weakened the entrepreneurial spirit; for the companies often have good R&D and quality products, but they seem to miss out in produc-tion and in penetrating new markets. The people at Philips, for instance, lament the fact that "if it were purely a matter of research brilliance we would have beaten the Japanese hands down" (Lawrence 1986: 42).

More generally, the weaknesses of the Dutch economy are structural and attitudinal. A number of commentators have begun to argue that the successes of the second half of the eighties have led to self-satisfaction and a lack of urgency.

> Holland is missing chances: our contribution to world trade is diminishing. The once so creative and innovative thinking Dutch tradesman is, spoilt by years of success, becoming short-sighted and in many cases even complacent (De Jonge and Kops 1990: 36).

Although exports were a record in 1989 (228 billion guilders with about a further 40 billion for services), this was 3 per cent less than had been forecast by the O.E.C.D. Indeed, in 1975 the Netherlands had 4.2 per cent of world trade whereas this had diminished to 3.4 per cent by 1989. Growth had remained low throughout the eighties at an average of 1.6 per cent.

Furthermore, the vast majority of exports go to neighbouring countries (particularly Germany and Belgium). There is low penetration in Eastern Europe, Africa, the Far East, and the "Newly Industrializing Countries" (with some particular traumas in China and a failure to compete in India where companies from Germany, Japan, and Italy are much more in evidence).

Diagnoses made by major institutions such as O.E.C.D., I.M.F. and W.E.F. (World Economic Forum, Geneva) point to a worrying shortage of flexibility, a limited dynamism, and too little innovative power. The old ills of high government spending (39 per cent of GNP), high taxes and social security provision, a high number of non-actives among the potential workforce (the highest of all countries represented in O.E.C.D.), and slow growth reappear ominously.

The general lack of flexibility is in striking contrast to the tendency to more flexibility elsewhere (according to the O.E.C.D. "economic outlook" of June 1990). The W.E.F. produces, furthermore, a world competitive index. Between 1981 and 1986 the Netherlands climbed from the 19th to the 9th position on the scale; but by 1990 it had slipped to 14th place. Overall the performance was not bad; there was a 4th for efficiency, a 5th for financial dynamism and for socio-political stability, and a 7th for international orientation. However, Ireland, Spain and Austria were considered to have more "dynamic" economies than the Netherlands and the four Scandinavian countries (Sweden, Norway, Denmark and Finland) also preceded it on the rankings (based on a wide range of socio-economic variables). The report was particularly critical about the economy, about re-educating personnel, and about government interference.

At the beginning of the nineties, then, there is a growing measure of concern about the prospects of the Dutch economy. Traditional ills—high government spending and national deficit, high personnel costs, high taxation, undue regulation, increasing absenteeism, and so on—have resurfaced and have been given a sharper edge by fears of slow growth, of the inability to create sufficient new jobs (particularly for the increasing number of women entering the work-force), the lack of home investment (capital flight), and by deficiencies in the systems of vocational and higher education, and by lack of dynamism. For instance, in 1990 absenteeism due to illness was estimated at 9.1 per cent of the full-time labour-force (in 1988 it was 8.5 per cent); while people receiving some form of sickness benefit rose to approximately 660,000 in 1980 to over 846,000 in 1989 (*De Volkskrant*, 23 March 1991). There is also a perception that the economic centre of Europe is moving south—with its links loosely connecting Munich, Milan, Lyon and Barcelona—and that new communication trajectories (such as the Channel Tunnel with North–South road and rail links) will increasingly disadvantage the Netherlands with its more northerly position.

In the post-war period, the Netherlands developed a relatively stable economy and a strongly considerate society. There can be no doubt that both elements are potentially threatened and that the Dutch economy will have to face some stiff challenges in the nineties; and it remains to be seen if it will display its usual resilience.

Industrial Relations

The Dutch inclination to reconcile opposing interests and to create balances between them is reflected in the *institutions* that have been created to regulate economic activity. In order to grasp the importance of the institutional framework, within which managers have to operate, let us first take a look at its output.

As we have already seen, the Dutch economy is a relatively prosperous one. To a considerable degree, the socio–economic institutions of Dutch society are closely concerned with the *distribution* of the fruits of that economic activity. This, of course, reflects itself in the distribution of income between different societal groups. First of all, the state is rechannelling roughly one third of the GNP into an extensive social security system that provides income to a vast array of groups (Veldkamp 1978; Talsha-Schulp 1991). Included are state pensions, arrangements for disabled workers, subsidies for inexpensive housing, allowances for unemployed workers, and so on. The distributive process has called for an elaborate system of organizations that apply the rules for granting particular allowances. The art of governing this system has become so intricate that it is even possible nowadays to acquire an academic degree in social security. The amount of money involved in granting a particular type of allowance is determined on the basis of changes in the salaries earned in the private sector. The same is true for the salaries of civil servants and employees of governmental funded institutions (as for instance in universities). The social and political construction of economic connections between social security systems, costs of government and the salaries of the private sector is based upon the cultural definition of "reasonableness" that pervades policy and decision-making. It has resulted in one of the most complicated distributive systems around.

It is important to notice that the different distributive activities are all tightly linked to their respective interest groups. Politicians cannot easily afford to propose changes in the system, because almost one third of the population is dependent upon the functioning of the distributive system. In practice, political life is condemned to minor adaptations and thereby to the promulgation of even more rules, necessary to handle each individual case in a justifiable way. Needless to say, this state of affairs has a choking effect on several societal dynamics: for example, wage-earners have a limited amount of money to spend which has a negative effect upon domestic consumption, while the functioning of the labour market is impaired by high labour costs and by social security regulations. Because of the open character of the Dutch economy even minor changes in the international economy call for regulatory action on the national level in order to restore balances between the different spending categories.

One of the explanations that have been offered to account for this tendency to install nation-wide distributive mechanisms refers to the evolution of the Dutch *system of industrial relations* to whose institutions, pivotal as they are in terms of the regulation of economic activity, we now turn (Visser 1990). Industrialization took a fairly long time in the Netherlands. Whereas the industrial revolution started in earnest early in the nineteenth century in Britain, the industrial structure of the Netherlands only began to develop in the fifties and sixties of the nineteenth century (Windmuller and van Zweeden 1987; Peper and van Kooten 1983). This meant that the traditional crafts disappeared quite gradually and, as a result, they did not become the organizational fundament of the emerging labour unions. Labour unions organized themselves from the beginning of the 1860s onwards around the evolving industrial sectors in a context of considerable poverty and social stagnation. Because of the weak position of labour, the unions tried to influence the elites of their respective "pillars" (catholic, protestant and socialist organizations) and to improve labour's position through parliamentary action.

It is said that these conditions were conducive to the definitive *centralist* characteristics of the system of industrial relations as they still prevail today. The pillarized structure of Dutch politics translated the tendency to move issues to the national level into a structure which especially reflects Roman Catholic corporatist thought. In the aftermath of World War II there was wide societal consensus on issues of national social and economic recovery from the devastations of war. In this climate, a *corporatist* structure was erected in which government, employees and employers could participate on equal terms. A typical example is the SER (Social Economic Council); it is a consultative organ that continually brings employers, employees and members appointed by the crown (effectively the government) together. The members are not elected and are not accountable to parliament. Yet no one objects to it and its deliberations on social economic policy are treated with the utmost seriousness.

This corporatist structure penetrated deep roots in every branch of industry. Later on it became apparent that the heterogeneity of economic life made it impossible for the corporatist invention to remain viable. Almost only the top structure is still alive today, together with reporting organizations that are rooted in traditionally conservative sectors of the economy (such as agriculture). At the same time, employers and employees constructed a private foundation to discuss their concerns at the national level without the government being able to "spy" upon them (in the "*Stichting Van de Arbeid*"). This Foundation of Labour is used by the associations of employers organizations and by the federations of labour unions to try to reach agreements at the national level. These agreements are used to set parameters' for subsequent negotiations at the branch level.

As the economy prospered during the sixties and matured during the seventies the national consensus on which the workings of these institutions was based, quickly disappeared. Because of the connectedness of different spending categories it became more difficult for the federations of unions to formulate a centrally viable negotiating agenda: increases of salaries of employees in the private sector for example would lead to increases of the salaries of civil servants and those on welfare.

The connectedness of issues at the national level had other consequences as well. Employers and unions knew that failures to reach agreements at the national level would force government to intervene and to determine the available scope for increases of the wages in the private as well as the public sectors. During the seventies, every cabinet, regardless of its political constitution, faced the necessity to intervene. The deterioration of the position of Dutch industry, a development that can be traced back to the late sixties, was only fully acknowledged in the late seventies. The effects on employment were masked by an excessive growth of the public sector. When eventually an influential committee, chaired by former Shell president Wagner (1981), made recommendations to improve Dutch industry, part of the proposals were concerned with preventing employers and unions from shifting the burden of their responsibilities towards government. In order for government to achieve this, it had to stop intervening in the negotiations between unions and employers.

Until now, government has largely abided by this new rule of the game, but it must be said that the connectedness of issues can still force government to step into the negotiating field. At the national level, a lot of lobbying and mutual consulting takes place; parties continually test out each other's negotiating space. Furthermore, many of the issues, that in other countries are agreed upon between employers and unions, have a legal basis in the Netherlands. Thus, when an agreement is reached between employers and unions at branch level, the minister of social affairs will declare the collective agreement valid for even the non-participating companies within that particular sector (Reynaerts 1987).

To summarize: the Dutch system of industrial relations traditionally is a centralized system in which government plays an active role. Labour agreements are made at the branch level. Individual companies, except the large ones, are only able to influence the outcomes of negotiations through their employers' organizations. For management it often means that the shaping of personnel policies has to take place within margins that are set elsewhere. How, then, does management cope?

Managing Within Margins

> The good Dutchman is *handig*. If you look up *handig* in the dictionary it gives
> it as clever or handy, but in the context of the successful manager it means a
> little more—able to convince and persuade, "sell" things to people, get
> agreement, do deals, bring people together. As one respondent put it
> . . . . "One is always in a bargaining situation. The successful manager
> is always a good bargainer. A sound integrator. We say *hij is handig*, he
> makes good manoeuvres, not Machiavellian, not just social integration, and
> certainly not just task oriented, but *handig*" (Lawrence 1986: 67).

Of course, it is difficult to discern a distinctive Dutch managerial style. Management styles in the Netherlands are as varied as anywhere else (with Lawrence 1986 reminding us of the resilience of regionalism in providing variety in the patterns of Dutch business and management). The Dutch context, however, is more conducive to styles that allow for *participation* than to more authoritarian styles; ("It appears that Dutch society is saturated in consultative institutions. Consultation seems to run in the Dutch blood"; Arjo Klamer in *De Volkskrant*, 23 3. 1991). One might be inclined to say that Dutch managers are forced to adopt a participative style because of the rather extensive legislation about participation at work.

Most companies, in fact, are obliged to have a "work's council" (*"ondernemingsraad"*). The work's council is an independent body within the company. Its main task is to advise management on important decisions regarding the company. Management is legally obliged to ask the work's council for advice when, for example, it wants to close a plant, or when it wants to sell part of the company. All major decisions are subject to advice from the work's council. However, the decision-making is done exclusively by management. The council's main rights are to be informed about major management decisions and to be asked for advice regarding those decisions. Possibilities for actual co-determination, however, are virtually absent. In spite of extensive legislation, it is estimated that only in a limited number of companies have employees learned to fully exercise their rights.

The social expectation to create balances between possibly opposing interests, however, forces management to allow for participation, even when it is convinced that participation will not improve the quality of decision-making. Quite a lot of participative procedures seem to function more as an after-the-fact legitimation of decisions that already have been taken. These procedures can considerably slow down processes of decision-making and implementation. They also force management to engage in, and to accept, a lot of "talking around".

The context of industrial relations and internal organizational processes becomes intertwined in varied and intricate ways: extensive laws on hiring and firing, on social security and the participation "circus" narrow down the "zone of acceptance" for nasty decisions to a rather large degree. Of course, managers are part of the same national culture as their employees; many managers have adapted to this style of managing and taking decisions. They continually anticipate the expected acceptability of their proposals by subordinates. This can undermine their propensity to take risks and to develop new courses of action. On the macro-level this reflects itself in a certain lack of innovation.

Although this analysis might lead the reader to rather sombre conclusions, there are also positive effects of participative management. Many Dutch companies are characterized by the existence of strong informal relations. Authority is not so much connected with position as with personal credibility. Employees often do not ask themselves whether a particular assignment falls within the limits of their formal task description. They do what they think is necessary. One could argue that this places even a greater burden upon management's shoulders: assignments in many cases are only accepted if management has succeeded in convincing employees of the reasonableness of a request. Many managers use participatory procedures to convince employees. Once employees are convinced they often do not need many or detailed instructions to execute their tasks. This greatly adds to the adaptiveness of many Dutch organizations.

Motivation

An issue that never fails to puzzle foreigners is the motivation of Dutch employees. The rather centralized system of labour relations traditionally produces salary systems that are more concerned with a reasonable distribution of income than with the creation of performance-related incentives. The fringe benefits for many employees are more than excellent: it is normal for Dutch employees to have at least 25 working days for holidays per year. Many companies have well-developed pension plans. The social security system provides nearly full coverage against the risks of unemployment and illness. If one relates these facts to the existence of considerable barriers for firing people the question arises: why would the Dutch even bother to work? Yet, obviously, they do work: indeed, productivity rates are among the highest in the western industrial world.

One explanation points to the traditional values of Calvinism, but that hardly suffices. Why should Calvinist values continue to hold out in competition with decades of luxurious regulations? Another explanation, offered by sociology, would focus upon the relationship between employees and their work, and, indeed, this relationship seems to be different from the relationships typically found in the Anglo-Saxon world. Whereas in Anglo-Saxon companies the relationship between employer and employee seems to be defined primarily as an *exchange relationship*, the typical Dutch employee identifies him-/herself to a substantial degree with the company he or she is working for. This does not mean that there are no exchanges. The point we want to make is that exchanges take place within a context of a perceived *social unity* in which both employer and employee play their role. The degree to which identification takes place varies from branch to branch, between levels of the hierarchy, etc.

This feature of Dutch organizational culture brought an American observer to the statement that the Dutch and the Japanese seemed to have a lot in common, meaning that both countries seem to have a collectivist culture. In our opinion, this observation is readily made on superficial acquaintance with Dutch social life but, as we hinted earlier, it is inaccurate because the limits to collectivism are quite different in the two societies. The typical Dutch employee is continuously testing the relationship. Quite unlike his Japanese counterpart, he assesses whether management is still operating within the zone of acceptance mentioned above. Outside this zone, the typical Dutch employee can be said to be even more "disobedient" than his Anglo-Saxon colleague. It is the *connectedness* of regulations that seduces foreign observers to interpret organizational life as being more collectivist.

In fact, the value systems in the Netherlands are fairly liberal and depart from the puritan belief system held by many in the Anglo-Saxon world. Many Dutch employees live in a voluntaristic world in which the exercise of free will is embedded in regulations that serve as an expression of the longing for an all-pervading "reasonableness". As a result of all this, managers see themselves confronted with the question of how to reward and to stimulate employees, because government regulations and collective labour agreements at the branch level often keep management within narrow limits. As employees work for a wide variety of reasons, not influenced simply by material rewards, managers look for other rewards. Although there is a tendency towards more differentiated performance-based reward systems, it is along the non-material dimensions of work and motivation that Dutch management has to be particularly creative. Basically management is continually trying to influence the balance between a variety of individual goals and the objectives of the organization. This is why Dutch organizations tend to be characterized by a lot of negotiations, resembling a political arena rather than an army-like command structure.

The positive effects are clearly visible: a consistently low level of industrial conflict, a high degree of unity and consensus on what is to be achieved, and a well motivated work-force. The negative effects are also there: the institutionalized care for employees results in the experience of feeling entitled to a comforting protective shield that takes away the propensity to take risks and that hides employees from the necessity to perform as well as they can. Where a single-minded commitment to high performance is called for, a lot of Dutch organizations will be confronted by a culture that stimulates an attitude "not to overdo it". There are, however, striking examples of organizations that have succeeded in overcoming this attitude, for precisely the reasons mentioned above: they knew how to utilize the sense of community among their employees. Indeed, they induce almost a sense of membership in an occupational community, but one which also respects a high measure of personal privacy and freedom.

Management

Where does this leave management? All managers are, to a certain extent, schizophrenic because they have to cope daily with the discrepancy between paper reality, and formal institutional demands, and the messiness of the shop floor reality. Dutch managers, we would maintain, carry with them not just a micro-induced ambivalence but a macro one as well. This is because they have to wrestle with tightly-coupled elements at the structural, and even societal, level in addition to continual minute adjustments at the work level that stretch their resourcefulness and their role-playing agility (Lawrence 1986: 67).

In general, we can also assert that Dutch managers are among the best educated in Europe. The majority of managers at the executive board level have a degree which will typically be in Economics, Engineering or Law. According to Lawrence (1986), who has conducted research on managers in several European countries, this makes the Dutch manager closer to his German counterpart than to say a British manager. Production is important and has high status and this is reflected in an emphasis on deadlines, delivery, and reliability. Marketing has also been strong and more recently finance, and even personnel, have taken on much more weight. Since the early eighties it has been possible to gain an MBA degree in the Netherlands, but the alumni of such programmes have yet to prove themselves. Many Dutch managers will have studied abroad, either early on in their career at an American or European graduate programme, or else later in life at advanced management development programmes at prestigious universities.

This is relevant for a further positive characteristic of Dutch management, namely its capacity to operate under difficult circumstances and then particularly abroad. Examples are construction companies that specialize in roads, dams, dykes, and harbours—often in inhospitable third world environments—and the salvage companies that await dangerous and financially risky escapades on the high seas. Most Dutch managers have a reasonable command of two or more languages—although there are critical voices which argue that language ability is diminishing because of developments in high-school education—and enjoy a favourable reputation for operating across borders. Many will have lived abroad at some time in their career and, with more than 60 per cent of GNP represented by exports, there are few firms that do not have an international dimension, however limited. When abroad, Dutch managers are particularly praised for not being overtly chauvinistic; they are seen as competent, businesslike, reliable and sober and, if sometimes they are a bit stiff and lacking in flair, they are somehow politically and culturally neutral and do not impose themselves as heavily and bombastically as the Germans, French, and British are accused of doing (and that is not to mention the Americans!).

There is a downside too. Dutch management is used to a "politicized" way of decision-making; that is, it is accustomed to the involvement of many parties within the company when a decision has to be taken. Many managers are used to playing a *moderating* role in these processes. When quick, sometimes radical decisions are called for, Dutch management often does not feel very comfortable. Being teamplayers *"par excellence"*, and stressing the virtues of consensus and community, they also tend to remain outside the floodlights of publicity and public life. Dutch managers in general lead hidden private lives; they exercise restraint with respect to their public behaviour. If a Dutch manager possesses an extravagant yacht or a number of race-horses he is likely to harbour the former in some Mediterranean port and to seek stables for the latter in Belgium. This is generally not seen as hypocritical, but as respecting norms that even the privileged should behave "normally". In turn, their private lives are largely their own affair. Unlike some Japanese and American corporations, the Dutch firm does not usually trespass across an accepted border to impose itself on private and family life. No Dutch firm would ever endeavour to influence the political choice of its personnel as some American companies unashamedly do; and certainly no Dutchman would allow his firm to dictate his style and location of holidays as happens in Japan. Indeed, by constantly moderating possibly opposing interests, and subtly balancing private welfare with the social desirability of sobriety, many managers are so deeply embedded into the social fabric that to be even slightly deviant is almost immediately interpreted as devious.

What we would like to argue here, then, is that managers tend to be overly integrated into existing social patterns. This can prevent them from being truly innovative. Rather the emphasis is on team-work, on suppressing prima donnas, on restraint, on a co-operative disposition, and on not making unnecessary waves (Lawrence 1986: 81). There are centuries of proverbs against originality, initiative, pomposity, and vanity. This might appear to suppress excellence, yet it is clear that there are excellent managers and excellent companies. It is a matter of style; the high-performer must not transcend group norms and must behave in a restrained way while seeing his achievement as oriented to the collective. You can be bright but not difficult with it, because that threatens social networks. There is a rejection of the stereotypical U.S. model of tough leadership, self-promotion, contest-excellence, and an orientation to individual results. The leadership style, then, of top Dutch management is restrained, competent, and self-confident. It simply does not produce the likes of Iacocca, Trump, Branson, Murdoch, Tapie, de Bennedetti, Berlusconi, or, for that matter, a Milken or a Maxwell.

Of course all this is in flux, as European unification and globalization have an increasing impact on Dutch business and management. However, the values and style upheld by Dutch society and Dutch business have proved remarkably long-standing and they are not likely to change overnight. It is not as if by listing the weaknesses of management that this will readily lead to their elimination, because those "weaknesses" are generated by deeply engrained social habits and by relatively stable infrastructural features. Perhaps self-confidence slides over into complacency, a low emphasis on brazen individual excellence into grey mediocrity, and decades of social legislation into lack of entrepreneurship. On the other hand, there is a new generation of managers, relatively young and working in companies not yet well-known, who are able to afford themselves considerably more latitude in many respects. In 1990, it was particularly the small companies that did well and then in areas such as services, consulting, maintenance, security, and retail (while a record number of companies—91.4 per cent—were profitable).

To be clear, the point we are endeavouring to make is not that there is a general lack of innovation within Dutch industry and business. On the contrary, technical innovation is happening everywhere (and it leads to a stream of patents that dwarfs those produced until now by Japan). It is at the point where the innovation enters the organization of a factory, or when it begins to affect existing relationships between departments and people, that the propensity to balance group interests (instead of making choices) often waters down the possible gains of renewal (Metze 1991).

As in all European countries, management in the Netherlands is being buffeted by all sorts of forces. Our opinion is that it will absorb, adapt, and accommodate and will become more open, more international, and more cosmopolitan, and yet will also remain remarkably similar. We suspect that it will continue to exude a number of values that the Dutch as a trading nation (with their curious mixture of expediency and principle) have exemplified for some four hundred years.

Conclusion

In this necessarily condensed sketch, we have attempted to afford the reader a number of insights into a small, complex, and widely misunderstood society. Currently the Dutch economy is under critical scrutiny, from the IMF and from its own Central Planning Bureau, and Dutch business and management will face tough challenges and painful choices throughout the nineties. Clearly it will not be alone, but there are certain features of Dutch economic life—centralism, consultation, tight-coupling, and considerateness—that will have to face up to the new adages of liberalism, flexibility, individualism, deregulation, and openness in the new European thinking. Will the Dutch be able to retain their identity within this new framework and maintain their remarkable performances?

There can be little doubt that Europeanization and globalization will lead to a dilution of connectedness in government regulation and in the centralist framework of industrial relations, to new patterns of ownership and control, and almost certainly to new styles of multi-cultural management. Our feeling is that Dutch business and management will manage to retain a fair amount of its identity and that the economy will display its traditional resilience. There can be no complacency in a global economy with tougher competition and an increasingly turbulent and less predictable environment. Certainly we have all been made acutely aware of this by the dramatic and hectic currency fluctuations of September 1992 which were generated by political uncertainty surrounding the future path of the European Community and by gloomy news on the economic front. Nevertheless, there are indications—providing the Dutch government, business and education respond sensibly and with foresight—that these conforming deviants will survive, and that this small country will remain an almost disproportionately strong trading nation in the new world economy.

References

Baene, Duke de (1966): *The Dutch puzzle*. Den Haag: Boucher.
Bagley, C. (1973): *The Dutch plural society*. London: Oxford University Press.
Geyl, P. (1958): *The revolt of the Netherlands*. London: Benn: (first published 1932).

Gladdish, K. (1991): *Governing from the centre: politics and policy-making in the Netherlands*. London: Hurst.

Goudsblom, J. (1967): *Dutch society*. New York: Random House.

Harvard Business School (1985): "The Netherlands and the Dutch Disease". Teaching Case 9–385–317. Boston, MA.: Harvard Business School.

Heerinkhuizen, B. van (1982): "What is typically Dutch?" *The Netherlands Journal of Sociology* 18: 103–125.

Hofstede, G. (1984): *Culture's consequences*. (abridged version). Beverly Hills, CA.: Sage.

Hofstede, G. (1987): *Dutch culture's consequences*. Maastricht: University of Limburg, inaugural lecture.

Huizinga, J. (1960): *De Nederlandse natie (The Dutch nation)*. Haarlem: J. Enschede.

Jacobs, D., T. Broekhorst and W. Zegveld (1990): *De economische kracht van Nederland (The economic strength of the Netherlands)*. The Hague: SMO.

Jong, H.W. de (1990): "Frau Antje en de diamant", *E.S.B.*, 19–26 December.

Jonge, C. de and H. Kops (1990): "Voorheen: Hollands glorie" ("Gone: Holland's glory"). *Elsevier* 46/31 (4th. August), 37–40.

Kousbroek, R. (1987): *Nederland: Een bewoond gordijn*. Amsterdam: Meulenhoff.

Lawrence, P. (1986): "Management in the Netherlands: a study in internationalism?" Unpublished typescript. Loughborough: Loughborough University of Technology.

Lijphart, A. (1968). *The politics of accommodation: pluralism and democracy in the Netherlands*. Berkeley, Los Angeles: University of California Press.

Metze, M. (1991): *Kortsluiting* (Short-circuit). Nijmegen: SUN.

Oijen, A.L. van (1990): *The Netherlands in the world*. Groningen: Wolters-Noordhoff.

Parker, G. (1979): *The Dutch revolt*. Harmondsworth: Penguin.

Peper, B. and G. van Kooten (1983): "The Netherlands: from ordered harmony to bargaining relationship" in S. Barkin (ed.), 111–145. *Worker militancy and its consequences*. New York: Praeger.

Phillips, D. (1985): *De naakte Nederlander (The naked Dutchman)*. Amsterdam: Bert Bakker.

Reynaerts, W.II.J. (1987): "Collective arbeidsovereenkomsten" ("Collective labour agreements") in W.H.J. Reynaerts (ed.), *Arbeidsverhoudingen: theorie en praktijk*, Vol. 2, 75–80. Leiden: Stenfert Kroese.

Schama, S. (1987): *Embarrassment of riches*. London: Collins.

Schendelen, M.P.C.M. van (1987): "The Netherlands: from low to high politicisation", in M.P.C.M. van Schendelen and R.T. Trackson (eds.), 95–83. *Politicisation of business in Western Europe*. London: Croom Helm.

Smidt, M. de and E. Wever (1987): *De Nederlandse industrie: positie, spreiding en struktuur. (Dutch industry: location, distribution and structure)*. Assen/Maastricht: Van Gorcum.

Talsha-Schulp, E. (ed.) (1991): *Praktische informatie over de sociale zekerheid. (Practical information about social security)*. Deventer: Kluwer.

G.M.J. Veldkamp (1978): *Inleiding tot de sociale zekerheid en de toepassing ervan in Nederland en België. (Introduction to social security and its application in the Netherlands and Belgium)*. Deventer: Kluwer.

J. Visser (1990): "Continuity and change in Dutch industrial relations" in G. Baglioni and C. Crouch (eds.), 199–242. *European industrial relations*. Beverly Hills, CA.: Sage.
Windmuller, J.P. (1969): *Labor relations in the Netherlands*. Ithaca, N.Y.: Cornell University Press.
Windmuller, J.P. and A.F. van Zweeden (1987): *Arbeidsverhoudingen in Nederland (Labour relations in the Netherlands)*, 6th ed. Utrecht: Het Spectrum.

Reports

Centraal Planbureau (Central Planning Bureau) (1990): *Economisch beeld 1991 (Economic survey 1991)*. The Hague: State Publishing Company.
OECD (1989, May): *Economic survey of the Netherlands*. Paris: OECD.
Ministry of Economic Affairs (1990): *Economie met open grenzen (Economy with open borders)*. The Hague: Ministry of Economic Affairs.
Intermediair (1990): "Hoe Flexibel is de B.V. Nederland?" ("How Flexible is the 'Corporation Holland'?"). *Intermediair* 25: 40 (special supplement).
OECD (1990): 'Progress in structural reform". *Economic Outlook* 47: June.
"Wagner Commission" (1981): *Adviescommissie inzake het industriebeleid; Een nieuw industrieel elan (Advisory Committee on Industry Policy: towards a new industrial elan)*. The Hague: Ministry of Economic Affairs.
W.E.F. (1990): *World Competitiveness Report*. Geneva: World Economic Forum (WEF).

Chapter 11: Portugal

Management in Portugal

Afonso Pereira Inacio and David Weir

Portugal, a Developing Country

The Portuguese economy has developed since 1985 within a stable social and political environment. Even so, it has not yet been possible to control the major structural problems of the economy. There is a rather high inflation level, more than 9 per cent in 1992; agriculture remains relatively backward; industry is under-developed technologically, and compared with most EC countries, there is a lack of qualified personnel.

Tables 1, 2 and 3 give economic indicators for 1991. These are followed by a list of other key features which provide a background to the analysis of management in Portugal.

Table 1. Main Indicators of the Portuguese Economy

	1991 (in %)	1992 (in %)
G.D.P. (mp)	2.5	1.5 2
G.F.C.F.	3.25	4.5–6
Domestic Demand	5.25	3.25
Exports (Goods and Services)	1.25	2.0
Imports (Goods and Services)	5.0	3.75
Inflation Rate	11.5	9.25
Prime Rate	19–20	18–19
Private Bonds (inv. grade)	19.5	17.5–18.5
Public Bonds (fixed interest — 5 years)	14.7	14.0–13.0
Unemployment Rate	4.2	5.00
GNP per capita (US$)	4.800	–
Population	10,337,000	
Area (Km^2)	91,985	

Source: QUANTUM—Ministry of Finance

Table 2. Total Foreign Investment in Portugal (in M. US$)	
1986	163,777
1987	437,434
1988	959,007
1989	2,019,024
1990	3,567,917
1991	5,300,000

Source: I.C.E.P. (Ministry of Commerce)

Table 3. Sources of Foreign Investment in Portugal (1980–1990) (in %)	
E.C.	66.5
U.S.A.	8.4
Brazil	5.2
Japan	1.6
Others	18.3

Source: I.C.E.P. (Ministry of Commerce)

– Notwithstanding developments since the mid-1980s, Portugal remains one of the poorest countries in the EC. The population of Portugal is only 3.2 per cent of that of the Common Market, but 6.2 per cent of its people are defined as "poor" by European Community norms.

– By the 21st Century, the Portuguese population will be the youngest in the EC. Portugal and Ireland share the characteristic that 30 per cent of their populations are under twenty years old. However, the birth rate has been decreasing and at the moment it is almost equivalent to the EC average.

– Pollution and traffic congestion in Lisbon are expected to increase, for Lisbon has one of the highest densities of population in the Community. Throughout the country as a whole, the inadequacy of the road network poses severe problems for mobility and distribution. It is only in the last few years that the two major cities, Lisbon and Oporto, have been linked by a fast motorway.

– The income per capita in Portugal is higher than in Greece and Ireland, the other two members of the poorest group of nations in the EC. However, surveys indicate that Portugal has greater development prospects than either of these other two nations. The real GNP per capita, although it remains very low in comparison with the EC average, has been increasing satisfactorily during the past few years.

– Portuguese hourly salary rates are still among the lowest in Europe and are on a par with the Pacific Rim "tigers" of Korea, Taiwan and Singapore. This clearly offers an attractive opportunity for inward investment in manufacturing.

– Portugal and Spain are the two countries in the European Community with the highest number of female employees engaged on temporary labour contracts. This figure currently stands at 18.5 per cent of the working population compared with Spain's 22 per cent.

– Portugal has one of the lowest absenteeism rates in the EC—only 5.7 per cent of the total working hours. There are, however, significantly more public holidays than in many countries in Northern Europe and the

Table 4.   Size and Distribution of Firms in Portugal

Number of People Employed	Number of Firms	%
1 to 4	207,656	74.0
5 to 9	37,870	13.4
10 to 19	18,519	7.0
20 to 29	6,011	2.0
30 to 39	3,098	1.0
40 to 49	1,863	0.6
50 to 99	3,157	1.1
100 to 199	1,526	0.5
200 to 499	847	0.3
500 to 999	220	0.08
+ 1000	125	0.04
Total	280,892	100

Source: I.N.E. (1990) (Statistical Institute of Portugal)

absenteeism figures may be affected by the acceptance of the *"ponte"* or bridging day which is conventionally taken as holiday if it falls between two official public holidays.
- The percentage of the population in education is rising, but nevertheless only 63 per cent of the age group between 5 and 24 is currently in education, compared with 82 per cent in France.
- Various indicators of social welfare in Portugal show the country in a rather unattractive light, compared with other EC members. For example, the country boasts the lowest ratio—2.9—of hospital beds per 1,000 inhabitants.

This overview of the current situation indicates that Portugal has many favourable features, with a market offering considerable opportunities. Manufacturing is still relatively important and provides 42 per cent of employment whilst the importance of tourism and foreign earnings is indicated by the 25 per cent employment in wholesaling, retailing, restaurants and hotels. The country appears to be relatively better placed than in the past to profit from a vigorous and dynamic policy of both domestic and foreign investment. Foreign investment has been increasing, spread over tourism, financial services, and manufacturing.

A key feature of the Portuguese economy is the high percentage of small and medium-sized familial-based companies. Table 4 indicates that 74 per cent of registered firms employ less than five people; 0.04 per cent of the companies employ over 1,000 and there are only 125 such firms. Only 59 companies show annual sales above 132 million US dollars. Most are at a

relatively low level of technological development characterized by weak
financial structures, poorly developed technology, relatively unqualified
managers and employees lacking professional training.

Various official reports highlighted the dominance of small firms, and
the Government has now instituted several development measures, most
notably a special agency to provide investment and training support for this
sector, IAPMEI. However, the problem persists, and Portugal has far to
go if it is ever to enter the faster track of developing nations in Europe.

Historical and Psycho-sociological Aspects of Portuguese Society

Portuguese national culture and character form a unique combination of
characteristics. It is a matter of the greatest annoyance to most Portuguese
that they are sometimes lumped together in some Iberian mélange by
uninformed outside observers. The Portuguese feel, and with considerable
justice, that they are as different from the Spanish in attitudes and
behaviour as the English are from the French. Winston Churchill once
characterized the Americans and the English as "two nations divided by
the possession of a common language". We may say of the Iberian Peninsula that "Portugal and Spain are two neighbours divided by their proximity". Portugal is at once a less extreme, more integrated, more friendly,
less proud, and less assertive society than Spain.

Historically, Portuguese society has shown considerable resilience and
assimilation. These have never been better demonstrated than in the brief
but relatively untraumatic progress of the Portuguese Revolution after the
overthrow of dictatorial control. Portugal effected a massive societal transition in the late 1970s with minimal violence. Outside observers may not
have realized the intense swings of political colour of the Governments
which followed in bewildering succession after the Caetano government
was deposed in 1974. There were real possibilities of the country going
Communist at that time and, indeed, it was under Communist domination
for a while.

The relatively middle-of-the-road centrist and social democratic policies
of the governments which held power in the late 1980s owe much to the
moderate and reconciliatory policy of leading politicians but also to the
historically developed resilience and phlegmatic realism of the Portuguese
people: it has been no mean achievement. It remains to be seen whether
the countries of Eastern Europe will cope as well.

Historically, Portugal has been characterized by a profound and consistent drive for independence. The Portuguese saw the departure of the invading Romans, the Moors, and the oppressive Spanish, the leaders of whose colonial administration were hurled from a first floor balcony in what is now the Praca Do Comercio. It was Portugal, a relatively poor country on the extreme fringe of Europe, which achieved a lead in exploration and discovered and colonized the most far flung parts of the earth. Recent archaeological investigation in Southern Australia, on the coast of Victoria, may prove that it was actually the Portuguese who first discovered and possibly circumnavigated Australia as well as establishing the Cape route to India.

However, this independence of spirit towards outsiders was counterbalanced by a dependency culture within the national framework. Dias' analysis of the Portuguese national character identifies the typical Portuguese as looking at the future with past eyes.

> He is a mixture of dreamer and action man or, better put, an acting dreamer with a practical mind capable of facing facts. The Portuguese activity is not supported by a cool will but it is sustained by imagination and dreaming. The Portuguese is rather an idealist, an emotional and creative man and a thoughtful man. He does not work towards, as the Spaniard does, a strong abstract ideal. The Portuguese is, above all, deeply human, sensitive, lovely, kind without being weak. He does not like to hurt and avoids conflicts, though he has a strong faith in miracles.

This state of mind makes the Portuguese think with the heart, leading to impulsive decisions which may later be regretted. Meditation and planning have never been strong features of the Portuguese approach. Of course, there have been calculating Portuguese leaders, but it is more typical of the Portuguese approach to avoid planning and programming and to face the future with a certain sense of adventure. The Portuguese also tends to have a somewhat messianic spirit and to modify enthusiasm with a sense of fatalism. It is characteristic to leave for tomorrow what should have been done today.

Time management and timekeeping have traditionally been the subject of Portuguese jokes against themselves. The term "à Portuguesa" when applied to matters of time would lend a delicious indeterminacy to the arrangement. Thus, to meet at 10.30 "à Portuguesa" may well imply that the person who more seriously wants the appointment will arrive at 11.00 and the other party at 12.00. Nevertheless, the visitor would do well to arrive at the planned time, just in case! However, these older traditions are changing.

The Portuguese tells with relish the widely known joke (also told in Ireland) when asked to translate the Spanish term "mañana". On being informed that the word means "tomorrow" the Portuguese demurs on the grounds that his language has no noun denoting quite such a degree of urgency. In fact, Portuguese colloquialism does indeed embrace "tomorrow"—"*amanha*", and "tomorrow, tomorrow" "*amanha, amanha*". The supportive beliefs and practices of an essentially non-industrial culture provide social justification for inaction and delay rather than decisiveness and decision-making.

Portuguese have a high respect for the individual and for individual beliefs. After the Portuguese Revolution, the rediscovered parliamentary democracy, evidenced by debates in the Assembly, was the subject of daily television broadcasts. Characteristically, however, the star of these daily performances was the sole representative of an extreme left-wing party, the MRPP. The Portuguese accepted this as proof of their fundamental attachment to free speech and the rights of the individual, though these were not especially noticeable elements of the political platform of the parliamentarian concerned. It was all taken in the best possible spirit, with a wry smile. However, the mass of the population are under-educated and, lacking access to political institutions, dependent. The typical mode of management is a relatively benign paternalism. As in other Mediterranean societies in which politics is both a matter of cafe discussion and of behind-the-scenes intrigue, intellectuals are more prominent than their actual performance and relevance might justify. Where analphabetism prevails, imagination and will remain dormant. If a small coterie of erudite performers then succeed in monopolizing political discussion and exerting unfettered control over people's destiny, a mass political gelding is achieved.

In psycho-analytical terms, with the ending of the "long dark night", of Salazar's traditional and authoritarian regime, the father figures, the *pater familias*, also disappeared. The punishing or protective father left the scene, leaving the vast bulk of Portuguese feeling like orphans or rebels, submissive, complaisant, and childlike.

The long obstructive political cycle which influenced and held back the cultural and technical development of Portuguese society has also kept it behind other countries less fettered by a long tradition which emphasized the traditional values of family life.

The exponential increase in the techno-structure within the world economy gives the Portuguese both advantages and disadvantages. They are very able extemporizers, a capability which makes them well able to face difficult, unpredictable and unknown situations. On the other, their tendency to take time to understand and assimilate complex historical processes leads to a slow pace of development, as they have not been prepared or trained in a way that enables them to profit from open, risky situations. Extemporization, and the capacity to manage complex interpersonal situations do not altogether substitute for a lack of technique and formal knowledge.

When Mayo wrote: "We are at the present time technically skilled as no other age in history has been, yet we combine it with a total social inability", he was describing the Americans. Perhaps the inverse is true of Portuguese management; their social competence is exceedingly high, relative to their lack of technical business skills. This combines to leave the Portuguese poorly placed in terms of general business and managerial capability so the basic cultural matrix is not especially favourable for business and managerial success. As pointed out earlier, there is a very high illiteracy rate; a relatively aging working population, though this will change as the next century approaches; a poorly developed professional capability due to outdated education; and a lack of professional skills. Management itself is rooted in paternalistic rather than professional and technical values, which has led to a lack of variety in managerial styles. Technology is relatively undeveloped and labour legislation lags behind current practice in other EC countries. However, the new political situation in Portugal and the confrontation with other European societies is starting to bring forth significant results.

The Historical Evolution of Management in Portugal

We can consider the historical evolution of management in Portugal under three periods: (a) before 25 April 1974; (b) between 25 April 1974 and 1986; and (c) after 1986.

The Period before the Portuguese Revolution of 25 April 1974

During this period, Portuguese management was not in a healthy condition. Excluding two or three important private economic groups such as C.U.F., which controlled a major bank as well as the world-famous Lisnave and Sevlénave shipyards, few companies were concerned with professional management and state-of-the-art management practices. The leading private economic groups such as C.U.F. did provide management training for their leaders and, in due course, some of these organizations as well as the Armed Services provided the basis for the new cadre of professional managers which emerged after the Revolution. The Espirito Santo group was another large conglomerate of firms with good professional management and organization.

The bulk of the Portuguese economy, though, was made up of small companies, mainly familial in ownership and control, relatively under-capitalized and controlled by owner–managers who lacked professional qualifications. Thus, managers in the conventional corporate sense did not exist in these companies. Some owners evidenced strong powers of intuition or ability in production and commerce, while others continued to manage their businesses on a more or less traditional basis, allowing one season to follow another. Such companies maintained little international contact and little inter-national awareness. The Portuguese economy was fenced off and protected from the effects of international competition. Most of the business was thus between Portuguese firms and with ex-Portuguese colonies. Even internally, there was little competition because of the legal and formal limitations imposed by the protectionist policies of the Government, in the form of the Industrial Protection Law.

The combination of this state protectionism and an archaic financial system led to a relatively subdued managerial environment. Creativity was neglected. During this period management behaviour and practices were not based upon authentic managerial theory and knowledge. The manager or owner functioned as a short-term supervisor, bounded by a repetitive perspective formed within a formal, closed economic environment which was unreceptive to change.

A typical manager of this period was thus an owner, poorly qualified in terms of both professional knowledge and experience, with little creativity and relatively unchanging habits. He was not exposed to, nor concerned with, the implementation of new technology. This technological obsolescence reinforced the other limiting factors. Moreover there was little or no concern with the training and development of human resources in this period.

A large agricultural sector, employing a very great number of poor, low-paid workers, gave the Portuguese economy a negative synergy. There was outward migration of both unskilled and poorly trained workers from the rural areas to industry. More significantly, about two million workers out of a population of eleven million opted to leave Portugal altogether, migrating to France, Germany, South Africa, Luxemburg and across the Atlantic to the United States and Canada. The workers who remained were trapped in a low-wage economy. Most of the population was thus truly living in poverty; others were dependant on remittances from expatriate relatives employed as cheap labour in the more advanced economies of Western Europe and North America.

There were very few graduates in the management cadres. The number of young people attending university was also rather low, and on graduation, they tended to enter the public sector or one of the few leading economic groups. For these reasons, management in Portugal between the 1950s and the 1970s was not a significant political or industrial force, and the working class was ill-educated and bereft of qualifications.

The social and political strains of a protracted colonial war in Africa lent considerable force to the tensions existing within Portuguese society and to the frustrations of a generation of young people whose training horizons were bounded by the expectation of four or more years' military service in a colonial war in the Tropics. Thus it was no surprise that this social and political situation, combined with a weak economy, fuelled the Leftist Revolution of 25 April 1974, which ousted the dictatorial regime. The Revolution was founded on the principles of democracy, liberty and fraternity, but the lack of a coherent political agenda almost inevitably allowed the Communists, whose consistent ideals represented an apparently coherent political programme, to gain strength. Yet out-and-out Communist principles also failed to offer a societal mandate to the managerial classes. This was not a Burnhamite "managerial revolution". Owner–managers had contributed to the Revolution by their failure to develop the economy and they were perceived as exploiters of an unqualified and underpaid working class.

The Period from 25 April 1974 to 1986

The political turmoil of the post-revolutionary period was accompanied by overt persecution of the owners of those private firms which survived. This confrontation between Communists and socialists on the one hand and the sources of private capital and entrepreneurship on the other, led to a political stand off and an apathetic response from the bulk of the population. In some cases, companies were expropriated and came under the control of the workforce. In others, the original owners maintained their responsibilities but had to operate within a structure of almost total constraint. Many owners, as well as some of the skilled workers and technicians, left the country to offer their services to the more vibrant economies of Brazil or Spain, thus further impoverishing the Portuguese business environment.

During the worst period of political confrontation there was a desperate struggle between democrats and hard-line Communists who wished to turn Portugal into an Eastern European-type economy, in effect a satellite of the USSR. The whole financial sector comprising the banks, insurance companies and financial institutions was nationalized, as were the main companies in the industrial sector. Land in the Alentejo, in the southern part of the country, was confiscated.

When the owners of companies were removed, they were replaced by a new class of managers who were, in the main, political appointees with no formal management skills. The Portuguese economy, already feeble, continued to decline. The budget deficit suddenly worsened and the inflation rate rose to over 30 per cent. The reduction of foreign debt became a political preoccupation. Portugal thus entered the 1980s with a non-competitive economy, based upon low salaries and unqualified managers and suffering from the adverse consequences of a period of overt politicization.

From the beginning of the 1980s onwards, support for the Communist and Socialist parties gradually declined. Since 1980, Portuguese government policy has been largely guided by moderate Socialist principles. The intervention of the World Bank and the emphasis on the financial disciplines which would permit the Portuguese economy to re-enter the international community has imposed rules, with generally positive results. However, the long crisis of Portuguese management continued through most of this period. The typical Portuguese company still evidenced a lack of leadership, proper management and motivational systems. The lot of the typical manager in private companies was that of coping with persistent and almost perpetual crisis. Public companies still formed a significant part of the economy, but their poor performance created a set of wasting assets at its heart. Managerial groups also lacked a political focus, until the electoral success of the Social Democratic Party in October 1985 led by Professor Cavaco Silva.

The Period after 1986

Since 1986 and the entry into the EC, political and economic conditions in Portugal have changed significantly. The spectre of Communism has been virtually eliminated and greater trust in government has led to economic development. EC entry has been critical in creating an openness to information, an increase in domestic and foreign competition and access to Common Market funds and programmes. Portuguese firms, therefore, have begun to adopt more modern management principles and have taken growing responsibility for strategies at the company level. They have shown a new sense of responsibility for the professional development and training of employees.

It has been recognized that to survive in the increased competition of the Common Market and to take advantage of the opportunities presented, a greater number of dynamic, productive and organized companies is required, based on proper management knowledge and expertise. There has been a growth of interest in management techniques, in management consultancy and in the hiring of management expertise. The status of the manager has therefore increased. The sluggish management practices of the public sector companies will improve now that the privatization of these companies has commenced, which offers new opportunities for professional management. A new generation, graduating either from Portuguese or foreign universities, has brought modern management concepts to Portuguese companies and a greater awareness of contemporary ideas. Of course, these trends are not universal. Many small and medium-sized companies, especially in less technically advanced sectors such as footwear and textiles, have not yet encountered this new generation. However, there is an increase in consultancy work with companies in these sectors and this should stimulate change.

Inevitably, in such a period of rapid development, there have been mistakes, such as the misuse or mis-application of techniques and funding mechanisms. The lack of cash and the heavy demands on the well qualified have also meant work for the less well qualified and the incompetent. New ideas have tended to influence the top managers first and many middle managers are still not yet properly trained. Without qualified middle managers, human resource systems and technological productivity will continue to lag. Although there is still much to be done, prospects are more encouraging than at any time in the past two decades. The universities have profited from international aid so that teaching programmes are now in line with good practice in foreign universities, and experienced professional and technical staff have returned from abroad.

A Review

Specific historical conditions have created a unique configuration, including cultural traits, which characterizes Portuguese society and infuses the behaviour patterns of both managers and workers. The salient features are:
– Portugal has never been a rich country and, despite its early colonial empire, it has never developed the imperial characteristics and large, centralized civil service and governmental bureaucracies of other colonial and trading nations such as England, France and Spain. Portugal is traditionally a country of farmers and seafarers, whose behavioural patterns and cultural expectations have been recreated in its colonies.

It is sometimes argued that of all the former colonial nations, the Portuguese speaking nations have been the least racist, the least exploitative, and the most inter-married with native host populations. The enormous flexibility, generosity and sympathy of the Portuguese people in this respect is, perhaps, well illustrated by the country's absorption of some three million *Retornados* from the former colonies of Angola, Mozambique, Goa and Timor, especially from the first two, during the years following the granting of independence. It is arguable that Portugal coped better with this large influx of returning expatriates than, for example, France, when assimilating its *pieds noirs*. However, the assimilation was at a relatively low standard of living. When there is less to share, perhaps it is easier to share.

- The financial incentive structure in Portuguese companies has been relatively unrelated to ability and performance. The hierarchical, and in some cases feudal, nature of enterprise has meant that rewards have been more closely linked to kinship, through behaviour which may be described as "deferential" or, more pejoratively, as "complaisant" or even "servile".
- In spite of a constricting tax regime, and relatively high taxes for the middle classes in recent years, there is an absence of good state services in the field of education, welfare and infrastructure and a parallel lack of private sector alternatives.
- During several decades, and for different reasons, investment in education and professional training and in cultural activity and the arts has been neglected. It is only since entry to the EC in 1986, which encouraged a changed political strategy and a positive determination to orient towards current practice in the rest of Europe that this situation has started to change.
- In common with several other Western economies, there has been a tendency towards short-term investment in technology and hardware. After the long period of social stasis of the Salazar regime, sometimes referred to as the "long, dark night", the succession of Left Wing governments also penalized long-term investment.

These factors have been compounded by the relative isolation of the Portuguese economy from the rest of Western Europe.

The Resistance to Change of the Current Generation of Portuguese Managerial Leaders

Some of the command posts of the economy are still in the hands of members of the older generation who are imbued with traditional Portuguese behaviour patterns. In these organizations, there is a widespread lack of professional assertiveness, which is paralleled by similar behaviour in other sectors, such as the religious, military, political, and education systems. Managerial boards tend to behave in paternal, autocratic ways. A strong us–them sentiment, inability and unwillingness to communicate and authoritarianism have led to a dated style of management in which production has continued to be the main concern and human resources have been largely neglected. This stance may be characterized as "passive" authoritarianism.

The general state of cultural ambiguity tends to lead to a withdrawal from leadership roles of those who are qualified to occupy them. There is a general unwillingness or inability to participate and contribute towards the managerial dialogue. Training and management development are shunned by such managers, who are "present though absent" in the corridors of managerial power. However, it is important to avoid an extreme characterization or to identify managerial behaviour in a polarized, either/or fashion. Portugal is not a country of extremes. What we have attempted here is to describe what is predominant or characteristic in managerial behaviour.

Particularly in the years since the Portuguese Revolution, there has been a state of flux in terms of rules, ideals, usages, and conducts, a questioning of once universally accepted truths. The education of young people is particularly disputatious, but there are real signs of greater participation and an upsurge of creativity. The classroom is becoming more closely linked with the factory and the office. There is greater participation, too, on the part of organizations, more dialogue and exchange of new ideas and a functional mobility instead of inactivity and immobility.

In this flux of change, a particular responsibility rests on top and middle managers to find ways of demanding more from the work force. There is widespread awareness that knowledge dates at an increasingly rapid rate. There is now an ongoing dialogue on the nature of management development and training, acknowledging the modern paradigm represented by Peters and Waterman (1982), among others, who say "Our duty is to provide professional training as well as developing chances for our professional personnel who should improve their ability, to enlarge their prospective career or just to complete their overall knowledge". However, as well as a more lively dialogue of ideas about education and training, it is also important to match the appropriate managerial systems and practices to new situations.

It is clear that Portugal has many things going for it. A stable country in political terms, its working class is well disciplined, traditionally oriented and politically rather well integrated, and there is a marked improvement in the status of women. With appropriate leadership, based on relevant professional training, it is capable of achieving considerably higher rates of productivity. The government has created an environment of confidence and faith in the future. There is a growing increase in foreign investment, mainly from the European Community, but also from Japan, and a rapid improvement in management philosophy and practice can be foreseen.

Reference

Peters, T.J. and R.H. Waterman (1982): *In search of excellence*. New York: Harper and Row.

Chapter 12: Spain

The Revolution from Outside: Spanish Management and the Challenges of Modernization

Max H. Boisot

Introduction

On 17 November 1990, the *La Vanguardia*, a Barcelona-based national newspaper, reported the findings of a study carried out by the *Instituto de Estudios Económicos* for the CEOE, the Spanish Employers Federation, on the competitiveness of Spanish firms in the looming single market. In the study, "*Empresa Española: Estructura y Resultados*" its author Eduardo Bueno painted a gloomy picture. Spanish firms, he claimed, are far too small relative to the European average, are stubbornly turned inwards towards the domestic market, and by most measures are uncompetitive, being oriented towards short-term results rather than long-term development. The result is a concern with current production rather than innovation and an increasing reluctance by Spanish banks to support firms in financial difficulty. They thus become easy prey for foreign purchasers. For José María Cuevas, the president of the CEOE, the report constitutes the writing on the wall for Spanish firms: in his view they are out of the European race before it has even started.

A month following the publication of the *La Vanguardia* article, the business magazine *Dirigente* echoed the theme. In an article headed "*La gran crisis Empresarial*", an EC Commission report on the prospects for the Spanish economy was cited, in which concern was expressed over the lack of preparation of Spanish firms for the single market. The Spanish firms surveyed by the report, in contrast to, say, French or Italian firms, perceived the advent of the single Market in 1992 as a threat rather than as an opportunity, and only a few of them had articulated any kind of strategy in preparation for it. Indeed, only 12 per cent of firms surveyed had indicated any willingness to contemplate an investment outside their home country, a far lower percentage than German, British, or French respondents.

Is all the gloom being overdone? The years from 1985 to 1989 have given the country the best rate of growth, capital formation and employment creation that contemporary Spain has known. In 1991, real GNP growth was forecast to be 2.7 per cent, or 8 per cent higher than it was in 1990. How can the future prospects of a country, which in 1960 could still be described as "pre-industrial" (Términe et al. 1979) and which only joined the European Community on 1 January 1986, possibly be assessed by ranking it against Europe's mature industrial economies? Can the country's past, or even its present, serve as a guide to its future?

In this chapter we take a closer look at the Spanish firm and its managers in order to shed further light on its competitive prospects. Since the analysis will proceed as much at the level of cultural attitudes and values as at that of "structure, conduct, and performance"—to borrow terms from industrial economics, it will be important to dig into the past a little in order to understand how such attitudes and values came to be shaped over time. The next two sections of the paper, therefore, offer a bit of context building, the second section at the level of national history, and the third section at the industrial level. Through them, we briefly survey the histori- cal forces that shaped the process of industrialization in Spain. The fourth section then constructs upon this base an eclectic image of the contempor- ary Spanish firm out of material drawn from industrial data, anecdotes, comparative studies, etc. The managerial "environment" in Spain is des- cribed, followed, in the next section, by a discussion of managerial behaviour and attitudes in relation to that environment. The exercise makes no claim to rigour and is merely intended to tease out suggestive patterns from the data; patterns which, in the concluding section, can be used to interpret—or perhaps re-interpret—the pessimistic forebodings that currently hover over the Spanish firm.

The Nations versus the State

The traditional Aragonese oath of fealty to a new ruler runs as follows: "We, who are as good as you are, swear to you, who are no better than we, to accept you as our king and sovereign lord provided you observe all our statutes and laws; and if not, no" (Atkinson 1960). The conditional nature of the commitment illustrates a problem that has plagued the Spanish nation throughout its history: centrifugal forces have undermined state building, often before it could even get underway.

Centrifugalism in Spanish history has its origins both in the geography of the Iberian Peninsula, and in the particular circumstances in which men found themselves at different moments in time. Acting as a bridge between

Europe and Africa—only 12 miles separate the two continents—the Peninsula became the natural route for an Arab conquest that was only stopped by that land barrier that separates Spain from the rest of Europe and gives it its "apartness" from the rest of the continent: the Pyrenees. Average altitudes in the Peninsula are second in Europe only to those of Switzerland and, with the exception of the Ebro Valley to the east, the Tagus–Guadania and Guadalquivir valleys to the west, and a narrow coastal belt, upland prevails. Of the upland itself, something like half is mountainous, with the hills in many areas coming almost down to the sea. Such terrain poses formidable challenges of communication and has done much to foster regional particularism—that loyalty to the *patria chica* (the "little fatherland") that has made state building so difficult in Spain (Atkinson 1960).

The Muslim invasion of the Peninsula that took place at the beginning of the 8th century AD was unleashed on a divided realm. However, the Arab forces, which were to stay on Spanish soil for nearly eight centuries, themselves lacked the manpower to settle and effectively hold the middle reaches of the peninsula. This was one of the reasons why their occupation of Old Catalonia was only to last for less than a century—Barcelona fell to Charlemagne's son Louis in 801—and it helps to explain that region's distinctive cultural identity.

The different Christian kingdoms—Asturias–Leon, Castille, Aragón, Navarra, Portugal—that participated in the re-conquest of the Peninsula from the Muslims did so on terms that weakened rather than strengthened the royal authority, depriving it of revenues and reliable allegiances. The settlement of re-conquered territories was encouraged by the granting of *fueros*, charters defining the relationship of individual citizens and communities to their overlords. The conditions on which fueros were granted varied considerably from one region to another and were thus to compound further the difficulties imposed by geography in building up a unified system of laws and administration at a later date.

Spain's attempt to build a modern bureaucratic state starts with Ferdinand II of Aragon (1479–1516) and Isabelle I of Castille (1474–1504) and in many respects pre-dates the Tudor and Valois efforts in this direction. The country's failure to do so is due to the conjugation of two causes. The first might be described as the prevailing concept of kingship which made of the kingdom a monarch's personal and disposable estate, a concept that was to last up to the nineteenth century and is incompatible, in its arbitrary exercise of power, with the bureaucratic rationality and the rule of law required by the modern nation state. The second cause, greatly exacerbated by the first, was the recurring tendency for royal expenditures to outrun revenues in the pursuit of ambitious foreign adventures. The wealth of Peru's silver mountain, the Potosi, discovered in 1545, instead of being used to strengthen state institutions constantly subject to centrifugal

forces, was channelled—where it was not diverted en route to England—
into ever more expensive European commitments. The time came when
consignments of gold and silver arriving from across the Atlantic at
Seville's *Casa de Contratación*—its Trade House—were immediately tran-
shipped to the coffers of German or Italian banking houses.

Given the mismatch between royal ambitions and royal resources, the
bureaucratic centralization brought about by Philip II (1556–1598) as he
sought to control his empire from a desk in his newly created—and many
would say arbitrarily created—capital in Madrid, quickly overwhelmed the
country's still fragile administrative machinery. Spanish dilatoriness
became a byword throughout Europe—"if death came from Spain", quip-
ped a Viceroy of Naples, "we should wait a long time" (Atkinson 1960).
The result was a weak autocratic centre, a rebellious periphery, and the
onset of a secular decline that was accelerated by every attempt to restore
past imperial greatness. The Hapsburgs, in pursuit of the mirage of empire,
had over-extended themselves and had consequently failed to provide the
national unity that could counter the centrifugal forces still pulling the
country apart.

A new stimulus to national unity was given to the country by the
Napoleonic invasion and the Peninsula wars. Instead of leading to coherent
state building and political development, it quickly led back to personal
autocracy, and, with the arrival of Ferdinand VII (1803–1833) on the
throne, to a reign of abuse and privilege. The first half of the 19th century
in Spain was characterized by a permanent crisis in public finance provoked
by the Peninsular wars and subsequent loss of the colonies gained in that
century. The state was unable to create a competent administration for the
collection of tax revenues and, in turn, lacked the tax revenues necessary
to create a competent administration. Mis-government at the centre made
it ever harder to secure the allegiance of the regions and those with the
greatest relative wealth—Catalonia and the Basque country—were always
the first to reject Madrid's incompetent leadership.

Nineteenth century Spain, unlike Britain and France, failed to develop a
viable parliamentary system founded on liberal principles. An attempt to
set one up was made after 1876, but although it was modelled on the
British system, it turned out to be quite ill-suited to the needs of the
country and never really functioned properly. Absolute personal rule,
from the top of the political hierarchy right down to the local *cacique*,
except in the newly urbanized centres of Madrid and Barcelona, remained
the characteristic style of political leadership.

This situation continued right up to the second half of the twentieth
century. As Temine et al. have pointed out (Términe et al. 1979), even in
fascist Europe, no dictatorship was ever as complete as that imposed by
Franco after the Spanish Civil War (1936–1939). In article 6 of the 1967
version of the "Organic Law of the Spanish State", for example, we read

that "The Caudillo is the supreme representative of the nation; he personi-
fies national sovereignty".

Atkinson, writing in 1960, pointed to a fundamental reality of Spanish
history which is not obscured by a mere change of regime, namely that
Castille is centralist in essence, and consequently authoritarian, whereas
the peripheral regions are centrifugal in outlook, and hence egalitarian.
Indeed centralism has been considerably muted since the arrival of
democracy after Franco's death. In a country which has known so many
tensions between the centre and the periphery throughout its history,
those who dream of a new social order continue to perceive the state as
something to be abolished rather than taken over—hence the particular
flavour of Basque and Catalan separatism, different as these are from each
other.

In contemporary Spain, the conflict between order and progress has
often proved acute and has tended to be framed as a choice between
hierarchy and anarchy. One reason for the persistence of this conflict into
the twentieth century, is that the country did not participate in a unique
European phenomenon that could have alleviated it, and that goes by the
name of *modernism*; a legacy of the revolution in science that proclaims a
belief in mechanism, rationality, the secularization of thought, and, above
all, a belief in progress.

The echoes of a loyal address given at the University of Cervera in 1823,
which began with the words "Far from us the dangerous novelty of thinking", have only just died out, but today its attenuation allows a new
discourse to be heard.

Industrialization

The failure of state building in Spain coupled with the absence of an
appropriate framework of values and beliefs and the persistence of a fis-
siparous regionalism, retarded the country's industrialization and ensured
that when it did occur it would do so largely as the result of foreign
initiatives and hence would remain something of an alien phenomenon.
Agricultural surpluses which in Britain and France were to form one of the
bases of industrial capital, in Spain were either channelled into the coffers
of the church, or into those of a landed aristocracy more concerned with
gracious living than with productive activity. A rising but tiny professional
bourgeoisie was co-opted and absorbed by this landed aristocracy, whose
values and lifestyle it adopted. Not surprisingly, its scarce capital went into
land rather than industry and it found itself with little motivation to seek
out a new order consistent with industrialization.

What industrialization did take place can be divided into three phases. The first occurred between 1856 and 1866 when a first railway network was created. The second coincided with the first decade of the Restoration of the Monarchy (1874–1884); during that phase the railway network was completed, the mining industry began to develop, and the foundations of a steel industry were laid in the Basque country. The third phase occurred at the beginning of the twentieth century and was characterized by an accelerated rate of investment in the mines of Asturias and the gradual spread of industrialization to new sectors.

Just how modest this effort at industrialization turned out to be can be gauged from the figures given for railway construction. By 1923 Spain had as its main transport infrastructure 7,150 miles of railway track. Great Britain, by contrast, a country with less than half of Spain's land area, had just under 24,000 miles of railway track by 1914, in addition to a fully developed road and canal network which Spain did not have. Furthermore, not only was the railway network in Spain of mediocre quality, but it did not generate the multiplier effect on which the growth of industrial activity depends.

Industrialization was not an indigenous phenomenon. By the middle of the nineteenth century, it had become obvious to enlightened Spaniards that the country would not be able to modernize on its own and that outside help would be required. This meant foreign capital, and, in particular, British and French capital—Spanish capital, when it was available, remained essentially speculative and short term in its orientation, in spite of government incentives to encourage long-term investment.

Foreign investment in Spain focused on three areas, banking, railways, and mining, and although over time it emerged that investments in mining were benefiting foreigners more than Spaniards, investments in railways, in spite of the fact that they ultimately failed to integrate regional markets, did give the country a minimal network. Far from blocking the development of Spanish enterprise, foreign investment in Spain in the second half of nineteenth century effectively created the infrastructure necessary for economic renewal.

However, this infrastructure was not in itself sufficient to bring about the country's modernization. For a start, Spain lacked the technical traditions and skills that had proved so indispensable to economic take-off in northern Europe (Broder et al. 1989). Even as late as 1860, no more than 20 per cent of the Spanish population could read and write. Second, the transport infrastructure proved to be too light or irrational in its distribution to integrate regional markets into national ones, so that the entrepreneurial opportunities that go with large market size and technological economies of scale remained extremely modest. Finally, want of opportunity and lack of transport also conspired to keep peasants on their unproductive land, with the result that outside Catalonia—the only region in the country to undergo a credible process of industrialization in the nineteenth century—and the region around Madrid the rate of urbanization also remained extremely low.

The industrialization of Catalonia itself was a mixed blessing since it appeared to foster a kind of economic dualism by drawing productive activities away from poorer regions, thus further exacerbating existing regional inequalities. Since it was a peripheral centre that was undergoing development—i.e., Barcelona, rather than a centrally situated city such as Madrid—such industrialization as did occur hardly contributed to nation building and political stability; indeed Barcelona became the centre of an anarcho-syndicalist movement drawing its inspiration from the ideas of Bakunin and the vision of a Catalonia freed from the oppression of the Spanish state.

In short, the dismantling of the Ancien Regim in Spain in the 1830s did not create conditions favourable to industrialization, in contrast to the French experience. Capital did not accumulate so that it could be applied to productive purposes; there was no growth of an entrepreneurial class—Catalan capitalism, for all its vigour, remained a marginal phenomenon—; and the advent of the railways did not succeed in creating a national market (Benassar 1989). It was only in the mid-twentieth century, following the ravages of the civil war, that economic take-off occurred. It did so on the back of a transport infrastructure quite inadequate to the task—even today the railway line from Barcelona to Bilbao is only single tracked and a motorway linking Madrid and Barcelona is still on the drawing board—, an economic culture that had never really known market competition, and an industrial structure either fragmented along regional lines or bureaucratized by the state.

Spain's industrial profile at the end of the twentieth century remains closer to that of Portugal, Greece, and Ireland than to the more industrialized countries of the economic community. Yet its growth over the past three decades—income levels in Catalonia are now on a par with those of the U.K.—make it a "late developer" par excellence (Dore 1973). The dynamism of late developers make it difficult to capture their prospects through snapshots which can only describe them statically. This should be borne in mind when reading the next section in which an industrial organization framework is adopted in order to examine the kind of environment to which Spanish managers and organizations have to respond. How the next section is read will depend to some extent on what interpretative models are applied to the data presented. Two are discussed in the concluding section and the reader will be left to choose between them and thus to make up his or her own mind about this late developer's future prospects.

The Managerial Environment

Spanish industry inherits an anticompetitive bias from its past. The temptation for the state to direct economic affairs has often proved hard to resist. Spain had what would be called an industrial policy from the end of the civil war in 1939 up until 1963. Prior to this period, the state was still present but it used legislation more discreetly to affect resource allocation by becoming indirectly, rather than directly, involved in "picking winners". In order to mitigate the destructive effects of competition, for example, barriers were legally constituted to entry into 23 key industrial sectors by the Royal Order of the 4th of November 1926; they remained in force for twelve years before being extended to industry as a whole by the Decree of the 20th of August 1938, and then remained on the statute books until 1963. Even after this date, the allocation of resources was still very strongly influenced by the state and it was not until 1980 that regulations specifying the minimum size of investment allowed in a given sector were finally abolished.

If the State's protectiveness towards certain sectors failed to elicit the required investment response, the state itself stood ready to step in with an investment vehicle fashioned for the purpose, namely, the *Instituto Nacional de Industrial* (I.N.I.), created in 1941 and modelled on the Italian I.R.I. As with many State-sponsored investment organizations—the British National Enterprise Board furnishes us with another example—the I.N.I.'s mission became, more often than not, one of protecting existing jobs and the status quo rather than initiating entrepreneurial activity.

Given such a corporatist environment one would expect Spanish industry to be characterized by high degrees of concentration and oligopolistic patterns of behaviour. The figures presented by Buesa and Molero, however, suggest only a modest degree of market concentration: only 23 out of 133 industrial sectors show a high degree of concentration at the four firm, or eight firm, level (Buesa and Molero 1988). Aguilo, in a 1983 study, shows that concentration ratios in 1971 and 1981 for the largest 10, 25, 50, 75 and 100 firms are much lower than for the U.S. or even the U.K. (Aguilo 1983). This cannot be explained as the effects of Spain's antimonopoly law, which was devised somewhat in haste under foreign— especially U.S.—pressure in 1963, because it was always under-resourced and never much applied. More likely, the apparent absence of industrial concentration is due to the narrowness of the country's industrial base, with no more than a dozen sectors accounting for more than half of all industrial value added.

Moreover, low levels of concentration do not automatically translate into high levels of competition. The evidence, direct and indirect, points to a high degree of inter-firm collusiveness in many industrial sectors

Table 1.   The Nationality of the Top Hundred
European Non-financial Firms by Market

United Kingdom	42
(West) Germany	20
France	14
Switzerland	6
Italy	5
Sweden	4
The Netherlands	3
Spain	3
Belgium	2
Norway	1

Note: The first of the Spanish Firms, Repsol, is
in 47th position; the second, Telefónica, is in
67th position; the third, Endesa, is in 80th
position.
Source: Mercado, No 467, 17/12/90

(Maravall 1976; Aguilo 1983) with reduced levels of market entry and exit.
Buesa and Molero hypothesize that some 39 per cent of industrial value
added arises in sectors that can be characterized as collusive and to this
consideration must be added the fact that until 1983, over 24 per cent of
industrial value added was subject to price controls by the state (Brunet
1986).

Strangely, collusiveness and oligopolistic behaviour do not appear to
have led to particularly oligopolistic market structures. Spain remains one
of the EC's member states with the least amount of integration between
industrial sectors. It also displays a lower degree of specialization than
countries such as France, Germany (pre-unification), Italy, or the U.K.—
indeed it suffered a further loss of specialization between 1970 and 1980—
whilst remaining more closed to trade.

One possible explanation for the low levels of industrial concentration at
the national level, is that the country's continuing lack of an adequate
transport infrastructure conspires to keep markets regional rather than
national in most sectors. Although we cannot provide conclusive evidence
on this score, one indicator points strongly in this direction, that of the
average firm size.

Firms in Spain, both large and small, are smaller, on average, than their
counterparts in other European countries. Table 1 gives the distribution by
nationality of the hundred largest firms in Europe. The table shows that
Spain, with a population of 40 million, has three firms in the largest hundred, whereas Switzerland, with a population of 5 million, has six. Berges

and Perez Simarro (1985), show that of the 5,000 larger firms in Europe, only 160 are Spanish—i.e., 3.2 per cent—and that in 1982 these had sales levels representing 59.3 per cent, and employment levels representing 58.95 per cent of the sample mean. Only the large firms of Italy, Belgium and Denmark were of a smaller average size than the Spanish ones.

Small firm size in Spain, unlike say, in Italy, is not associated with dynamism and entrepreneurship. In a report on small- and medium-sized firms in Spain produced by the *Instituto de la Pequeña y Mediana Empresa* (I.M.P.I.) in association with the firm of Ernest and Young, it was shown that the median level of sales of the Spanish firms sampled was 1,276 billion pesetas whereas the median level of sales for Italian firms in the sample was 1,7889 billion pesetas, or nearly 50 per cent higher. This is in spite of the fact that the average size of firms in Italy appears to be smaller than in Spain (*Empresa y Futuro*).

I.M.P.I.'s data indicates that, depending on how one classifies firms, between 90 per cent and 99 per cent of Spanish firms can be classified as medium or small. They tend to be concentrated in very few regions—around Madrid, Barcelona, Valencia, and the Basque country—and typically, they tend to be small family firms, plagued, according to the report, with the usual litany of woes that afflict small firms everywhere: an ill adapted organizational structure, outdated methods of production, under-qualified employees, a lack of interest in exports, poor access to credit for expansion, and, alarmingly for the authors of the study, little or no interest in the looming single market.

In a competitive market environment, the small and medium firm sector is usually an important source of dynamism and innovation in which individual entrepreneurs, following their bent, and answerable to no one but themselves, are willing to take risks that larger firms with an eye on the expectations of institutional stockholders would be unwilling to absorb. The small- and medium-sized firms in Spain, however, do not operate in such an environment, and on any measure of innovativeness it is clear that the rate of innovation leaves much to be desired.

As far back as the 1780s, Joseph Townsend, an Englishman travelling through the Iberian Peninsula was struck by the total absence of technical progress in Spanish agriculture (Benassar 1989: 27). Today, the industries in which the country appears to enjoy some measure of competitive advantage are those characterized by low levels of technological complexity (Buesa and Molero 1988). The small size of firms is certainly a factor in this since, generally speaking, small firms cannot afford to support R & D activities. In 1983, for example, only 8.8 billion pesetas (93 million US dollars) was spent on R & D by Spanish firms and, in total, they em-jeployed 3,525 qualified researchers—fewer than many individual multinational firms employ in their research laboratories. However, size is obviously not the whole story, since, as shown by Braña, Buesa and

Molero (1984), the large state-owned firm in Spain has demonstrated as much, if not more, dependency on imported technology than the private ones. The authors go on to argue that the state, far from acting as a stimulus and a support to innovation by firms, has actually detracted from it.

The lack of innovative capacity in Spanish firms can be gauged from Tables 2 and 3. The first table gives Research and Development expenditure as a percentage of GNP for the countries of the O.E.C.D. and of Latin America. The second table gives the volume of Patent applications for different countries for selected years from 1963 to 1985. From the figures, it can be seen that not only does Spain spend far less on R & D than other industrialized countries, but also that the volume of patent applications has, if anything, been declining—for example, it was 33 per cent lower in 1983 than 18 years previously. The figures on patent applications look even worse if one then distinguishes between patents applied for by Spaniards and those applied for by foreigners in Spain. Whereas patent applications by foreigners declined from 9,541 to 7,777 between 1965 and 1983, those made by Spaniards over the same period went down from 4,089 to 1,369, a decrease of nearly two thirds. To adjust these figures for variations in the size of countries, Table 4 gives the average number of patent applications per 100,000 inhabitants of different countries. The figures appear pretty conclusive: in 1983 the average number of patent applications per 100,000 inhabitants, itself averaged over O.E.C.D. countries as a whole, was 47; for Spain, the figure was 4.

Although small, conservative, inward-looking firms in a closed economy spell backwardness and stagnation, Spain is no longer closed and has, in fact, modernized with astonishing speed, using foreign investment as the lubricant.

One can distinguish three phases in the involvement of foreign firms with the Spanish economy. The first, as we have already seen in the previous section, occurred in the second half of the nineteenth century when French and British financiers, such as the Pereire brothers and the Rothchilds, invested in the construction of the railways and the opening of mines, as well as in the creation of utilities for a rising urban population. A second phase, nationalist in outlook, sought to keep foreigners out. It was characterized by a strong protectionism originating within the country's rural bourgeoisie, but also within Basque steel interests and those of the Catalan textile industry each of which considered the country as a whole as "its" market. A third, liberal phase occurred in the 1950s following the establishment of a U.S. military presence in Spain as a result of the Treaty of Madrid. The period from 1956 to 1960 saw a spectacular growth in the number of U.S. firms investing in Spain—from 21 in 1956 to 92 in 1960. They were followed by French, German, British, and Italian firms, which, together with U.S. firms, powered much of the country's economic growth

Table 2. R & D Efforts in Spain, Other OECD Countries, and Latin America

Country	R & D Expenditure as a % of GNP	No. of R & D Researchers	R & D Personnel as a % of Working Population	GNP per capita in 1981 US Dollars	Industry's Share of GNP in 1981
Austria	1.24 (83)	6,712 (81)	5.6 (81)	10,210	39
Denmark	1.10 (81)	5,988 (81)	6.2 (81)	13,120	32
Finland	1.32 (83)	9,421 (83)	7.9 (83)	10,680	36
France	2.15 (83)	85,500 (81)	11.0 (83)	12,190	35
FRG	2.54 (83)	128,162 (81)	13.5 (83)	13,450	46
Greece	0.21 (81)	2,624 (81)	1.3 (83)	4,420	31
Ireland	0.71 (83)	2,636 (81)	4.4 (83)	5,230	–
Italy	1.12 (83)	52,060 (81)	4.9 (83)	6,960	42
Japan	2.56 (83)	392,625 (81)	12.1 (83)	10,080	43
The Netherlands	2.03 (83)	19,436 (81)	9.9 (83)	11,790	33
Norway	1.42 (83)	7,496 (81)	7.9 (83)	14,060	41
Portugal	0.35 (82)	3,019 (82)	2.0 (82)	2,520	44
Sweden	2.46 (83)	15,035 (81)	10.5 (83)	14,870	31
U.K.	2.28 (83)	104,445 (78)	–	9,110	33
U.S.A.	2.72 (83)	683,700 (81)	–	12,820	34
Spain	0.44 (83)	14,229 (83)	2.3 (83)	5,640	36
Brazil	0.60 (82)	32,508 (82)	–	2,220	34
México	0.20 (74)	8,446 (74)	–	2,250	37
Argentina	0.50 (80)	9,500 (80)	–	2,560	38
Venezuela	0.30 (81)	3,673 (80)	–	4,220	45

Note: The figures in brackets are the years to which the data refers.
Sources: INE. (1986), O.E.C.D. (1986) and U.N.E.S.C.O. (1985)

Table 3. Patent Applications per Country

	1965	1970	1975	1980	1981	1982	1983
U.S.A.	94,629	103,174	101,014	106,218	108,673	12,234	106,314
Japan	81,923	130,829	159,821	193,779	219,877	238,880	256,528
F.R.G.	66,470	66,132	60,095	66,765	66,926	11,262	73,334
France	47,793	47,283	40,437	45,081	47,190	47,496	49,330
U.K.	55,507	62,101	53,400	59,643	62,356	62,721	63,241
Italy	29,308	31,828	24,151	29,943	32,007	31,961	32,894
Canada	30,093	30,510	25,652	24,974	25,498	25,293	25,707
Spain	13,630	11,810	10,522	10,877	10,227	10,201	9,146
Australia	15,150	16,443	14,082	14,781	18,092	18,084	18,368
The Netherlands	17,284	19,109	15,267	21,263	23,790	24,339	25,887
Turkey	739	636	610	661	525	511	—
Sweden	17,079	17,858	14,799	21,334	23,159	23,715	25,477
Belgium	16,810	17,187	13,224	16,621	18,046	20,085	20,594
Switzerland	18,180	19,406	16,940	21,086	22,842	23,281	24,377
Austria	11,832	11,786	9,911	15,693	17,925	17,959	19,584
Yugoslavia	2,193	3,214	3,448	3,358	3,156	2,984	2,532
Denmark	6,713	6,637	5,958	6,590	7,323	7,190	7,539
Norway	4,899	5,007	4,431	4,738	5,724	5,733	6,507
Greece	1,964	2,672	2,981	2,898	3,154	3,260	3,211
Finland	3,145	3,528	3,761	4,218	5,099	5,651	6,067
Portugal	1,176	1,995	1,476	1,823	1,933	1,826	1,851
New Zealand	3,450	3,573	3,322	3,438	3,457	3,533	3,739
Ireland	1,363	1,662	2,844	2,749	3,110	3,110	3,094
Iceland	—	78	48	77	93	80	94

Source: O.E.C.D. (1985a)

Table 4.   National Patent Applications per 100,000 Habitants

	1965	1970	1975	1980	1981	1982	1983
U.S.A.	37	37	30	27	27	27	25
Japan	62	97	121	142	163	178	191
F.R.G.	65	54	49	50	49	50	52
France	36	28	23	21	20	20	21
U.K.	45	45	37	35	37	37	35
Italy	14	13	11	11	—	—	—
Canada	9	9	8	7	8	8	8
Spain	13	9	5	5	5	4	4
Australia	35	31	31	45	42	44	45
The Netherlands	20	19	14	14	15	15	15
Turkey	0	0	0	0	0	0	—
Sweden	62	54	49	50	48	49	52
Belgium	19	14	11	10	9	10	9
Switzerland	96	95	91	68	63	65	65
Austria	37	30	33	31	32	30	32
Yugoslavia	4	5	6	6	6	6	6
Denmark	24	17	16	19	21	21	23
Norway	23	24	19	18	17	17	20
Greece	10	16	18	14	13	13	13
Finland	18	19	25	28	30	34	35
Portugal	1	2	1	1	1	1	1
New Zealand	30	32	40	37	33	31	34
Ireland	5	7	10	12	13	12	16
Iceland	—	9	6	8	6	8	14
O.E.C.D. (Average)	36	39	39	41	43	45	47

Source: O.E.C.D. (1986)

in the 1960s and 1970s. Today, foreign ownership remains high in the economy's most dynamic sectors—indeed, the chemical, automotive, electrical, electronic, mechanical, and steel industries are more than 50 per cent in foreign hands. Table 5 gives the proportion of the 960 largest firms in Spain that are either under state or foreign control, and Table 6 presents a broader picture of the impact of direct foreign investment on Spanish industry.

In the 1960s, foreign firms invested in Spain in order to exploit the newly liberalized domestic market. By the middle of the 1970s, as the economy continued to open up, the country began to be used as an export base offering inexpensive labour and an improving infrastructure. In recent years, the pace has quickened. In the period between 1975 and 1981, the volume of direct foreign investment was three times what it had been for the period 1960 to 1975, and from 1982 to 1985 authorized investment was double the volume for the whole period from 1960 to 1981. If anything, since 1986, with Spain's entry into the European Community, the country has proved even more attractive to foreign investors.

Spain's entry into Europe, in addition to bringing more foreign firms into Spain, might be expected to broaden the horizons of Spanish managers and to make them more willing to venture outside their own territory. In the past, Spanish firms had tended to resort to exports only sporadically, in order to get rid of products that could not be moved in the domestic market. There are signs that this is now changing and that a number of firms—for example Conservera Campofró, Dragados y Construcciones, Lois, Chupa-Chups, Pedro Domecq, Freixenet, Alsa, Amper, El Corte Inglés—are developing a distinctly multinational orientation. Interestingly, not all of these firms are large; Freixenet, Chupa-Chups, the Lois Group and Alsa are, in fact, quite modest in size. It remains generally the case, however, that few Spanish firms invest abroad and if, at 166 billion pesetas (1.76 billion US dollars) direct foreign investment by Spanish firms in 1990 turned out to be 22.5 per cent higher than in 1989, that figure is still fourteen times smaller than the direct foreign investment carried out by French firms in the same year (*La Vanguardia* 2–1–91).

Managerial Culture

In the preceding section, managerial behaviour in Spain was largely inferred from the structure, conduct, and performance of Spanish firms. The emphasis was on the industrial and enterprise environment to which managers had to respond and which, through their own values and behaviour, they helped to shape. This section will focus on the values and behaviours themselves. What does a Spanish manager or entrepreneur consider important in the execution of his task and how does he express this in his actions?

Since we are essentially concerned with description in this chapter, we shall not ask whether the structural features of the managerial environment described in the last section are the causes or the effects of the values and behaviour patterns that we shall present in this one. We shall content ourselves with outlining cultural characteristics of Spanish management for correlation with what has been discussed so far and leave it to the reader to assess in which direction causality flows. Given the paucity of empirical work on Spanish management and organization (Anzizu 1989), we shall

Table 5. Control of the 960 Largest Industrial Enterprises in 1981

Origins of Capital	Number of Firms	%	Sales (millions of Ptas.)	%	Number of Employees	%	Net Assets (millions of Ptas.)	%
1. Foreign capital	191	19.9	1,095,456	17.4	185,789	23.7	914,612	10.0
2. State capital	75	7.8	2,041,025	32.3	215,533	27.5	2,822,419	31.0
3. Private domestic capital	557	58.0	2,421,445	38.4	287,456	36.6	4,346,004	47.7
4. Private and state domestic capital	13	1.3	135,888	2.1	5,917	0.8	443,133	4.9
5. Private domestic and foreign capital	116	12.0	586,604	9.3	85,998	11.0	539,592	5.9
6. Private domestic, state and foreign capital	8	0.8	30,150	0.5	4,274	0.5	50,412	0.5
Total	960	100.0	6,310,568	100.0	784,967	100.0	9,116,172	100.0

Source: Adapted from MINER: '*Las grandes empresas industriales en España, 1980–81*'. Barcelona, 1983

Table 6. Levels of Direct Foreign Investment in Spanish Industry

Structural and Performance Indicators	Level 'A' Foreign Participation = 0	Level 'D' Foreign Participation 50%	Level 'A' / Level 'D'
Social capital	23.17	105.37	4.54
Physical capital	50.71	231.39	4.56
Physical capital/Social capital	2.19	2.20	–
Sales	79.02	644.35	8.15
Purchases	51.15	375.27	7.34
Sales/Purchases	1.55	1.72	–
Personnel expenditures	16.49	157.16	9.53
Number of employees	28.81	183.81	6.38
Imports	5.78	75.77	13.11
Invisible earnings	6.14	80.25	13.07
Exports	5.18	111.86	21.59
Invisible payments	7.37	228.81	31.05
Rate of coverage—visible trade	1.12	0.68	–
Rate of coverage—invisible trade	0.83	0.35	–

Figures given in millions of Pesetas except for invisible earnings and payments, which are in thousands of dollars.
Source: Puig Rojas (1980)

initially address the subject at the broader cultural level and then, armed with the necessary insights, apply them to the managerial level.

In a popular book on Spanish culture published in 1972 and entitled *El Español y los Siete Pecados Capitales*, Dáz Plaja observes that:

> The Spaniard lives within a society but is never immersed in it. His personality is covered with "spines" that stand dangerously on end when faced with collaboration in any undertaking. In science, such collaboration is called "teamwork" and the absence of it has long been recognized as a determining factor in the slowness of Spanish progress. . .

Horizontal collaboration requires individuals to acknowledge an authority that resides in the nature of the task itself and that dictates the need for interpersonal coordination. Authority in Spanish society, however, is perceived as residing in persons who are hierarchically ordered and who often have to forcefully impose themselves to establish their legitimacy. Montaner (1976) claims that "Spain is a country in which hierarchical violence is practiced in a terrible way. In all classes, in all castes, in all the institutions, authority is felt. It makes itself felt". Messeguer notes that "the way of distributing power in our country has always been authoritarian. We have an authoritarian tradition. There have been only three republics in the course of two thousand years, all of which have died shortly after birth" (Messeguer 1976). For Anzizu, such authoritarianism breeds an emotional dependency by subordinates on their hierarchical superiors and also the kind of conformism that is evidenced in social surveys such as the one reported in February 1974 by the journal, *Cambio 16*.

The need for a strong leader and a hierarchical order, however, does not necessarily give the enterprise manager the kind of mandate that would allow him to play a proper coordinating role: he is not easily accepted as a substitute for the missing task-driven coordinator. Echevarría has highlighted, through empirical analysis, the low level of social legitimacy enjoyed by Spanish managers (García Echevarría 1984a, b). In one survey, only 16 per cent of the sample granted him any legitimate role and this reduced to 11 per cent for graduate respondents in the sample. In a more informal work, Abad (1974) has claimed that managers and entrepreneurs in Spain are perceived as speculators and exploiters by the man in the street, as tax evaders by the State, and as sinners by the church—the last-mentioned point might help to explain the extensive involvement of religious institutions in management education. The major business schools in Spain such as ICADE, ETEA, ESADE, IESE, or "DEUSTO", are all directly or indirectly linked to one of the religious orders. Marzal (1983) feels that the problem of managerial legitimacy is one that afflicts Latin culture as a whole since there, the economic dimension is perceived to be little more than an expression of the political one. Given such conflict-

laden perceptions, participative relationships inside the firm become particularly difficult to achieve, and more often than not give way to over-
centralization. The consequence is a managerial style much closer to
Theory X than Theory Y (Anzizu 1989) and a low degree of decision-
making rationality (Ferrari 1974; Losada 1990).

The difficulty in achieving a productive level of social integration may
not be the only obstacle in the way of rational decision-making. Figure 1
indicates that to a far greater extent than his U.S., Scandinavian, Central
European, or even Greek counterpart, the Spanish manager believes that
fate is pre-ordained, lying largely outside his control. Losada hypothesizes
that religion could have something to do with it, but that probably such
beliefs reflect the constant influence of often arbitrary government intervention in economic activity.

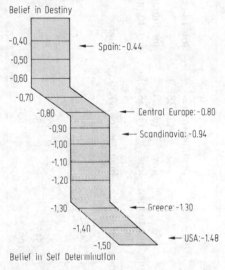

Figure 1. External versus Internal Control

Source: Cummings, Harnett, Stevens and Veciana (1989)

On-the-job fatalism may not explain, but is certainly consistent with, other
features of the Spanish managerial style. Echevarría, in a study of decision-
making in Spanish firms, in addition to finding it short term and highly
centralized, has observed that only 25 per cent of his sample had any kind
of written objectives to work to, or operated an annual budgeting process
(García Echevarría 1984b). Furthermore, there is evidence that Spanish
firms remain psychologically and operationally much more closed to their
external environment than their counterparts elsewhere in Europe (Losada

Figure 2. Hofstede's Culture Variables Applied to Europe

Culture Variables:	Individualism/Collectivism	Power Distance	Uncertainty Avoidance	Masculinity/Femininity
Groups of Nations:				
Anglo-Saxon Europe	individualist (98,...)	medium to low (35,28,...)	low to medium (35,35,...)	masculine (66,...)
Germanic Europe	,, /medium (67,...)	low (35,,...)	medium to high (65)	masculine (66,...)
Nordic Europe	individualism medium to high (74,80,...)	low (18,38,...)	low to medium (23/53)	feminine (16,43,...)
Latin Europe (including Spain)	individualism medium to high (76,71)	high (68,60,50,63)	high (86,75,104)	medium masculine (31,43,...)
EC average	(66,4)	(46)	(68)	(48)
Single Nations				
United States	(91)	(40)	(46)	(62)
Spain	(51)	(57)	(86)	(42)
Catalonia	(66)	(53)	(72)	(27)

Notes: 1. The values in brackets are those given by both Hofstede (1980) and Filella (1990) for different countries in each grouping. Each nation's score is the mean of respondents from that nation.
2. The figures for Spain include Catalonia, but the latter was also studied separately by Filella i Ferrer (1990).

1990). They fear change (Ricardi 1966) and resist it (Barraneche 1981) and because of this they are much more reluctant to operate outside Spain in an international environment with which they are unfamiliar and which they consider threatening.

The managerial values and beliefs just described are echoed in more systematic and comparative studies of organizational culture such as those published by Hofstede in 1980. Figure 2 abstracts those applicable to Europe from Hofstede's findings (Losada 1990). Spain clusters in the diagram with other Latin cultures—Italy, France, Belgium, Portugal—and appears to share with them a low tolerance for ambiguity (uncertainty avoidance) and a tendency to centralize power (power distance). In the Spanish case, García Echevarría (1984a) argues that such a cultural profile makes for a lack of flexibility and breeds intolerance, thus sapping the ability to innovate and adapt to new circumstances.

If the foregoing description of Spanish managerial practice makes bleak reading it is because, like all summary descriptions, it has had to concentrate on average values and measures. In a stable situation, average values allow some plausible extrapolations as to the future states of a system, whether physical or social. In an unstable situation, however, when the system is undergoing rapid transformations, average values can be grossly misleading as to future states and it is to the margin of the system that one must look in order to assess its evolutionary potential (Nicholis and Prigogine 1989). This last observation certainly applies to Spain, one of the few countries in Europe to have experienced Asian growth rates in recent years, and to have undergone profound transformations since the death of Franco. According to Anzizu, in 1960, only 0.7 per cent of the Spanish population had benefited from university studies. By 1975 the estimated number of students in full-time higher education was 450,000. In the last few decades, Spain has witnessed the rise of a new middle class that has not known the bitterness and desolation of the civil war. The country's new generation of managers is much closer in its values and attitudes to the European average than the generation of senior managers currently in charge of firms. Generational changes may take time to work their way through the system, but they will come, nevertheless. The question is, in which direction? We shall briefly address this issue in the concluding section.

Conclusion

In his most recent work, *Scale and Scope* (1990) the Harvard business historian, Chandler, distinguishes between three different kinds of capitalism. The first, managerial capitalism, is a product of the U.S. institutional environment, the ideological commitment to market competition joined with the separation of enterprise management and control. Managerial capitalism is associated with the rise of the large industrial enterprise operating worldwide through professionally managed autonomous divisions. The second, personal capitalism, is a product of Great Britain's earlier industrial and imperial inheritance, and is characterized by the absence of separation of management and control and a commitment to a "live and let live" attitude towards market competition and a subsequent failure to build a professional managerial class. It is the institutional commitment to personal capitalism, according to Chandler, that is responsible for the tardy appearance of the modern industrial enterprise in Great Britain. The third kind of capitalism identified by Chandler, cooperative capitalism, expresses a German-like commitment to technical excellence, education, and cooperation rather than competition in product markets. Cooperative capitalism allowed the emergence of the large industrial enterprise in Germany but endowed it with quite different cultural and operating characteristics from its U.S. and British counterparts.

From a Chandlerian perspective, the future belongs to the large global firm and to those countries whose industrial and cultural traditions enable them to breed such firms. Britain's early failure to produce such firms, according to this view, can be explained by its continuing commitment to a personalized non-professional managerial order in which idiosyncratic ownership preferences worked to undermine the full exploitation of strategic potential.

Applying Chandler's reasoning to the Spanish case would lead us to some fairly pessimistic conclusions. The industrial tissue is made up of mostly very small family firms managed in a highly personal way and with little reach beyond the local market. The few large firms are only large by Spanish standards—not by those of their international competitors—and are either the artificial creation of the Spanish state, or of foreign concerns. Even more daunting for Spanish industry, the advent of the single market will require an even greater organizational capacity by Spanish firms if they are to survive.

The case for the large firm however, is by no means waterproof, and organizational capacity does not automatically translate into organizational size. Piore and Sabel in their book *The Second Industrial Divide* (1984) put forward an organizational paradigm quite at odds with the one defended by Chandler, a paradigm in which small firms compete, but also collaborate with each other in ways that achieve large firm effects. Here, personal capitalism survives and thrives because it is embedded in an institutional structure responsive to its potential: the region or industrial district. Two of the most successful applications of what we might term *regional capitalism* described by Piore and Sabel were in Latin cultures such as those of Italy and France, until at least, in the case of the latter, a centralizing state bent on imitating U.S. practice eroded its structures

Spain, a country of small firms and strong regional identities, might well find this second organizational paradigm better suited to its possibilities. The challenges confronting Spanish managers—innovation, coordination, participation, decentralization—would in no way diminish, but they would be different challenges, more realistically attuned to the country's cultural and institutional potential. More important, perhaps, is the challenge that such an organizational paradigm would pose to a traditionally centralizing Spanish State, because within it, the regions emerge as important economic actors in their own right, inspiring, guiding, and assisting local firms in ways that can only be described as entrepreneurial. In the large industrial enterprise, the innovative and coordinating function of the entrepreneurs is internalized by the firm itself. In the new organizational paradigm, at least a part of it is internalized by a local territorial authority operating at a regional or an urban level. How one views the prospects for Spanish firms in the new Europe, and what managerial skills the exploitation of these prospects will require, will depend on which of these two organizational paradigms is used to focus one's vision.

References

Abad, A. (1974): *La empresa y el empresario ante el desarrollo*. Madrid: Editorial Index.

Aguilo, E. (1983): "Movilidad y cambios de identidad de las grandes empresas: una aplicación a la industria española". *Cuadernos económicos de ICE*.

Anzizu, J.M. de (1989): "Cultura organizativa. Su incidencia en el funcionamiento y desarrollo de la empresa". *Apuntes de clase IESE*, Barcelona.

Atkinson, W. (1960): *A history of Spain and Portugal*. Middlesex: Penguin.

Barraneche Martínez, F. (1981): "Tipos de dirección empresarial". *Alta Dirección* – 96 (ESCE).

Bennassar, B. (1989): "Les resistances mentales" in B. Bennassar (ed.), *L'Espagne: De L'immobilisme à l'essor*, 131–145. Toulose: CNRS.

Berges, A. and R. Pérez Simarro (1985): *Análisis comparativo de las grandes empresas industriales en España y en Europa*. Madrid: Ministerio de Industria y Energía.

Braña, J., M. Buesa and J. Molero (1984): *El Estado y el cambio tecnológico en la industrialización tardía. Un análisis del caso español*. Madrid: Fondo de Cultura Económica.

Broder, A., G. Chastagnaret and E. Témine (1989): "Capital et croissance dans l'Espagne du XIXe siecle" in B. Bennassar (ed.), *L'Espagne: de l'immobilisme à l'essor*, 75–95. Toulouse: CNRS.

Brunet, (1986): "Contribución al análisis de la regulación pública de precios en España". *Información comercial Española*, No. 638 (October). Madrid.

Buesa, M. and J. Molero (1988): *Estructura industrial de España*. Madrid: Paideia.

Cambio 16 (1974): "Estilos de vida en España 1973". *Cambio 16* (February), 119.

Chandler, A. (1990): *Scale and scope*. Cambridge, Mass.: Harvard University Press.

Cummings, L., D. Harnett, O. Stevens and J. Veciana (1989): "Riesgo, determinación, espiritu conciliador y confianza" in J.M. Veciana (ed.), *Papeles de economá Española*, No. 39.

Dáz Plaja, F. (1972): *El Español y los siete pecados capitales*. Madrid: Alianza Editorial.

Dore, R. (1973): *British factory—Japanese factory*. Berkeley: University of California Press.

Ferrari, S. (1974): "Cross cultural management literature in France, Italy and Spain". *Management International Review* 14/4–5.

Filella i Ferrer, J. (1990): "Gestión intercultural de una empresa multinacional". *Apuntes de clase*. Barcelona: ESADE.

García Echevarría, S. (1984a): "La dirección empresarial en España: Es necesaria una nueva orientación". *Alta Dirección 116*.

Garcá Echevarrá, S. (1984b): "Capacidad directiva: el caso español". *Alta Dirección 115*.

Hofstede, G. (1980): *Culture's consequences: national differences in work related values*. Beverly Hills, CA: Sage.

Losada, C. (1990): "Cultura de empresa y liderazgo empresarial en España". ESADE Working Paper, May.

Maravall, F. (1976): *Crecimiento, dimensión y concentración de las empresas industriales españolas (1964–1973)*. Madrid: Ed. Fundación INI.

Marzal, A. (1983): *Análisis político de la Empresa*. Barcelona: Editorial Ariel.

Messeguer, R. (1976): *Los Españoles en grupo*. Dirosa.

MINER (1983): Las grandes empresas industriales en España, 1980–1981. Madrid.

Montaner, C. (1976): "España: Una intepretación freudiana". *Diario El Universal de Caracas*.

Nicholis, G. and I. Prigogine (1989): *Exploring complexity*. New York: Freeman.

Piore, M. and C.F. Sabel (1984): *The second industrial divide*. New York: Basic Books.

Ricardi, R. (1966): "La dirección de la empresa española en el período 1961–1966". *Boletín de estudios económicos* (September).

Términe, E., A. Broder and G. Chastagnaret (1979): *Histoire de l'Espagne contemporaine*. Paris: Editions Aubier.

Veciana, J.M. (ed.) (1989): *Papeles de economía Española* 39.

UNESCO CASTALAC II (1985): Conferencia de Ministros Encargados de la aplicación de la ciencia y la tecnología al desarrollo en América Latina y el Caribe, SC-85/CASTALAC II/Ref. 3, Paris.

Chapter 13: Sweden

A Modern Project, a Postmodern Implementation

Barbara Czarniawska-Joerges

Meetings Between Strangers

The task of describing a country's specific approach to the issues of management is not an easy one, and this is not just because there are such obvious problems as completeness and representativeness. After all, nobody can reasonably expect one person to describe a country's management in a way that will cover all the relevant issues and, what is more, stand the test of time. Management is a set of actions that are shaped as they happen and all we can achieve is a glimpse in passing. What accounts for the main source of uneasiness, though, is that such a task puts one dangerously close to such notions as "national culture" or, even worse, "national character", which inevitably bring in the moral ambiguity connected with a reified, manipulative use of such concepts.

What is culture, after all? In spite of many intense attempts to arrive at new definitions, the old one, produced by Kluckhohn and Kelly (1945), still stands. Culture is "all those historically created designs for living, explicit and implicit, rational, irrational and nonrational, which exist at any time as potential guides for the behavior of man" (1945: 87)—and woman, we should add at this point. A national culture—if we leave aside the doubtfulness of using "states" for cultural borderlines (see Leach 1982)—is ways of acting and giving meaning to action which are often taken for granted and are therefore "invisible". They emerge only when challenged, that is, confronted with different ways of acting and different ways of accounting for acting. Daun, a Swedish ethnographer, begins his book on "Swedish Mentality" (1989) by assuming that only a *contrastive* approach to national cultures makes sense. There is no way to describe a culture as such: it can only be done from the standpoint of another culture.

Culture is therefore an explanatory concept which emerges when strangers meet, or rather, when they perceive each other as strangers, and their ways of going about things as problematic in the sense that the personality of the one is not readily understood by the other. In this article,

I shall focus on the images of "Swedish management" which emerge from such encounters.

Basically, there are two types of encounter. One is when a foreigner becomes acquainted with Swedish organizations—as a manager in a multinational company, as a researcher coming from abroad, as an immigrant living in Sweden (which is my case), or as a consultant called in from abroad. Take an example of the last situation:

> There are many misperceptions about the U.S.A. among Swedes, says Michael Maccoby. For example, that U.S. companies are more hierarchic than the Swedish. As a matter of fact the Americans are more egalitarian, they do not have any great respect for bosses—hence some hierarchy is needed to achieve any order at all. According to Maccoby, it is the Swedes who have a deeply rooted respect for bosses and formal authority, in spite of what we ourselves tend to think. (*Ledarskap/Ekonomen* 1986).

Maccoby is no novice to Sweden. He visits the country regularly and cooperates with the Swedish Council for Management and Quality of Working Life and has, among other things, presented a fascinating portrait of Pehr Gyllenhammar, the Chief Executive Officer of Volvo, in his book *The Leader* (1981). His utterance is a typical example of an intercultural dialogue that continuously takes place where mutual stereotypes stand corrected (or are exchanged for newer ones, as the case may be).

The article in *Ledarskap/Ekonomen* (Leadership/Economist)—the Swedish leading monthly concentrating on management issues—points to another source of images of Swedish management: the Swedish managers (helped by researchers and journalists) themselves. These self-presentations are also constructed against encounters with other cultures. Usually written in English (which after World War II became the main foreign language in Sweden), they present Swedish organizational reality either as directly sketched by the Swedish authors or as related by visitors.

In what follows, I shall be using both sources to arrive at a picture of Swedish management. There is no clear pattern that separates them: the foreign reports are often much more enthusiastic than the Swedish ones (for a good example see Clegg and Higgins' description of wage-earner funds, 1987), as self-presentations are often masochistically self-critical (see Zetterberg's "The Rational Humanitarians", 1984), but the reverse is also possible.

One question might, however, bother the reader. If these are all pictures, or social representations, produced in far from ordinary encounters, how can one be certain that they accurately represent Swedish reality? A social constructionist answer is: one cannot ever be certain! However, even if the Swedes behave quite differently when nobody is looking, what difference does it make to the global economy? Put less facetiously, it is these representations which are the basis for action and interaction, for foreigners and Swedes alike.

I start by characterizing the present socio-political climate in Sweden on the assumption that it contains the most relevant elements of the organizing context (history will be called in when appropriate). I will then proceed to characterize organizational life within the two economic sectors, the private and the public, also following the popular image in this differentiation. Finally, I shall examine the image of Sweden as a country where organizational design is supermodern and organizational performance is based on knowledge of a postmodern type. However, before engaging in analytical endeavours, let us first take a quick glance at what Sweden and the Swedes are like, as portrayed by the Swedish Institute, a government-financed foundation whose aim is to propagate knowledge about the country abroad.

Sweden for Foreigners

Brochures claim to present facts. There is no reason to quarrel with this, but it is important to remember that facts presented always denote facts omitted; that, as semiologists point out, it is possible to say something only by not saying other things. This is why reading brochures is both important and interesting. The one I am going to use here (*Sweden*, Stockholm 1990[1]) is no different in this respect. Each paragraph (of which I am going to quote only a few) emphasizes a trait that is seen as positive but at the same time defies popular critical stereotypes about the country.

> Sweden is located so far north in Europe that the Arctic Circle slices through its northernmost province, Lapland. But it's not an Arctic country. Thanks to the winds that blow from the warm Gulf Stream in the Atlantic, Sweden has a rather mild climate considering its location. . . Half of Sweden's surface is covered by forests. The country also has plentiful supplies of water. Nearly 100,000 lakes are connected in a lacework of waterways, and many large rivers flow from the northwestern mountains through the forests to the sea.

Thus Sweden is an "exotic" country, with many tourist attractions (notice the poetic "lacework of waterways") but, contrary to the popular prejudice, it is not a cold country. What, then, about the people?

> For many centuries, Sweden was ethnically very homogenous with one exception—the Sami (Lapps), an indigenous minority in the north. Today there are about 15,000 Sami, some of them still making their living by herding reindeer. During the 1960s and 1970s more than half a million immigrants moved to Sweden to work, mostly Finns but also Yugoslavs,

Greeks and others. In addition, Sweden has accepted refugees from many troubled corners of the world and still accepts refugees in acute need of protection.

While the information about the Sami is still of a touristic nature, it also serves as a bridge towards information with a more political slant. Sweden is proud of its immigration policy—notice, however, the wording "acute need" in the last sentence, subtly indicating a recent tightening of Swedish acceptance policy. Let us carry on reading to find out what this heterogeneous nation does.

Statistically speaking, each inhabitant of Sweden has 54,000 m² to move around in.² People are accustomed to having plenty of space and to having access to rather unspoiled nature. Most of the population live in cities and towns, especially in the three major urban regions of Stockholm, Göteborg (Gothenburg) and Malmö.

In other words, yes, Swedes love nature (and have enough of it to share with appreciative foreigners), but no, it is not true that they are asocial and inclined to a peasant lifestyle—the life of contemporary Sweden is urban and urbane.

Foreign accounts of Swedish history invariably begin with the Vikings. The Viking Museum in York, England gives prominence to the Viking activities in England, not to mention the competition with the Danes and the Norwegians. The Swedish account thus turns to what is undoubtedly special to Sweden:

(It) is one of the oldest kingdoms in the world. At the same time, it has ancient democratic traditions.

For our purpose, however, the main historical tale is more recent, and is indicated by the headings "From poverty . . ." ". . . to prosperity": from the depressed thirties to the prosperous eighties.

Five main themes representative of the eighties are then developed. "Life in Sweden" confirms the Swedish reputation for being the foremost welfare state in the world (the brochure cites "from cradle to grave", that venerable social policy slogan). "Leisure activities all year round" contrast the suspected puritanity and severity of Swedish life style with a picture of continuous festivities ("Midsummer" in June, "Walpurgis Eve" in April, "Crayfish Holidays" in August and "Lucia" in December complement the standard Christian holidays). "Cultural life" reminds us of Bergman, opera singers and glass artists while not letting us forget the role of the State as the mecenas. Under the theme "Business and labour market" it is claimed that Sweden went a long way in a short time. Statements such as "from raw material production . . ." ". . . to advanced technology", "from agrarian to postindustrial society" convey pride in the Swedish tradition of technical inventions (Nobel and dynamite!). Finally, "Sweden in the world" is a tribute to one time Prime Minister Olof Palme's dream of transforming Sweden's claim to glory from a military force in the past to a force of peace in the future.

So much for a static picture of the country. At present, however, Sweden is very far from being in a stable state and the brochures will have to be amended more than perfunctorily every year.

Europa ante portas

In 1992 the mass-media buzzed with one main topic: Swedish entry into the European Community! The issues to be cleared up are the following: whose idea was it (and therefore who is responsible) and who is going to carry the burden of the consequences? There are no simple answers to these questions.

To begin with, the idea of joining the rest of Western Europe basically came from the non-socialist parties and it was first opposed and then enthusiastically espoused by Social Democrats. This appropriation was made easier by the fact that the Centre Party, representing the Swedish farmers, is, not surprisingly, wary of the idea. As to the consequences, the picture is unclear. Veterans of Swedish politics foresee that, even though the Social Democrats lost the elections, they will still be held responsible for the decision, whereas the consequences (which, one may expect, will tend to be negative initially) will be attributed to the winning coalition. The citizens are ready for more socialist measures, as usually seems to be the case when a non-socialist coalition comes to power, and vice versa: the present campaign against the wastefulness of the public sector and an on-going marketization of public services was initiated by the Social Democrats. As to the mass-media, they keep to the spectacular as a rule (Edelman 1988) and paint two pictures of "Sweden after EC": that of a hell and of a paradise. There is little mention of actively forming one's fate—the reader gets the impression that the day the agreement is signed the fate of Sweden will be determined forever. In one version, it is going to be a paradise of cheap booze and free market creativity. In the other, the unemployed women will weep in the remains of the Swedish forests (there is something to that last vision, not so much because of the Common Europe but because of acid rain blowing across the North Sea).

Contacts with the executives in private and public organizations do not confirm these dramatic versions. Most of them expect no dramatic changes as an automatic result of joining the EC. They look forward to the opportunities that might be created and foresee the need for an active representation of local interests (perhaps following the Danish example, whose participation in the European Parliament is judged by Bryder 1989 as "parochial").

The opportunities and challenges resulting from drawing nearer to the continent are expected to take place initially in the know-how markets, rather than in the traditional industries (pulp and paper, cars and trucks, shipyards). The concept of *kunskapsföretag*—the "knowledge producing company"—was coined in Sweden (Sveiby and Risling 1986). This small country actively participates in international education programmes and sells services all over the world. Will it be competitive without the shelter of the internal market? ask the pessimists. How can it become even more competitive in the new situation? inquire the optimists.

The Demise of the Swedish Model

The Swedish public sector experienced a long period of economic expansion that came to a halt only in the late 1970s. Since then there has been a continuous campaign aimed at making it more effective. In 1990 a government crisis took place, something as alien to the Swedish political scene as it is normal in Italy, due to the failure of the programme designed to control inflation. Wildcat strikes and problems with the renewal of central labour agreements tended to be labelled as a "legitimacy crisis".

The partners of the "historical compromise" (symbolized by the agreement signed in Saltsjöbaden in 1938 after a long and bitter fight between employers and labour) are changing their positions. The Swedish Employers' Federation announced a retreat from the practice of collective bargaining. In relation to this, its Chairman, Ulf Laurin pronounced that "After a long-term illness, the 'Swedish model' is dead" (*SAF-tidningen*, 16 February 1990).

The Study of Power and Democracy in Sweden, a 5-year interdisciplinary research programme, could be seen as performing the task of peacefully burying the "Swedish model". In the final report (1990), the Swedish model both acquires a definite form (as Luhman, 1986, points out, a period can be properly characterized only when it has ended) and is given a farewell treatment. Basically, the argument is that a package of solutions, half a century old, cannot be expected to function as it did when first introduced—and that new solutions are in sight, together with new problems.

One of the basic assumptions of the Swedish model was the open interplay between the parties on the labour market—free from state intervention. However, the practice of industrial relations was influenced by the fact that the State and the municipalities are among the main employers, which then found an institutional expression (the pay stoppage and a special mediating organ, both introduced in the Spring of 1990). To counter yet another stereotype, one should add in passing that the state and the municipalities, though major employers, are not owners. Jointly, they own 5 per cent of the stock market in Sweden (*Demokrati och makt i Sverige* 1990).

This free play in the labour market arena was supported by specific institutions. The parties were represented centrally by a few homogeneous organizations. Nowadays, however, "organizations are neither few, centralized nor homogeneous" (*Demokrati och makt i Sverige* 1990: 390). Local pay negotiations became legitimate even within the public sector organizations.

These changes reflect the fading of the "historical compromise". The Swedish wage-earner funds, an initiative proposed by the Congress of the Trade Union Confederation in 1971, designed to increase employee participation in capital formation, turned out to be an issue that led to a strong polarization in political opinion. According to the original proposal formulated by Rudolf Meidner, the large private companies should transfer a certain percentage of their profits annually to "wage earner investment funds" (Åsard 1980). The long (10 years) and bitter fight between the protagonists which followed, cast a shadow on the consensus culture, previously proudly presented as a "Swedish characteristic". The report points out that if consensus continues to be a pragmatic technique for handling difficult interactions, it is mostly its normative value which has changed in public opinion, which nowadays prefers more critical attitudes, where consensus-seeking is termed "conflict-avoidance", and the fight for equality has been renamed "a pressure for uniformity". There seems to be a suggestion underlying the discussion that a half-century-old national image, no matter how positive, must invariably reach a point where it is no longer adequate, useful or even flattering.

A new identity is needed – and according to the report, looked for. The potential sources of both the rebellion and the new model(s) are women's and immigrant problems on the labour markets, and growing differentiation in terms of economic standards, perceived influence and access to knowledge. All in all, it is not a question of a crisis, but of a turning point. Besides, as usually happens, actual practices still cultivate the old virtues, especially in the private sector, which has not been under direct attack (so far).

The Swedish Quality: Reason, Consensus and Reform

A "Swedish Management Style"?

Before an attempt can be made to sketch the changes which are taking place, it would be well to look back to an established picture of "the Swedish style of management". As perceived by executives in multinational companies, the organizational structure of Swedish corporations is ambiguous—which is sometimes interpreted as a preference for complicated matrix structures, and sometimes simply perceived as chaotic (Forss et al. 1984). The decision-making processes are slow (Axelsson et al. 1991)—which, again, is interpreted by some authors as a result of striving for technical perfection, and by others as a routine aimed at preventing action (Brunsson 1985). Control processes are experienced as informal but tight, paradoxically enough (Forss et al. 1984). Finally, the importance of reaching consensus is always noticeable, whether interpreted as a cultural trait (conflict-avoidance, Hofstede 1980), or else as a conscious choice of democratic procedures (Lawrence and Spybey 1986).

The ambiguity of such perceptions can be best described as oscillating between ritualistic and rationalistic explanations. A visitor to Sweden usually faces one of these aspects first and believes that that is all there is to it. "No bureaucracy at all", sighs an Italian who cannot believe that a serious deal can be settled by a telephone conversation. "Why don't these people say what they mean?" wonders an American who participated in a typical consensus-reaching meeting, where everyone was speaking round the matter, looking at the walls or at nothing in particular, ending the meeting at, apparently, the same point where it began.

I do not know whether there is a "Swedish management style", but if I were forced to describe typical organizational practices in one word, I would choose "pragmatism". It means balancing rituals with rational choices, so that the former acquire instrumental uses (see, for example, Olsen's famous article on budgeting as a ritual, 1970. Olsen uses Norwegian examples, but organizational pragmatism seems to be a trait shared by all Scandinavian countries), while the latter—rational choices—express important values (for special accounting as a ritual of reason, see Czarniawska-Joerges and Jacobsson 1989).

One crucial element, however, would be left out from such a description: the value of change.

A Change of Doctrine

A series of studies conducted in leading Swedish companies concluded with a thesis of a change of doctrine in management thinking (Beckérus et al. 1988). The following is a summary of the authors' description of the changes taking place in Sweden.

Table 1.

The Old Doctrine	The New Doctrine
production in focus	business in focus
hierarchical organization	open dialogue
centralized decision-making	local negotiations
machines as the main resource	people as the main resource
leadership through command	leadership through ideas
industrial values	commercial values
financial rewards	participation and sharing
expert knowledge	local competence
priority: production development	priority: human capital

SAS, Ericsson and Eka Nobel were companies which served as examples of changing orientation from production to markets, of moving attention from inside to outside the organization, of focusing on customers' needs as defined by the customers and not by the companies. Volvo was then used as an illustration of how the changed attitude towards markets influenced the process of production as such:.

> In relation to their business strategy, both Volvo companies (under study) demonstrate a move from a relatively simple notion of efficiency to a holistic view of effectiveness, better fitted to a situation characterized by many incompatible demands and with a strong imprint of variability. (Beckérus et al. 1988: 83).

Consultants stand for knowledge production, whereas leaders (Percy Barnevik from Asea Brown Boveri, Jan Carlzon from SAS and Pehr G. Gyllenhammar from Volvo) stand for charismatic performances in the mass-media. The weight of large companies is compensated by the increasing attraction of small companies and entrepreneurship in general. Last but not least comes the clearly formulated demand for a balanced life, resulting both from women's attainment of more and more demanding positions and men's wish to participate in family life.

Is this "change of doctrine" anything new, one may ask, and is it specific to Sweden? Compared to the picture sketched by Forss et al. (1984), mentioned before, it seems to contain similar traits—flexible service orientation rather than structured production organization. One possible—and obvious—interpretation is that the "new doctrine" is an emerging picture of processes that have been taking place for quite some time now. One could, indeed, find the same type of description in any issue of *Harvard Business Review*.

It is the second question—is this something specifically Swedish—that is more problematic. One possible interpretation is that Sweden is catching up with the business *Zeitgeist*—or, perhaps, it is the *Zeitgeist* which is catching up with Sweden. Without excluding either of those interpretations, I would like to concentrate on one meta-phenomenon: the value of change.

The Wonderland of Reforms

I have borrowed this title from my own article (Czarniawska-Joerges 1989) which concentrates on public sector reforms as an empirical example. The phenomenon, however, is typical of the whole of Swedish organizational life. Change is important, and keeping up with the times is *very* important. Let me illustrate this by another cross-cultural experience.

At international conferences, we usually exchange not only research papers but also other experiences in our professional lives. What is often striking for a Swede, especially in encounters with the British and Dutch colleagues, is the difference in the teaching curricula for practitioners. In Sweden, academics teaching practitioners rarely have a substantial advantage over the practitioners' own awareness of current issues, whereas teaching programmes in e.g. Great Britain seem to have remained about 10-20 years behind the current research concerns (Carter and Jackson 1991). An apocryphal story has it that a well-renowned international strategy guru was sent packing by a group of Swedish general managers because "he was too rationalistic" and so was seen to be behind the times. On another occasion, a lecture on cognitive barriers in decision-making was interrupted from the audience by a person who claimed that the theory was too old-fashioned: she wanted to hear about the organizational uses of chaos theory.

Is it change as such which is ascribed a high value? The studies show that it is the idea of planned change, called "reorganization" in the private sector and "reform" in the public, which is seen as attractive. The attraction lies in the fact that planned change implies a possibility of exercising control, of intentionally shaping history, whereas it excludes, as threatening alternatives, both randomness and revolutionary changes (Brunsson and Olsen 1990).

It has also been pointed out that the change often starts—and seemingly ends—with a change in rhetoric (Rombach 1986). Swedish organizations are very sensitive to fashions and trends which influence, in the first place, the metaphors and labels used for organizational ideas and ideologies (Czarniawska-Joerges 1990). This is, on the one hand, denounced as "illusory changes", and on the other, is praised as a preference for "pragmatic solutions".

There are, indeed, rules even for introducing changes. Organizational change is strongly institutionalized. Thanks to it, there is room for new ideas, but the rules protect organizational processes from excessively extreme swings. Consequently, reformers (usually administrators) become irritated with the "organizational inertia", whereas the performers (usually professionals) are able to protect their activity from too many whimsical changes.

If it seems that I am describing the best of possible worlds, two caveats must be made. Naturally, the professionals do not always manage to protect themselves from overzealous reformers, and the reformers are not always wrong. Additionally, the process is much more balanced within the private sector than in the public domain.

The Swedish Public Sector: In Search of an Identity

At the end of the 1970s, the Swedish public sector was placed in a pillory and it has remained there ever since. The public (as represented in and by the mass-media) is constantly criticizing and giving advice. The situation is not, however, quite unique. One can say, indeed, that the Swedish public sector fell victim to a climate which is generally unfavourable to public sectors, with its source perhaps in the U.S.A. This climate was perhaps best expressed in the Grace Report (an investigation ordered by Reagan in 1984) which claimed

> (1) that the private sector is far more efficient than the public sector and is the repository of all management wisdom, (2) that the public and private sectors are similar enough that the former can be dramatically transformed by techniques imported from the latter, and (3) that the reform efforts of the past have little to teach present-day reformers (Downs and Larkey 1986: 219).

As mentioned before, in political terms, there is talk of a legitimacy crisis, but in terms of public administration it is perhaps better to speak about an identity crisis. The old identity (public authority as controller, public sector as wasteful spender) is rejected. In the search for a new identity, the private sector is one source of inspiration, but not the only one.

An Organizational Identity

After Meyer (1986) I assume that individual identity is a modern, Western institution which is committed to encouraging coherence and continuity in an individual's activities, across that person's working life (Brown 1987). Individualism is supported and complemented by two other modern institutions: that of the state and the market. The focal elements of modern individuality, says Meyer (1986), are self-respect, efficiency, internal locus of control and a labile commitment, which signifies creativity and flexibility. All these are important for the roles of citizens and of buyers/sellers, who are the building stones of the state and the market, respectively.

To fit this major institutional pattern, organizations are also given the attribute of individual identity. Organizations become "Super-Persons" who learn, make decisions, are born and die, populate both organizational theory and popular thinking. It is precisely this modern identity that the public organizations in Sweden are searching for—once again. Once again, because the previous version has lost its legitimacy. In it, self-respect was revealed to be self-righteousness, efficiency an urge for control, internal locus of control as a breach of communication with the clients, and flexibility as political opportunism. The search is to find new contents for those forms.

The problem is that it is not only the identities that are in turmoil, but practically all relevant institutions as well. On the one hand, there is a burden of "old identities", the very identities that put such organizations in a pillory, but which still feel legitimate and true. On the other hand, these organizations cannot get much outside help, because the whole institutional field has become blurred.

Tentative Identities in a Blurred Field

In terms of the structuration of organizational fields (DiMaggio 1983; DiMaggio and Powell 1983), one can depict the process of building new identities as a repetitive performance by certain actors in society which is recognized as consistent and therefore invokes consistent reactions from other actors. In this way, a typification arises creating a basis for an institution: actors of type X usually perform actions of type A (Berger and

Luckmann 1966). Even if the process is mutual (acts create identities and identities stabilize interactions), there is usually some part of an organizational field that is more stable than others and therefore helps the ongoing structuration. Most studies analyze cases of new actors creating new fields or of new actors entering already existing fields (March and Olsen 1989; Meyer et al. 1987; Olsen et al. 1989; Sahlin-Andersson 1989).

In the case under discussion, the situation is complicated by the old identity lurking behind new attempts and by the uncertain rules of the whole field. The actors can compose their identity in the course of an intellectual process, or, more correctly, under an internal process of negotiation of meaning. However, their newly constructed identity must be recognized and confirmed in concrete interactions in the field.

Let us take a typical example of what is happening now in many Swedish municipalities under a name of *bolagisering* (*bolag* means a company), which I shall call "corporatization". Basically, it means that part of a municipal activity (usually of a clearly technical character) acquires the status of a company (owned wholly by the municipality). Such a company, however, assumes a double identity from the very beginning. It is a business enterprise, but in the service of the local community. This expresses a wish to assume different identities on different occasions. In practice, however, it often leads to a confused identity. The municipal "companies" are treated as administrative units when they want to appear "business-like", and vice versa when they do not. To begin with, they acquire their physical equipment from their local governments at outrageous prices ("economic thinking" wins the upper hand with the local politicians). In the next round, however, when the resources are allocated in the budgeting process, the newly born "company" is treated as any other department and told to cut its budget according to municipal instructions. This leads, in the longer run, to the "company" exaggerating its "business-like" image, which creates internal conflicts and does not do much to promote the "company" on the real market (Czarniawska-Joerges 1991).

Additionally, there are no clear rules as to what is acceptable and what is not, and more, what is legal and what is not. A pragmatic attitude towards the law (which emerges from accumulating precedents) makes the situation very risky for those who are first in the field. Several directors of municipal finances have found themselves in court charged with illegal stock market speculations. The speculations did not involve any personal gain, but did incur severe losses. Apparently, it is legal to make profits with the tax-payers' money but not losses, municipal executives ironically remark. Clearly, the State has created a new space for experiments, but the rules of the game will emerge only when the game has been played for a while.

I took those examples to illustrate the on-going process and not to present conclusions. It is very difficult to foresee what will be the result of those change processes, which identities will emerge and what structure the renewed field will have. Additionally, all these changes are taking place on a visible stage where the public is not exactly supportive. Nevertheless, there are good chances that the Swedish public sector will emerge with a new set of identities and new patterns of interactions. Let me support my optimism with a historical example.

"Informalization"

There is a general feeling that the 1990s are bringing a re-formalization of social relationships in Sweden. Sales people are beginning to address customers in the second person plural (the polite form of address) and it is not shameful anymore to put "professor" in front of one's name. A new epoch is at the gates and therefore it is a proper time to describe the era that is ending. This task has been undertaken by a group of Swedish ethnographers (Löfgren 1988), who described the "informalization" which took place in Sweden in the 1970s.

Frykman (1988) depicts this informalization as a cultural renewal which became symbolic capital for one generation, those born in the 1940s. This was the generation that dominated the public sector organizations, where the number of employees grew by 800,000 between 1965 and 1981.

> Those who now write to you with a familiar form of address from your social insurance office are people who grew up in times when the society neither put a strong emphasis on junior/senior relationships nor on ascribed or acquired social identities. Their childhood was spent in a society where authority relations or other properties of a *societas* were not taken for granted (Frykman 1988: 30)

Indeed, they were the children of the generation that decided "to set life right" as Hirdman (1989) calls it in her book on the 1930s. Informality, claims Frykman, became their strategy, their way of marketing their own life-style as a model for everybody else.

Forming such a large group, they were able to halt the reproduction of old institutions. They stabilized the modernity of their parents and went even further—trying, in fact, not only to "set life right" but the whole world (what I mean here is Sweden's very visible presence in the international arena and in developing countries' programmes in the 1970s).

Why, then, is there now this tendency to re-formalize? To a certain degree it is, of course, part of a much wider phenomenon. Sales persons in Italy also address clients as *Signora* and *Signore* nowadays. Those born in the 1950s and 1960s address people formally, cut their hair short and wear double-breasted suits. It is often interpreted as their neo-conservatism, but much of it can simply be seen as "camp". However, the rebellion of the younger generations against the "1940-generation" is quite serious in Sweden. It has been pointed out that although there is an increasingly lighter tone used by the authorities in their dealings with citizens, the presence of the authorities is actually felt more and more. Mårtensson (1988) points out that within "informalization" two different things became mixed up: simplification and intimation. What started as a campaign against bureaucratic language came to the point of threatening personal integrity.

Yet I describe this historical anecdote in optimistic terms. It shows that it is possible to reform institutions—and create a new identity—during the life-time of one generation, if there is a collective will to do so; a new identity expressed not in new projects, plans and decisions, but in everyday routines.

A Museum of Modernity or a Pragmatist Paradise?

> To those who are observing political trends in this Northern Kingdom it may look as if the Swedish model is now changing, that the era of modernity and the rule of Social Democracy in the welfare state is terminated. "Being modern" is, however, not only a simple attitude that may change with the new fads and fashions. It is a matter of existence beyond political trends, especially if it has been a form of life for generations. It then turns into a condition deeply rooted in human mentality. In the Swedish case, modernism is closely linked to a special kind of mentality we may call "managerialism" (Guillet de Monthoux 1991: 27)

Guillet de Monthoux continues his argument by claiming that the conventional picture of "peaceful interorganizational cooperation" on the one hand and the dramatic contradiction between the public and the private sectors is not really relevant. What is most important for understanding contemporary Sweden is the managerial mentality permeating all Swedish organizations (which in turn, permeate the whole of Swedish society). Sweden is one big firm. Everything can be managed, when left in the hands of corporatist managers. This tradition is so strong that no legitimacy crises are going to affect it—"Sweden ... will probably become a cute little island of modernity in the European post-modern ocean" (Guillet de Monthoux 1991: 40).

There may be a great deal in this, especially as the Swedish kind of modernism has proved to be extremely successful, in spite of all pessimistic prophecies. "How bright are the Northern Lights?" asks Olson (1990) and answers comfortingly that "a society can, if its policies and institutions are intelligent, prevent destitution and even make fairly generous provision for its least fortunate citizens, yet still remain a prosperous and dynamic society" (p. 91).

Both Olson and Guillet de Monthoux see Sweden as a modern project through and through—the difference is whether they see it as a reason for optimism or for pessimism. Another possibility is to look for reasons for the survival and success of the modern project in its postmodern practices.

The postmodern condition, as described by Lyotard (1979/1987), is characterized not by a disappointment with the modern project (in fact, it can be seen as its inseparable part), but by a skepticism towards the legitimizing meta-narratives of modernism: that of functional system, as designed by experts and that of emancipating freedom, as created by a political consensus. People who populate organizations are well aware that experts represent only one voice in a polyphony, not to say cacophony of voices, and that a final consensus can never be reached. What is more, there is no greater danger to the system than its efficiency (Antonio 1979; Lyotard 1979/1989), whereas consensus can be seen as a condition for a dialogue rather than the purpose of that dialogue. One wonders whether the fact that Sweden is so well known for its inventions (dynamite, ball bearings, milk packs, AXE telephone exchanges and, recently, a claim to "cold fusion") has to do with the understanding of the fact that a consensus enables a search for creative solutions. This characteristic applies to both the internal and the external functioning of Swedish organizations. Much has been said about the collective policies of Swedish trade unions; less attention is dedicated to the unique capacity for collective action revealed by Swedish business (Pestoff 1991).

Berg (1989) claims that the key to an understanding of contemporary developments in the Swedish organizational context is through typically postmodern traits: "the deconstruction of organization structures, the rejection of grand strategies, the emphasis on expressivism, and the importance of coding" (p. 213). The results of my study of public organizations (1991) point in the same direction—towards the importance of postmodern knowledge, i.e. understanding that every organization hosts a multitude of little narratives, multiple interpretations, plural realities. These result from ideological and occupational differences, or generation and gender discrepancies. Paradoxicality is built into public sector organizations. To be able to act, one is forced to choose one version of the world upon which to act, but that does not make it permanent or valid, even in the future. The reality has to be constantly negotiated. The concept of a "negotiated economy" (Hernes 1978) is slowly acquiring a new meaning, as much or more in Sweden than elsewhere.

Notes

1. I am grateful to the personnel of the Swedish Institute for supplying me with the brochure.
2. The area of Sweden is 450,000 km^2 (174,000 sq. miles), the population 8.5 million.

References

Åsard, Erik (1980): "Employee participation in Sweden 1971–1979". *Economic and Industrial Democracy* 1/3: 371–393.

Antonio, Robert J. (1979): "The contradiction of domination and production in bureaucracy: The contribution of organizational efficiency to the decline of the Roman Empire". *American Sociological Review* 44 (December): 895–912.

Axelsson, Runo, David Cray, Geoffrey R. Mallory and David C. Wilson (1991): "Decision style in British and Swedish organizations: a comparative examination of strategic decision-making". *British Journal of Management* 2: 67–79.

Beckérus, Åke, Anders Edström, Claes Edlund, Göran Ekvall, Jan Forslin and Jan-Erik Rendahl (1988): *Doctrinskiftek: Nya ideal i svenskt ledarskap.* Stockholm: Svenska Dagbladets Förlag.

Berg, Per-Olof (1989): "Postmodern management? From facts to fiction in theory and practice". *Scandinavian Journal of Management* 5/3: 201–217.

Berger, Peter L. and Thomas Luckmann (1966): *The social construction of reality.* New York: Doubleday.

Brown, Richard Harvey (1987): *Society as text.* Chicago: University of Chicago Press.

Brunsson, Nils (1985): *The irrational organization.* London: Wiley.

Brunsson, Nils and Johan Olsen (eds.) (1990): *Makten att reformera.* Stockholm: Carlssons.

Bryder, Tom (1989): *Political culture, language and change.* Copenhagen: University of Copenhagen, Institute of Political Studies.

Carter, Pippa and Norman Jackson (1991): "Modernism, postmodernism and motivation: or why expectancy theory failed to come up to expectation". Paper presented at the "New Theory of Organizations" conference, Keele, England.

Clegg, Stewart R. and Winton Higgins (1987): "Against the current: organisational sociology and socialism". *Organization Studies* 8/3: 201–222.

Czarniawska-Joerges, Barbara (1989): "The wonderland of public administration reforms". *Organization Studies* 10/4: 531–548.

Czarniawska-Joerges, Barbara (1990): "Merchants of meaning: management consulting in the Swedish public sector" in Barry A. Turner (ed.) *Organizational symbolism*, 139–149. Berlin: de Gruyter.

Czarniawska-Joerges, Barbara (1991): *Styrningens paradoxer: Scener ur den offentliga verksamheten.* Stockholm: Norstedts.

Czarniawska-Joerges, Barbara and Bengt Jacobsson (1989): "Budget in a cold climate". *Accounting, Organisations and Society* 14/1–2: 29–39.

Daun, Åke (1989): *Svensk mentalitet*. Stockholm: Rabén and Sjögren.

Demokrati och makt i Sverige: Maktutredningens huvudrapport (1990). Stockholm: Carlssons.

DiMaggio, Paul (1983): "State expansion and organizational fields" in Richard H. Hall and Robert E. Quinn, *Organization theory and public policy*, 147–161. Beverly Hills: Sage.

DiMaggio, Paul and Walter W. Powell (1983): "The iron cage revisited: institutional isomorphism and collective rationality in organizational fields". *American Sociological Review* 48: 147–160.

Downs, George W. and Patrick D. Larkey (1986): *The search for government efficiency. From hubris to helplessness*. Philadelphia:-Temple University Press.

Edelman, Murray (1988): *Constructing the political spectacle*. Chicago: Chicago University Press.

Forss, Kim, David Hawk and Gunnar Hedlund (1984): *Cultural differences— Swedishness in legislation, multinational corporations and aid administration*. Stockholm: Stockholm School of Economics.

Frykman, Jonas (1988): "Fördelen att vara informell. Konsten att få ett övertag och behålla det" in Orvar Löfgren (ed.), *Hej, det är från försäkringskassan!*, 17–35. Stockholm: Natur och Kultur.

Guillet de Monthoux, Pierre (1991): "Modernism and the dominating firm—on the managerial mentality of the Swedish model". *Scandinavian Journal of Management* 7/1: 27–40.

Hernes, Gudmund (1978): *Forhandlingsøkonomi og blandingsadministrasjon*. Bergen: Universitetetsförlag.

Hirdman, Yvonne (1989): *Att lägga livet till rätta*. Stockholm: Carlsson.

Hofstede, Geert (1980): *Culture's consequences: international differences in work-related values*. Beverly Hills, CA: Sage.

Kluckhohn, Clyde and William H. Kelly (1945): "The concept of culture" in Ralph Linton (ed.), *The science of man in the world crisis*, 78–106. New York: Columbia University Press.

Lawrence, Peter and Tony Spybey (1986): *Management and society in Sweden*. London: Routledge and Kegan Paul.

Leach, Edmund (1982): *Social anthropology*. Oxford: Oxford University Press.

Ledarskap/Ekonomen 1986, No. 3.

Luhman, Niklas (1986): "Das Problem der Epochenbildung und die Evolutionstheorie" in H.U. Gumbrecht and U. Link-Heer (eds.), *Epochenschwellen und Epochenstrukturen im Diskurs der Literatur- und Sprachhistorie*, 11–33. Frankfurt: Suhrkamp.

Lyotard, Jean-Francoise (1979/1987): *The postmodern condition. A report on knowledge*. Manchester: Manchester University Press.

Löfgren, Orvar (ed.) (1988): *Hej, det är från försäkringskassan!*. Stockholm: Natur och Kultur.

Maccoby, Michael (1981): *The Leader*. New York: Simon and Schuster.

March, James G. and Johan Olsen (1989): *Rediscovering institutions. The organizational basis of politics*. New York: The Free Press.

Meyer, John W. (1986): "Myths of socialization and of personality" in Thomas C. Heller, Morton Sosna and David E. Wellbery (eds.), *Reconstructing individual-*

ism; autonomy, individuality and the self in Western thought, 208–221. Stanford: Stanford University Press

Meyer, John W., John Boli and George M. Thomas (1987): "Ontology and rationalization in the Western cultural account" in George M. Thomas, John W. Meyer, Francisco O. Ramirez and John Boli (eds.), *Institutional structure: constituting state, society and the individual*, 12–37. Beverly Hills, CA: Sage.

Mårtensson, Eva (1988): "Den familjära myndigheten. Intimisering av det offentliga språket" in Orvar Löfgren (ed.) *Hej, det är från försäkringskassan!*, 105–127. Stockholm: Natur och Kultur.

Olsen, Johan P., Paul G. Roness and Harald Saetren (1989): "Styring gjennom institusjonsutforming" in Johan P. Olsen (ed.), *Petroleum og politikk*, 94–120. Bergen: TANO.

Olsen, Johan P. (1970): "Local budgeting, decision-making or a ritual act?" *Scandinavian Political Studies* 5/3: 85–118.

Olson, Mancur (1990): *How bright are the Northern Lights? Some questions about Sweden*. Lund: Lund University Press.

Pestoff, Victor A. (1991): *The demise of the Swedish Model and the resurgence of organized business as a major political actor*. Stockholm: Stockholm University Studies in Action and Enterprise, PP 1991: 2.

Rombach, Björn (1986): *Rationalisering eller prat*. Lund: DOXA.

Sahlin-Andersson, K. (1989): *Oklarhetens strategi. Organisering av projektsamarbete*. Lund: Studentlitteratur.

Sveiby, Karl-Erik and Anders Risling (1986): *Kunskapsföretaget*. Malmö: Liber.

Zetterberg, Hans L. (1984): "The rational humanitarians". *Daedalus* (Winter): 75–92.

Chapter 14:

Many More Ways Than One

David J. Hickson

Diversity

The British—and I am one of them—speak of putting all your eggs in one basket. This proverb, like many others, is pan-European in one form or another. We all recognize it, and know that it means taking a risk that could lose everything. For if that one basket is dropped and all the eggs in it are shattered, then no eggs will have been safely kept somewhere else, away from risk. Yet that is what Western Europeans are doing, trying to make a single basket that can contain all their peoples and societies. It is that which prompts the writing of this book, though such a book would have been just as pertinent had there been no European Community, and were there never to be a European "United States". The same eggs are there and for a long time will be there, for societies change slowly in their basic elements.

This particular basketful is not so fragile as eggs usually are. Indeed, these are very hard boiled eggs. Over the course of history they have banged against each other again and again, they have spewed over one another, yet still they are sharply separable, different, eggs. Very different indeed. Bigger ones and smaller ones, older ones and younger ones, stronger ones and weaker ones, even multi-shaped ones, and certainly different tasting ones. It is their innermost cultures that keep them so.

Nowhere on earth is there greater cultural diversity in a relatively small space than in Western Europe. In his overview of the European cultural scene in Chapter 1, Hofstede, whose work has done more than anyone's to rouse interest in cultural understanding (Hofstede 1980, 1991), and who is by far the most cited authority in this book, shows how doubling the number of EC nations from six to twelve markedly increased the cultural differences within the EC. He suggests that the EC may have within it quite a large proportion of the differences in culture that can be found in the world as a whole.

Who can doubt this when an extensive survey of the values held by Western Europeans (Harding and Phillips 1986) finds that for children to be thrifty is said to matter much less in Britain than in Germany, and that bringing them up in a religious faith matters far less to Danes than it does to many Irish. Homosexuality is held to be much more acceptable to the Dutch than it is to the neighbouring Belgian (French-speaking) Walloons, and fighting with the police worries the French less than it does the neighbouring British. Italians say they trust others much less than the Dutch claim to do, and the Germans say they value responsible work which encourages personal development more than the French say of themselves; and so on, and so on, for many more values.

Furthermore, the preceding chapters in this book see the Belgians inclined (*inter alia*) to be pragmatic, the Danes to be indulgent, the English conservative, the French elitist, the Germans orderly, the Greeks patriarchal, the Irish loquacious, the Italians dependent, the Dutch reserved, the Portuguese resilient, the Spanish fatalistic, and the Swedes consultative!

Small wonder that there is such variety in the form and content of these chapters themselves. Partly it is the differences in the societies they analyze, perhaps more so it is the personal differences between the authors in their own cultural origins (see the Preface to this book, and the biographical notes at the end of the book) which will have led them to see their task in different ways. Whilst all chapters do give something of the history of a country that has brought it to where it is now, and examine its economic and political make-up and the essence of its culture as reflected in the typical approach to management, the chapters vary hugely both in style and emphasis. How else could it be?

Not all this variation between chapters is due to culture. More is probably due to the differing availability of published material. Whilst there is a substantial amount of published thought and empirical evidence on the cultural and managerial features of some West European countries, especially the larger ones, there is comparatively little on others, especially some of the smaller ones, so when writing their chapters, some authors faced the challenge of selecting from plenty, others of making something from scarcity. This unavoidably shaped what could be said about management in each nation.

Each chapter is therefore best regarded as if it were a picture portrait. No portrait can show everything that might be seen were it possible to view it from other angles. Some portraits are sketchy, others more detailed. All are limited in size and cannot possibly include everything. Like viewers in an art gallery, different readers will prefer different portraits. However, this book stands upon the premise that to see something is better than to see nothing at all, and that—to contradict another proverb—a little knowledge is *not* a dangerous thing, but a definite advantage.

Country and Culture

To return to culture, there is a sense in which West Europeans do have a great deal culturally in common. It is possible to attend a Beethoven symphony, a Moliere comedy, a Shakespeare tragedy, a Verdi opera, anywhere. That, though, is another meaning of the word culture, a meaning signifying artistic taste, sometimes better expressed by the German spelling "*Kultur*" than by the joint English/French spelling. It can also imply what may be regarded as social refinement; an elitist meaning.

The sense in which the word is used here is not this. The meaning here is given by Hofstede's definition in Chapter 1, the "collective programming of the mind which distinguishes one category of people from another". As the word culture is much argued over, defined and redefined, this way of putting it has the merit of simplicity, instantly conveying how it is that the nations covered in this book differ from each other. Since the people who belong to them differ in how they are formed mentally from childhood onwards, they differ, too, in what time they get up in the morning, in what they eat, in what they value, in their ways of managing and organizing, and in a great deal else.

Chapter 13 by Czarniawska-Joerges points out that we really only become aware of culture when we encounter another one. How come these strange people get up at such a surprising time in the morning, have such a peculiar breakfast, put such a value on punctuality, talk to their subordinates in such an odd manner, and organize in a way that is so difficult to understand? It is quite a step beyond this to realize that we ourselves, too, get up at a surprising time in the morning, eat a peculiar breakfast, etc. It is not they who are funny, it is me! We can spend the rest of our lives trying to grasp that.

People who travel around Europe encounter this shock over and over again, as they move from nation to nation. Or is it from society to society? These two words, nation and society, are widely used casually and interchangeably, and that is the way they will be used here, as if a society with a unifying culture was the same as a nation state. Though often it is not. People may see themselves as belonging to a society with a common culture which lies across the formal borders of nation states—there are Basques in both France and Spain, for instance—or which covers only part of a nation state, so in writing about Belgium, Mok (Chapter 2) has to cope with its division into Flemish and Walloon societies. Indeed, there are minorities throughout the European nation states. Bretons, Scots, Alsatians, Frisians, Bavarians, Lapps, and so many, many more. In this book, none of them are given their due, and as its Editor I feel this especially keenly. The more so since I am one of the English majority in my homeland, and Tayeb has carefully and honestly limited Chapter 4 to

English culture. She could not possibly have included also the Scots, Welsh, Ulster Irish, or our more recent minorities. It is, in itself, a comment on the diversity of Europe that it would have been quite impossible to consider all the minorities within this kind of book.

Hence this book perforce deals only with the predominant culture of each nation, the one that distinguishes a nation, overall, from others. We must leave it to future generations of authors to delve more sensitively into the even deeper subtleties of how "sub-cultures" shape managing and organizing.

Implicit Theory

Though the authors of each chapter were not asked to formulate any explicit theory on what they were writing about, nor was a theory imposed on them for fear it might cramp the contribution each had to make, there is an implicit theory or theoretical position underlying this book—a hazy one, but discernible, nevertheless.

It is that managing and organizing are not activities isolated from society, carried out by automatons in executive suits, in executive suites, according to universal management principles, in some glassed-in managerial sphere. Critics of contemporary management may feel this is so, seeing managerial lives often remote from the other lives far down at the bottom of the pyramids of power. Indeed there can be a similar managerialism, which could be called a worldwide managerial culture, extending through managerial elites everywhere. It is a research problem to detect how far this extends; how far managers everywhere do some things the same way. It is a practical problem for multinational corporations to find the common denominator among their managers. But first and foremost, each manager is a person in a society, formed by a society (or societies), and so the processes of managing and organizing are not separable from societies and their cultures. These processes are part of society, just as much as anything else is. If it helps the thinking process to conceive of a society's culture as shaping, or as causing, its managerial processes, thereby analytically distinguishing the one from the other, so well and good, but that is for analytical purposes only. In a fuller sense, the one should be seen as part of the other.

That is the way in which any particular piece of research should be interpreted. Even if in the report of the research a separation has been made between the cultural characteristics of a society and its managing and organizing, so as to explain the latter by the former, this should be interpreted just as a logical step in order that an explanatory argument may be constructed. Nor, incidentally, should research work which does not include societal culture be dismissively accused of neglecting or ignoring it. Quite likely, there was not enough time and money to include it, for studying culture is not a brief, lighthearted affair. Each chapter in this book is evidence of just how much there is to be known that is relevant to management and organization. The positive approach to research is to appreciate the achievements of those, including co-authors here, who have made the effort to encompass societal cultures.

The achievements of the chapter authors do not stop there. For insofar as these can be analytically distinguished from culture, the politico–economic frameworks of the twelve nations are also crucial. The differences that have been described are marked.

Some nations have pronounced state ownership and influence. This is especially so in Italy (Chapter 9) where there is substantial ownership by the state of both industry and services. Beyond that there are comparatively few large companies, and these are family owned, as in Greece, rather than owned by multitudes of impersonal shareholders, as is typical in Britain. In France, too, the State plays a prominent part both through direct ownership and indirectly, the French state having long been centred upon Paris which focuses education, careers, and transport (Chapter 5). There is a noticeable paternalistic element in French business, stemming from the strong figure of the President-Directeur General. In Germany there is not such an overt state involvement and regulation as in Italy and France, but the company system, stable compared to that in Britain, rests on direct bank investment to a considerable extent, and through this there is a doubly indirect stabilizing state influence (Chapter 6). In Ireland, the State came proactively in to a "late developer" economy after independence in 1921 (Chapter 8). Prior to that the British had encouraged co-operatives, primarily in the dairy industry. Now these, and a wide range of state-owned enterprises, continue alongside hi-tech, multinational firms which have given a recent impulse to the economy, as they have to other "late developers".

Britain (Chapter 4 is on England) has twice been mentioned as a contrast to the situation in other nations. This culturally very individualistic nation exemplifies the Anglo "law of the jungle" situation where company managements and marauding financiers are ever on the lookout for bargains, and hostile takeovers are commonplace. "In 1988 Britain accounted for 73 per cent of all takeovers in Europe" (Campbell and Warner, Chapter 6), a shifting capitalist battleground of a kind "frowned upon" in Germany, The Netherlands, and Scandinavia (Sorge, Chapter 5); though the French do engage in this sort of thing, too.

The impulse given to "late developers" by foreign investment can be seen in other nations besides Ireland. Though there was a sophisticated basis from which to begin, The Netherlands did not develop industrially on any scale until after World War II, and whilst it has large, well-known, indigenous firms, the economy contains a great number of foreign multinationals (Chapter 10), including the two Anglo-Dutch giants Shell and Unilever. The latest developer of all is Spain, a nation typified by small inward-looking firms serving regional rather than national markets (Chapter 12). Here, too, the multinationals have entered in force to boost the more dynamic sectors of the economy.

Sweden (Chapter 13) stands as exemplar of relatively steady development from an economy based on natural resources, the pulp and paper derived from the timber of the northern forests, to an advanced export orientated economy, many of whose brands are household names everywhere.

Even so, never let it be forgotten that throughout Europe the prevalent feature is small private businesses. There are far more of these than of any other organizational form. They are probably least significant in Britain, most in Italy, Greece, Portugal, and Spain, but everywhere they flourish.

Empires and Cultures

These politico–economic contrasts are part of societies many of whose contrasts in culture go back to three great influences which have left profound imprints across Europe. They were the Roman Empire, the Viking invasions and what, for want of any better term, must be called the Russian Empire.

The Roman Empire, of the last centuries B.C. and the first centuries A.D., though so long ago now, still leaves the most marked imprint. In Western Europe that imprint closely follows the line of the Rhine. Today's managers and employees differ according to whether they were born and brought up North or South of Western Europe's great river. South of it the Empire, which spread ever wider from Rome, left its strongest imprint. The grand, remote authority of Emperors, and the Empire's codified system of laws, reigned the longest. The Romans either never reached north of the Rhine, or their civilization there was more superficial and transient. True, Constantine was installed as Emperor when he was in the North of England, near where I live, but the Emperors never stayed long in this climate! "Barbarian" societies came and went without the vast hierarchic order that held sway, despite its internal struggles, further South. As the twenty-first century approaches, managing and organizing still differ according to whether they take place in societies characterized by Romance languages closest to Latin, by Roman-type legal systems, and by the strongest Roman Catholic churches, or in societies with mainly Germanic languages, varied and often less detailed and less all-embracing legal systems, and the strongest Protestant churches.

Towards the South, in what is generally called Latin Europe (and these are sweeping groupings, for no nation is purely Latin), there is a more personal approach to managing and organizing, personal authority counts for more, and personal relationships matter more besides the formal organizational connections. There can be a wider vision of what might be (which strikes Northerners as overstatement). What to organization theorists is Weberian bureaucracy, with layers of hierarchy, rows of specialist offices, and many written procedures, can become an over-formalized facade made to work as much by overriding or circumventing the rules as by bending them.

So whilst Spain is described (Chapter 12) as entering a time of rapid change, it is still very much a society in which authority on the job is seen as deriving from the boss personally, to whom others are inclined to show both emotional loyalty and dependency. Yet at the same time there is an offsetting distrust of authority in general. France, likewise, is inclined to prominent leader figures stamping their personal control upon organizations that can be highly bureaucratic, with relatively numerous layers of managers and supervisors, many departments and much written instruction and communication, yet constantly this is in tension with a tendency to reject domination by authority (Chapter 5). On the other hand, the French pursuit of high standards of professional practice may combine with personal flair to produce "elan" and managerial inspiration. Management in Italy gets things done by adopting strong "clientelismo" personal relationships and patronage, which carry into the workplace the importance of family relationships (Chapter 9). It is expected that superiors will have privileges just as do the elders of the family. Along with this goes a "sense of style" expressed in design, architecture, and corporate image.

In summary, these are the nations whose predominant societal cultures are characterized by Hofstede (Chapter 1) as comparatively high in power distance, and sufficiently family-oriented compared with the Northern societies to show some characteristics that are relatively collectivistic.

Turning towards the North, there is here a more impersonal approach to managing and organizing. On and off the job people are more distant and reserved. They often coldly ignore personal relationships with acquaintances or family that might interfere, as they see it, with their work responsibilities. Managers are inclined to a narrower vision of what might be (which strikes Southerners as understatement). Bureaucratic forms of organization can be made to work impersonally as defined in the original Weberian model, flexibly bending rules rather than circumventing them.

Germany is well known for its efficient forms of bureaucracy; its orderly and controlled organizations (Chapter 6). These have flatter hierarchies with fewer layers than those in Southern Europe, and are operated with less close supervision since subordinates can be relied upon to follow the rules. The Dutch, too, have something of the same, but with a particularly restrained, tolerant approach (Chapter 10). In the Netherlands, differing interests can be reconciled in a participative way so that there is a low level of industrial conflict, but stability can also mean inflexibility. Flamboyancy among managers is distasteful. Swedish management has, in turn, much in common with the Dutch, and its model national consensus between employer's and employee's organizations, supported by the State, has been widely envied for decades, although currently it appears to be breaking down (Chapter 13). There is a taste for teamwork and innovative ways of group problem-solving. Managerial decisions are talked around at length in a participative atmosphere. The English, on the other hand, are more deferential towards authority, though at the same time they "do not like to be ordered about" (Chapter 4). Organizations rest on a degree of trust between colleagues and between superiors and subordinates that allows them to run in a less bureaucratic manner with details less specified. This degree of trust goes with a cautious conservatism that slows down the forces of change.

Ireland, the only Celtic state in existence (Chapter 8), might have something of everything. It has what is probably the strongest Roman Catholic church, but the English language is spoken as much, if not more, than Irish Gaelic. Its own informal style of management, if that is what it may be, has yet to emerge and be recognized.

In summary, these are the nations whose predominant societal cultures are characterized by Hofstede (Chapter 1) as comparatively low in power distance, and relatively individualistic, the English being especially individualistic, as are all Anglo societies due probably to their origins in the British Empire.

A second notable influence upon present day managing and organizing were the *Viking invasions* of the ninth century. Sweeping seawards from Scandinavia, mainly from what are now Denmark and Norway, these people raided and eventually colonized coastlines and rivers around Western Europe. They even penetrated into the Mediterranean, though their influence there was minimal; but it is felt still in the Northern lands. Here in the North of England I do not look out of my study window across a valley, equivalent to the French "*vallee*", but across a dale, a Scandinavian/Germanic form of word, for here there was the "Danelaw" or some degree of Danish rule for several centuries. It has even been suggested that the English language in its present form could have begun here in Wharfedale where Anglo-Saxon speech and the then Danish language came together among farmers who were compelled to talk with one another to survive the harsh conditions in the Northern dales.

The Vikings seem to have reinforced the contrast with the imprint of the

Roman Empire, accentuating the characteristics of the Northern peoples. They had no elaborate Roman style administration, rather they had simple and more local hierarchies and laws, developed in largely independent self-reliant settlements. The traces of this can be sensed in the sketch of the contemporary Swedish way of managing and organizing, talking through decisions in a participative manner in a team setting (Chapter 13, and above). There is much of this in the English also, though obscured by being subsequently overlaid with Norman–French elitist feudalism (Chapter 4, and above). It blends with the English inclination to gradually feel the way forward, to procrastinate.

Hence, therefore, the greater likelihood of organizations with a Northerly base being managed by pragmatic gradualists, working things out bit by bit and move by move. Whereas organizations with a Southerly base are more likely to be managed with greater idealism, planning and promulgating with more vision and more optimism, even if hopes are not fulfilled.

In Chapter 1, Hofstede crystallizes this in the concept of uncertainty avoidance, showing that Southern cultures are more uncertainty avoiding and Northern cultures are more uncertainty tolerating. The former tend to try and lay down rules for the future so that the future feels more certain, the latter to muddle along and to wait and see.

Putting it in the most simple possible way, the contrast between the high power distance plus high uncertainty avoidance cultures of the Southern societies, and the low power distance plus low uncertainty avoidance cultures of the Northern societies, is at the heart of many struggles within the EC. It does not explain everything, far from it, but it lies beneath much of the difference between those who cry forward with proclamations of intent, and those who ask for time and remain uneasy, most conspicuously the obstinate British. It is a contrast familiar in the executive meetings of multinational organizations.

Most recent of the three great influences on contemporary Western Europe was the *Russian Empire*, one-time Tsarist and more recently and in the West more influentially Stalinist. Why should this be referred to here? It did not absorb Western Europe, and Western approaches to managing and organizing cannot be traced to it. No, but though reference to it is brief, it is too important to be ignored without mention. For the "iron curtain" that its Stalinist phase dropped across Europe heightened Western Europe's self-awareness. At least as much as the horrors of two European-created World Wars, it fostered the flickering identity that is responsible for the interest in similarities and differences that created this book.

Europeanness

Is there, then, a Europeanness in managing and organizing that could strengthen within an EC egg basket, all together? Western European diversity notwithstanding, Western European managers do not go about things in the same way as Americans do, or as Africans do, or as Asians do. Which implies that they have enough in common to distinguish them from their counterparts in other Continents.

First, they are Old World, not New World. Even though Europe spawned the New World, differences in management between the two are well known. Americans epitomize this best. Their more assertive and open style has long been recognized, and as citizens of a New World, they are future orientated, looking ahead to what can be achieved, eager to get on with what is new. To them "time is money", not to be wasted. Instructions should be clear, and acted on without delay (Hall and Hall 1990). Compared to this, and irrespective of the differences among them, European managers in general have been reared in societies with longer and deeper traditions and, by comparison, are more conscious of the past, more willing to take time in negotiations, and to proceed with care. They communicate with greater subtlety, assuming a greater implicit understanding of how things are done in a particular organization in a particular society.

Nor is this a difference with North America only. In South America, the Brazilians, who dominate in population and geography almost as much as the Americans do in the North, have similar attributes. They, too, optimistically look for change, and seek fast results, though they tend to be "immediatist" and want the pay-off now, more present-orientated than are the future-orientated Americans (Oliveira and Hickson 1991). Whereas the Portuguese who founded Brazil are seen as comparatively patient (Chapter 11).

The Brazilians have a semi "Developing World" economy, of course, and share many of the features which separate management in developing countries from that in most of Western Europe. Often trying to build on to the remains of a colonial administrative structure without a Western infrastructure of education and communications to support it, developing countries struggle to manage and to organize effectively. They wrestle with a degree of over-centralized formalistic bureaucratization, worked by personalism (who knows who) rather than run flexibly, which is only found here and there in Western Europe (Jaeger and Kanungo 1990).

Nor is Western Europe the same as Asia, to state the glaringly obvious. Even though the Swedes have been whimsically called "the blue-eyed Japanese of Europe", because of the stability of their organizations, this is rather far-fetched! Western Europeans, broadly speaking, would be hard put to equal the collectivistic approach of, say, the Japanese and the

Chinese (mentioning the Japanese and Chinese together does not imply that those very different peoples are otherwise the same). The Japanese commitment to work-group and organization, remarkable in comparative terms though neither absolute nor universal even in Japan, and the Chinese commitment to family and family business (Redding 1990), are renowned.

Thus, notwithstanding radical differences among them, Western European managements are liable to be more cautious than those in the New World, more sophisticated in methods than those in developing nations, and more individualistic in reward systems and careers than those in Asia.

Are they likely to become more and more similar? To share many features rather than just a few very, very general ones to which exceptions can always be found? It would be surprising if burgeoning air travel, telephone conversations, and fax and electronic mail messages, associated with the accelerating volume of trade within Europe and increasing collaboration and overlapping ownership between organizations, had no effect. Though someone else's means of doing business may be a trifle odd, it may also include a good idea worth copying. Continued association begets common norms of behaviour. There is a rapidly rising number of students who follow some or all of a management type education in a country or countries other than their own. There is a working "lingua franca", English, which the British like myself give as an excuse for not learning other languages.

Moreover, organizations throughout Europe operate under the same pressures which lead towards uniformity. As this century began, Weber (1947) was foreseeing the widespread growth of the now commonplace bureaucratic form of organization. Most obviously, common technologies require the same jobs: trucks require truck drivers, machine tools require skilled machine tool operators, electricity power stations require control room staff, and so on. Common markets, indeed a single common market, require similar modern distribution and marketing methods from each organization if they are to compete with the others.

The common pressures from growth in size and from widening interdependence between organizations have been expressed as a "culture-free hypothesis" (Hickson and McMillan 1981). Irrespective of which societies they are part of, if organizations get bigger they are likely to have an increasing panoply of specialist departments and the formal documentation or electronic records associated with them (in a word, bureaucratization). Larger size requires this means of ensuring (specialist) attention to what needs doing, and the routine co-ordination of everyone involved. Also, irrespective of society, organizations which in complex economies become more (inter) dependent upon other organizations are likely to centralize more decisions. As major contracts and ownership links with supplier and customer organizations increase, including links with governmental organizations, so the importance of these dependence relationships for survival raises to the top the growing number of decisions affected by them. Large commercial conglomerates have many organizations dependent upon them whilst, similarly, intervention by governments creates in other organizations a dependence on the State. In both situations the decisions of the dependent organizations become more centralized within them, and also above them insofar as decisions governing them come to be taken by the organizations on which they are dependent.

In short, the "culture-free hypothesis" says that, in all cultures, greater size brings greater bureaucratization, and greater dependence brings greater centralization. These fundamental relationships are likely to hold everywhere. Certainly they hold across quite a range of societies, including those of Western Europe (Donaldson 1986; Miller 1987).

So organizations in all the twelve nations included in this book are subject to a series of influences which tend to erode differences in managing and organizing, and to make these processes more and more alike. Greater political and business contact, more connections within management education, the use of similar technologies, common markets, the sameness in large and interlocked organizations, all lead in that direction — and yet . . . . . . ? Really?

Even the "culture-free hypothesis" on the effects of size and dependence does not mean that organizations would all be the same — not even if nothing else were happening. It postulates that different sized organizations are likely to have *differing* levels of bureaucratization, and differently dependent organizations are likely to have *differing* levels of centralization.

The differentiating effects of societal culture are even more pervading. They can even influence the two factors on which this hypothesis rests. Although the relationships of size and dependence to organizational features indeed may be substantially culture-free, size and dependence themselves are influenced by cultures. For example, an Italian preference for smaller family-based organizations may limit the size of Italian businesses. A German preference for stable relationships between businesses may sustain a high level of (inter)dependence.

Beyond that again, and overwhelmingly, how organizations are set up and used in managing and organizing processes is culturally "saturated". Even if organizations in two societies look much the same on an organization chart, similar organizational frameworks will be used differently. Moreover, even similar organization charts will, on detailed examination, show differences in the hierarchy and specialisms. This is what every single chapter in this book has been about, and what this chapter has attempted to draw together. The proof is not only in twelve different portrayals in twelve differing chapters, but in the strength of the minority cultures that were mentioned earlier. Cultures can fade away, and some do, but they can also be astonishingly persistent.

Nobody knows what the future will bring in Western Europe, but the chances must favour a gradual convergence in ways of managing and organizing, if only because so many influences lead that way, but—and it is a big "but"—it is likely to be a drawing together that will never completely come together. In other words there are likely to be more similarities, but differences will persist.

Simply Speaking

There can be no author of a chapter in this book who has not had misgivings about having to compress the essence of a society in its managing and its organizing into so few pages or, as I did in this final chapter, of having to take an equally compressed view of all twelve societies. Each of us has had to simplify simplifications.

Each one of us must feel uneasy about giving an incomplete portrayal; a biassed one, a distorted one, for any selection gives an over-prominence to what is selected by taking it out of the fuller context within which it would be seen in proper proportion. There is a great danger of stereotyping. Whilst these societies tend to have the attributes described, these are tendencies not absolutes, and broad tendencies at that. They appear more in some things that are done and said than in others, more at some times than at others. Vitally, these are tendencies viewed across societies as a whole. No one person in Belgium, Denmark, England, France, Germany, Greece, Ireland, Italy, the Netherlands, Portugal, Spain and Sweden will be quite like that.

Most of all, it should be remembered whenever this book is read that *everything is relative*. Society A is said to be such and such only because it is possible to see that Society B is less so. Everything has to be interpreted in a comparative way.

Nevertheless, despite the misgivings, we must hope that even simplifications provide a starting point from which to work, and that for those readers who wish to go further, the lists of sources with each chapter will help them to do so. Our aim is to foster an appreciative curiosity about other peoples, a respect for what seem to be their virtues, a better understanding of what seem to be their weaknesses, and an awareness that these apparent virtues and weaknesses seem so largely because of our own personal ethnocentrism. It is our hope that such a book might even contribute to better managing and organizing, whatever that may be for each of us.

References

Donaldson, Lex (1986): "Size and bureaucracy in East and West: a preliminary meta-analysis" in S.R. Clegg, D.C. Dunphy and S.G. Redding (eds.) *The enterprise and management in East Africa*, 67–92. Centre of Asian Studies, University of Hong Kong.

Hall, Edward T. and Mildred Reed Hall (1990): *Understanding cultural differences*. Chicago, IL: Intercultural Press.

Harding, Stephen and David Phillips (with Michael Fogarty) (1986): *Contrasting values in Western Europe*. London: Macmillan.

Hickson, David J. and Charles J. McMillan (eds.) (1981): *Organization and nation: The Aston Programme IV*. Aldershot: Gower.

Hofstede, Geert (1980): *Culture's consequences*. Beverly Hills, CA: Sage.

Hofstede, Geert (1991): *Cultures and organizations: software of the mind*. New York: McGraw-Hill.

Jaeger, Alfred M. and Rabindra M. Kanungo (eds.) (1990): *Management in developing countries*. London: Routledge.

Miller, George A. (1987): "Meta-analysis and the Culture-free Hypothesis". *Organization Studies* 8/4: 309–326.

Oliveira, Beto and David J. Hickson (1991): "Cultural bases of strategic decision-making: a Brazilian and English comparison". Paper presented at 10th EGOS Colloquium, Vienna.

Redding, Gordon (1990): *The spirit of Chinese capitalism*. Berlin: de Gruyter.

Weber, Max (1947): *The theory of social and economic organization*. New York: Free Press.

Notes on Contributors

Max H. Boisot is Professor of Strategic Management at E.S.A.D.E. in Barcelona and Senior Research Associate at the Judge Institute of Management, Cambridge University. He trained as an architect at the University of Cambridge, in management at M.I.T. and holds a doctorate in Economics from Imperial College, London University. From 1984 to 1988 he was director and dean of the China–EC Management Programme in Beijing and prior to that was Associate Professor at the *Ecole Superieur de Commerce de Paris*. His current research interests are at the confluence of three fields: culture, technology, and strategy. Max Boisot lives with his Polish wife and son in Sitges, 35 kilometers from Barcelona.
Mailing Address: ESADE, Avenida de Pedralbes, 60–62, 08034 Barcelona, Spain.

Adrian Campbell is a Lecturer at I.N.L.O.G.O.V., School of Public Policy, University of Birmingham. He has previously held research posts at Aston Business School, London Business School and the Henley Management College. He has carried out research at the International Institute of Management in Berlin, and the Leningrad Engineering–Economics Institute in what is now, once again, St Petersburg. His most recent publication (co-written with Malcolm Warner) is *New technology, skills and management* (Routledge, 1992).
Mailing Address: Institute of Local Government Studies, University of Birmingham, Selly Oak, Birmingham B15 2TT, England.

Barbara Czarniawska-Joerges holds an M.A. in Social Psychology from the University of Warsaw (1970) and an E.D. from the Warsaw School of Economics—then the Central School of Planning and Statistics—(1976). Until 1981, she was Assistant Professor at the University of Warsaw. She was temporarily associated with the Sloan School of Management, Cambridge, U.S.A., the Science Centre Berlin, the Swedish Working Life Centre and the Stockholm School of Economics. At present Barbara Czarniawska-Joerges is Professor of Business Administration at Lund University, Sweden. Her research focuses on control processes in complex organizations. She has published widely in the area of business administration in Polish, her native language, as well as in Swedish and English, including *Controlling top management in large organizations* (1985), *Ideological control in nonideological organizations* (1988), *Economic decline and organizational control* (1989) and *Exploring complex organizations: a cultural perspective* (1992). Her articles have appeared in *Economic and Industrial Democracy*, *Scandinavian Journal of Management Studies*, *Organization Studies*, *Journal of Management Studies*, *Accounting, Organizations and Society*, *Management Communication Quarterly* and *Consultation*.
Mailing Address: Institute of Economic Research, Lund University, Box 7080, S 220 07, Lund, Sweden.

Nic van Dijk studied Psychology, Economic Sociology and Business Administration, receiving his doctorate from Erasmus University, Rotterdam. He served as an Associate Professor and Deputy Programme Director on the faculty of Nijenrode, The Netherlands School of Business, and has been a visiting professor at the Graduate School of Management of the University of Oregon. He worked for Bank Mees & Hope as an advisor and also as interim manager of the Training Department. He is currently a partner at Intervisie, Consultants in Management and Strategy, Leiden, The Netherlands. His areas of specialization are strategic human resource management, business planning and management development.
Mailing Address; Middelmolen 30, 3481 AS Harmelen, The Netherlands.

Egil Fivelsdal is Professor of Organizational Sociology at the Copenhagen Business School. He was born in Norway in 1929 and has lived in Denmark since 1968. In 1969–70 he was Visiting Professor of Sociology at the University of Texas at Austin. He has carried out empirical research projects and published extensively within organizational sociology and political sociology. He is co-author of a text on organization theory which is used in Denmark, Norway and Sweden. His present interests include the sociology of management and general sociological theory.
Mailing Address: Copenhagen Business School, Institute of Organization and Industrial Sociology, Blaagaardsgade 23B, DK-2200 Copenhagen N, Denmark.

Pasquale Gagliardi is Director of ISTUD-Istituto Studi Direzionali (an Italian management institute situated at Stresa, on Lake Maggiore) and Professor of Organization Theory at the Catholic University in Milan. His research focuses on the relationship between culture and organizational order. He has published books and articles on this topic in Italy. In English, he has recently edited *Symbols and artifacts: views of the corporate landscape* (de Gruyter, 1990). Professor Gagliardi is a consultant to many large Italian corporations.
Mailing Address: ISTUD-Istituto Studi Direzionali, Corso Umberto I, 71, 28049 Stresa (Novara), Italy.

James Georgas is Professor of Social Psychology and Head of the Department of Psychology of the University of Athens. He was educated in the United States and has lived in Greece for the past 25 years. His areas of research interest are in the cross-cultural studies of values, group dynamics and the psychological effects of stress. He is the author of numerous publications in these areas and the deviser of various psychological tests. He is an industrial consultant in selection and evaluation techniques, personnel and management training, and in market research.
Mailing Address: Department of Psychology, University of Athens, Illissia 15784, Athens, Greece.

David J. Hickson is Research Professor of International Management and Organization at Bradford Management Centre. His principal research interests are how societal culture affects managerial decision-making in different nations, and what influences the success of major decisions. His previous research has included processes of managerial decision-making, power in organizations, and bureaucratization. He was Founding Editor-in-Chief of *Organization Studies* from 1978 to 1990. He has held appointments in Canada, the United States, and The

Netherlands, and has an Honorary Ph.D. from the University of Umea in Sweden. He is author, joint author, or editor of six books, and numerous journal papers and book chapters.
Mailing Address: University of Bradford Management Centre, Emm Lane, Bradford, West Yorkshire, BD9 4JL, England.

Geert Hofstede is Professor of Organizational Anthropology and International Management at the Department of Economics and Business Administration of the University of Limburg at Maastricht, the Netherlands, and Director of I.R.I.C., the Institute for Research on Intercultural Cooperation at this University. He holds an M.Sc. in Mechanical Engineering from Delft Technical University and a Ph.D. in Social Psychology from the University of Groningen. His occupational activities have varied from sailor, factory worker, industrial engineer, plant manager and personnel director to teacher and researcher at various academic institutions in Europe including I.M.D., I.N.S.E.A.D., E.I.A.S.M. and I.I.A.S.A. He has done extensive research in the area of national and organizational cultures and has published, lectured and acted as a consultant for public and private organizations in many countries in Europe and beyond.
Mailing Address: Faculty of Economic Sciences, Rijksuniversiteit Limburg, PO Box 616, NL 6200 MD, Maastricht, The Netherlands.

Afonso Pereira Inacio holds a degree in Finance from the I.S.E.-Technical University of Lisbon and has also undertaken professional studies in various Universities—Autes Etudes Comerciales de Paris, I.E.S.E. Barcelona, Massachusetts Institute of Technology, University of Texas (Austin), Scottish Business School, M.C.E. (Europe). Afonso Pereira Inacio is currently Professor of Management at the Portuguese Catholic University and is also a business consultant mainly in the areas of strategic planning, management control systems and productivity.
Mailing Address: Chairman, O.A.C.G., Lisbon, Portugal.

Brian Leavy is Senior Lecturer in Strategic Management at Dublin City University Business School. He obtained his B.Sc. and M.B.A. from University College Galway and his Ph.D. from the University of Warwick. His research interests centre mainly on the processes of strategy formation and strategic leadership, on competitive analysis and on manufacturing strategy. He has published in the *British Management Journal*, *Long Range Planning*, *Production and Inventory Management*, the *Handbook of Business Strategy* and in *Administration*. Prior to his academic career, he spent eight years with Digital Equipment Corporation as an engineer and engineering/quality assurance senior supervisor at the Galway manufacturing plant.
Mailing Address: Dublin City University Business School, Dublin City University, Dublin 9, Ireland.

Albert L. Mok is Professor of Business Policy and Organizational Behaviour at the University of Antwerp and Professor of Sociology of Work and Technology at the Agricultural University, Wageningen, Netherlands. A native of Amsterdam, Holland, he has lived in Belgium for over twenty years and is still amazed about the pragmatic solutions Belgians find in their everyday life. He has written articles on the quality of work, autonomy in professional work settings and comparative industrial relations, and books on service work, labour market segmentation (with Ray Loveridge), occupation formation, the principles of sociology (with Hugo de Jager) and the sociology of work. He participated in the research project which led to the book *Information technology in European services*, edited by Child and Loveridge (Blackwell, 1990).

Mailing Address: Department PSW, Universitaire Instelling Antwerpen, Universiteitsplein 1, 2610 Antwerpen (Wilrijk), Belgium.

Maurice Punch studied at the universities of Exeter, London, Cambridge, and Essex, gaining his Ph.D. in 1972. He taught at Essex University, University of Utrecht, S.U.N.Y. Albany, and Nijenrode, The Netherlands School of Business, where he is now Professor of Sociology. Fellowships from Nuffield and Leverhulme enabled him to visit the University of Amsterdam in 1973 and 1974, and he was Visiting Professor at the State University of New York at Albany, Rockefeller College of Public Affairs, School of Criminal Justice, for the Fall Semester 1981. In England, he specialized in the Sociology of Education and, in the Netherlands, he has researched the management of the police organization and is now concerned with corporate social responsibility, deviant behaviour, regulation and control in business. He has published in English, Dutch and American journals and has written several books.

Since joining Nijenrode in 1977 he has been chairperson of the Department of Business, Government and Society, Pro Dean of the Faculty, Director of Research, and Programme Director for the MBA.

Mailing Address: The Netherlands School of Business, Straatweg 25, 3621 BG Breukelen, The Netherlands.

Iette Schramm-Nielsen is an Associate Professor at the Copenhagen Business School, Integrated Modern Languages and Economics Centre, where she teaches in French on aspects of French economy and comparative management, as well as intercultural communication. She was born in Denmark, studied in France, worked in Iran, and has travelled extensively. Her professional career includes experience from a number of well-known Danish companies and a period as a free-lance French interpreter and translator in the Danish business community. In 1992, she published a Ph.D. dissertation on interaction between Danish and French managers and personnel. Her present research interest is comparative management in an intercultural perspective.

Mailing Address: Copenhagen Business School, Dalgas Have 15, DK 2000 Frederiksberg, Denmark.

Arndt Sorge has taught and done research on the organization and management of industrial enterprises, vocational education and training, personnel policy and industrial relations. In particular, he has taken part in international comparisons and covered the subjects mentioned, with specific respect to the development and utilization of new technology. Since 1972, he has held several university or research institute positions in Germany, his native country, as well as in England, France and the Netherlands. His main professional affiliation is with E.G.O.S., the European Group for Organizational Studies. Arndt Sorge taught Organization,

International Personnel Policy and Industrial Relations at the Department of Business Administration, University of Limburg, Maastricht (Netherlands), moving to Berlin at the end of 1992 where he is now Professor of Industrial and Organization Sociology at the Humboldt University.
Mailing Address: Humboldt-Universität, Institut für Soziologie, Ziegelstr. 13C, 0-1040 Berlin, Germany.

Monir Tayeb is a Lecturer in International Business at the Heriot-Watt University Business School, Edinburgh. Prior to coming to Britain in 1976, she worked as a financial executive in a state-owned company in Iran. She has been teaching organizational behaviour and international business at various British universities since 1980.

During the past sixteen years she has been involved in comparative studies of employees' work-related attitudes and values, organization structure, and leadership style at Oxford, Aston, Sussex and Heriot-Watt Universities. She is currently working on a project about cultural, political and economic challenges to British small business in the 1990s, and has just finished writing a book on international business and the global environment. Her publications include *Organizations and national culture* and over twenty-six articles and contributions to edited books.
Mailing Address: Business School, Heriot-Watt University, Riccarton, Edinburgh EH14 5AT, Scotland.

Barry A. Turner is Professor of European Business at Middlesex Business School. After reading sociology at Birmingham University, he carried out research into a variety of industrial and organizational topics, at Imperial College, at the Universities of Exeter and Loughborough and now at Middlesex. A former Chairman of the Standing Conference on Organizational Symbolism, S.C.O.S., he has a long-standing interest in cultural aspects of organizations and has published two books on this topic. He also conducts research into disasters and hazard management, work which enabled him to spend a year in Italy as a Visiting Scientist at the EC Joint Research Centre, Ispra, in 1989–90.
Mailing Address: Middlesex Business School, The Burroughs, London NW4 4BT, England.

Malcolm Warner is a Fellow of Wolfson College, Cambridge and a member of the Judge Institute of Management, University of Cambridge. He has taught and researched at Brunel University, the Henley Management College and London Business School. He previously carried out research in Columbia University and Stanford University in the US. His most recent publication is *How Chinese managers learn* (Macmillan, 1992).
Mailing Address: Management Studies Group, Department of Engineering, University of Cambridge, Cambridge CB2 1RX, England.

David Weir is Professor of Management and Director of the Bradford Management Centre. He was previously Professor of Organizational Behaviour at the University of Glasgow and has been a consultant for the World Bank, the Portuguese Government and U.N.E.S.C.O. Between 1976 and 1982 he taught regularly on executive programmes in Portugal and has consulted with Portuguese companies.

He is Managing Editor of the *European Management Journal* and author of several books including the *Modern Britain* series.
Mailing Address: University of Bradford Management Centre, Emm Lane, Bradford, West Yorkshire BD9 4JL, England.

Subject Index

Chapter 1: Europe

Chapter 2: Belgium

Chapter 3: Denmark

Chapter 4: England

Chapter 5: France

Chapter 6: Germany

Chapter 7: Greece

Chapter 8: Ireland

Chapter 9: Italy

Chapter 10: The Netherlands

Chapter 11: Portugal

Chapter 12: Spain

Chapter 13: Sweden

Chapter 14: Many More Ways Than One

Name Index